MARX: A HUNDRED YEARS ON

MARX: A HUNDRED YEARS ON

Karl Marx

Marx: A Hundred Years On

edited by
Betty Matthews

LAWRENCE & WISHART

Lawrence & Wishart Limited
39 Museum Street
London WC1A 1LQ

This edition first published 1983
© Lawrence & Wishart, 1983

Each essay © the author

Hardback ISBN 85315 565 8
Paperback ISBN 85315 566 6

Photoset in North Wales by
Derek Doyle & Associates, Mold, Clwyd
Printed and bound in Great Britain by
Camelot Press, Southampton

Contents

Illustrations

Preface

It is a measure of the vitality and resilience of Marxism that it has survived the combined attempts of the political and academic establishments to denigrate it or declare it redundant. That vitality springs from the contribution Marxism's theoretical framework and methodology makes to our understanding of past and present societies in their totality and as part of a historical process. This is what gives Marxism such political potency.

The influence of Marxism on various disciplines and fields of study is now widely recognized, and interest in it is increasing continuously. Over the past two decades the publication of Marx's own works, books about Marxism and books written from a Marxist perspective has been a growth industry. This volume of essays, to commemorate the centenary of Marx's death, pays tribute to the greatest revolutionary thinker of the modern age in the spirit he expressed in a letter to Arnold Ruge in September 1843, when he wrote: ' ... We do not confront the world in a doctrinaire way with a new principle: "Here is the truth, kneel down before it!" We develop new principles for the world out of the world's own principles.'

This book is therefore a refutation of the familiar caricature of Marxism as a rigid, determinist and closed system — a characterization compounded by its opponents' distortions and nurtured by trends within Marxism. As the reader will discover, the essays in it — written by more than one generation of Marxists — are not cast in a common mould, but express differing positions on a number of the subjects discussed. Controversial questions are raised, assessments made and views expressed which will doubtless prompt critical discussion.

While the content centres on Marx, Engels has a place in this volume, not only because of their fruitful partnership, but also because of his distinctive contribution to Marxist theory and to historical materialism in particular. And since theory is the product of real people, living and working in specific historical and social conditions, the volume also includes an essay about Marx in his family, which gives a vivid picture of the harsh and often tragic personal circumstances in which he produced some of his major works.

The history of Marxism has been neither smooth nor unproblematic. Periods in which it has been preserved in a deep freeze have had a stultifying effect, reinforcing dogmatism and resulting in a failure to respond effectively to historical change and to particular national conditions. Conversely, there have been attempts to revise Marxism out of existence. However, despite the vicissitudes of its history – or perhaps because of them – Marxism is very much alive today and is increasingly acknowledged as a vital point of departure in the study of society, past and present.

Contemporary Marxists face many challenges in making a contribution to the further development of Marxism, not least the need to avoid abstract theoreticism, which has been a tendency in recent years. A number of essays in this volume illustrate Marx's readiness and ability to make reassessments of his social and historical analyses in the light of change. In a similar fashion a hundred years on from Marx it is necessary for Marxists to confront and analyse the problems posed by changes in capitalism, the socialist countries and in the Third World. This volume points to some of the areas to be explored and clarified. A continuous relationship between theory and practice is essential for the fruitful development of Marxism and for the process of influencing movements to bring about the transformation of society.

Betty Matthews

Gwyn A. Williams

18 Brumaire: Karl Marx
and Defeat

With the exception of only a few chapters, every important section in the annals of the revolution from 1848 to 1849 carries the heading: *Defeat of the Revolution*!

What was overcome in these defeats was not the revolution. It was the pre-revolutionary, traditional appendages, the products of social relationships which had not yet developed to the point of sharp class antagonisms – persons, illusions, ideas and projects from which the revolutionary party was not free before the February revolution, from which it could be freed not by the *February victory*, but only by a series of *defeats*.

In a word: revolutionary progress cleared a path for itself not by its immediate, tragi-comic achievements, but, on the contrary, by creating a powerful and united counter-revolution; only in combat with this opponent did the insurrectionary party mature into a real party of revolution.[1]

Read this celebrated opening passage of Marx's *The Class Struggles in France 1848 to 1850* in parallel with an even more celebrated passage at the end of his *18 Brumaire of Louis Bonaparte*, written two years later after Napoleon's coup d'état:

But the revolution is thorough. It is still on its journey through purgatory. It goes about its business methodically. By 2 December 1851 [date of the coup] it had completed one half of its preparatory work; it is now completing the other half. First of all it perfected the parliamentary power, in order to be able to overthrow it. Now, having attained this, it is perfecting the *executive power*, reducing it to its purest expression, isolating it, and pitting itself against it as the sole object of attack, in order to concentrate all its forces of destruction against it. And, when it has completed this, the second half of its preliminary work, Europe will leap from its seat and exultantly exclaim: 'Well grubbed, old mole!'[2]

In both these passages, the underlying purpose is the same, to unmask that objective process, the revolution, which is remorselessly working itself out through all the contingencies and contradictions of political events. The two texts are close kin, also, in that they are both very dense and meticulous analyses of contemporary history in which Marx strains every resource of rhetoric at his command to relate events to the determinant realities of class. That rhetoric is shaped by its assumptions and purpose. A dialectical analysis demands a confrontation in virtually every sentence and a permanent revolution in demystification; its natural mode is paradox and its natural manner is irony.

The ever-present need to unmask, to expose, to bring to the surface, drives Marx to identify whole classes with individuals, to relate a class to its political expression with brutal directness, though this is more patent in the *Class Struggles* than in the *18 Brumaire*. It compels him, above all, to seize upon any element of *drama* that can be brought into play: a by-election becomes a revolution, a vote a coup d'état, the appointment of a minister a restoration. He imposes his own chronology, the chronology of Marxism, upon events and the punctuation points are invariably theatrical performances. The texts constitute a Drama of Revolution which, in the exposure of the contradictions of a bourgeois regime grounded in universal suffrage, becomes a Theatre of the Absurd.

The drama frequently evolves into melodrama, above all in the *Class Struggles*, where all the features of this mode of discourse are sharper, more direct and in the last resort more simplistic. For all the similarities between the two works, they are radically different. Consider the passages quoted. In the *18 Brumaire*, written two years later after Bonaparte's coup, the climax of the revolution is located in an indeterminate future. In the passage from the *Class Struggles*, the educational process seems virtually complete. In fact, the final sentence says that the revolutionary party is now mature.

While this stark assertion is qualified in the texts which follow and accompany it, it is, in truth, an accurate reflection of the mind of Karl Marx when he wrote it. The first three chapters of the *Class Struggles* were written as essays for a journal. They were published between January and March 1850, accompanied by surveys of current events. Interweaving with each other, these chronicle an intensifying drama in which Marx's expectations of a renewal of revolution and an outbreak of European war drove him to the rim of apocalypse. At that point, they collapsed. His fourth chapter was sheer anti-climax.

The *Class Struggles* and the *18 Brumaire* do not constitute a continuous text; there is a rupture. The latter is a revaluation. The former is fractured; the fracture occurs at the end of its third chapter.

Marx's original strategy was grounded in his perception of the essentials of the French Revolution: a revolutionary class which could present itself as the hero class of a society in revolt, a counter-revolutionary invasion which would ignite a people's war, a bourgeois order in total contradiction to the democratic political form which it required. These themes run as undercurrents throughout the *Class Struggles*. They had been incorporated in his newly minted materialist conception of history. He and Engels had evolved a strategy for Germany by 1846 which they tried to effect through the Communist League. German workers were to subordinate themselves to the bourgeois revolution while working towards an alliance with the peasantry and the petty bourgeoisie. Marx followed this practice as a revolutionary in Germany but by December 1848 realised there would be no bourgeois revolution. In the last, desperate days in 1849, he reversed his policy and threw himself into the formation of an independent workers' movement.

In exile in London, he worked to re-organise the Communist League in the conviction that the German bourgeoisie would never stage 'its own' revolution, that the unstable and deeply suspect petty bourgeoisie would take the lead in the struggle against the old regime and that the proletariat, despite its minority predicament, could work through this crisis to become the leader of a plebeian coalition and, in effect, the revolutionary hero class. He was no less convinced that the revolution was about to recommence and to merge into that European War of Liberation against the Holy Alliance which was the panacea of all revolutionaries and which Marx thought was imminent.

To this process, France in revolution was central and Marx moved into action in a sequence of related articles published in the *Neue Rheinische Zeitung Revue (NRZR)*, launched in Hamburg in January 1850. He wrote two interlocking series: surveys of current events throughout Europe which were intended to be monthly, and an historical analysis of France in monthly instalments which would inevitably converge with the former. It is the first survey, covering January-February 1850 and published in the second issue in the latter month, which fixes the context of the French articles which became the chapters of the *Class Struggles*.

The survey, dramatic in its account of an advancing counter-revolution led by Russia and a revolution intensifying in response, is taut with expectation of war. France is at the heart of the counter-revolution. The bourgeoisie, through an Assembly elected by universal suffrage, ruthlessly pursues its own interests; the wine tax which ruins half the population has been followed by police repression, attacks on teachers, the surrender of schools to the priests. It is hell bent on restoring the monarchy, but Legitimists and Orleanists cancel each other out, while the President, also elected by universal suffrage, is too weak to form a Bonapartist party.

In consequence, whole sectors of the plebeian population are being revolutionised …'the mass of the rural population has embraced the revolutionary party and professes a form of socialism, albeit still very crude and bourgeois'; the petty bourgeoisie follows its lead and its papers are going socialist. A grand coalition similar to that of the original revolution of February 1848 is building up, but this time 'workers have a deeper consciousness of their strength' and are moving centre stage. The abolition of universal suffrage has thus become essential to the bourgeoisie, but 'in this necessity, on the other hand, lies the certainty of an imminent victory for the revolution …'[3]

Women on the barricades near Porte St Denis, Paris, June 1848.

This process of polarisation Marx dates from an abortive *journée* of 13 June 1849, when the democratic republicans of the petty bourgeoisie were defeated. His job, then, in his history of France, is to bring the story up to that point. This he does in the issues of the *NRZR* in January and February in parallel articles which became the first two chapters of the *Class Struggles*.

The style of his history announces itself in its first words.[4] When at the moment of triumph in February 1848, the liberal Laffitte said that from now on, 'bankers will rule ... he betrayed the secret of the revolution'. Politics is certainly granted some autonomy: the republican fraction of the bourgeoisie represents no specific economic interests; Bonaparte bounces across the surface of classes like a flexible rubber ball; Marx immerses himself in an intricate scrutiny of particulars. But everything is referred back to the basic class realities which are generally marshalled in great blocs. The Legitimists are landed property, the Orleanists, finance and industry, the Montagne the petty bourgeoisie. Central to the whole business is the relative immaturity of capitalism in a France dominated by bankers and the ripple effect this produces ... 'In France the petty bourgeois does what the industrial bourgeois would normally have to do; the worker does what would normally be the task of the petty bourgeois. Who then does the task of the worker? Nobody. It is not accomplished in France; it is only proclaimed ...'[5]

The workers proclaim it at the very beginning in their heroic struggle during the June Days of 1848, to which Chapter One of the *Class Struggles* (January) is wholly devoted. In terms of Marx's analysis this is the essential preliminary. For all the often brilliant detail, the theme is basically simple. As the revolutionary government summons up reaction through universal suffrage and tries to create its ideal state, the workers storm into the scene in the cause of their own, inevitably premature, revolution. All other classes, including the vacillating petty bourgeoisie, mobilise; they dredge up the *Gardes Mobiles* from the lumpenproletariat and the workers go down in bloody defeat. The first necessity has been achieved. The Republic builds itself on the corpses of the proletariat. But their revolution, the authentic revolution of the present, has been proclaimed ... 'The present generation is like the Jews whom Moses led through the wilderness. They have not only a new world to conquer; they must perish in order to make room for the men who are equal to a new world.'[6]

In Chapter Two, published in February, Marx traces the resumption of that march as the Old Mole of Revolution starts his grubbing. In a biting and brilliant examination of contradictions, he poses the central question: ... 'the most comprehensive contradiction in the Constitution consists in the fact that it gives political power to the classes whose social slavery it is intended to perpetuate: proletariat, peasants and petty bourgeoisie. And it deprives the bourgeoisie, the class whose social power it sanctions, of the political guarantees of this power.'[7]

Upon this stage, the bourgeois theatre of the absurd performs.[8] The immediate inheritors of June are the republican bourgeoisie who promptly start building a political order fit for the mass of the royalist bourgeoisie, who are French capitalism, through the agency of an Assembly grounded in universal suffrage. In doing this job, it exhausts its credit and is given notice to quit. Its victims are the petty bourgeoisie and the peasants, the former crushed into bankruptcy by big business as a reward for deserting the proletariat in June, the latter hit by the 45 centimes tax and a myriad insults. But the democrats conjure up their own executioner. They decide on a President as the second head of their chosen polity and have him elected by that same universal suffrage which has so far served them well. In revenge, the peasants, supported by other disaffected plebeians, elect an adventurer, a clown, a Krapulinski who offers them false guarantees from a half-remembered past and an escape from the bourgeois juggernaut bearing down on them. The day of the election of Louis Bonaparte, declares Marx in his instrumental melodrama, 'was the day of the *peasant insurrection* ... 10 December was the coup d'état of the peasants who overthrew the existing government ...'[9]

There follows a long and particularised account of the endless duel between President and Assembly which is itself enmeshed in the developing European counter-revolution; through this maze of the contingent with its three major crises, an ironic commentary detects a remorseless polarisation of the fundamental classes of bourgeois society. It acquires political form in the elections for a Legislative Assembly in the spring of 1849. The bourgeois republicans are contemptuously dismissed, as Legitimists and Orleanists fuse into that Party of Order which is the instrument for monarchists to turn the republic into a shield for bourgeois social order against Bonaparte and the plebeians. Disaffected petty bourgeois and others gravitate back towards the proletariat in a minority but potent social republican party. As soon as the new Assembly meets, there is a confrontation. Ledru-Rollin, for the Montagne and the democratic petty bourgeoisie, moves the impeachment of the President for violating the Constitution and sending an army against republican Rome, to align the republic with counter-revolution. It is defeated. Negotiations with a resurgent proletariat reach stalemate and a half-hearted half-insurrection is suppressed.

The petty bourgeoisie have, in turn, staged their pallid imitation of the proletarian June of the previous year. That proletariat is left as the major protagonist. At the opposite pole, the royalist bourgeoisie takes full possession of the republic. It is precisely from this moment, which closes Chapter Two, that Marx dates the beginning of the truly revolutionary, because final, polarisation.

And that polarisation drives towards apocalypse. In the Review which accompanies the historical essay in February, the theme is war.[10] In every corner of Europe, the counter-revolution is driving the revolution back into action. Switzerland is becoming a focal centre of dissidence and Marx writes at length and in strictly military terms on the mobilisation of Prussia and Austria against the cantons. These tensions fuse with older national rivalries. Russia, entrenched in the heart of Europe on the ruins of revolutionary Hungary, must act now — against Turkey if it wants to fulfil its aims, against the Babel of Revolution in France, if it wants to save itself and its satellites. Any such war will drag in England whose colossal power will straddle the continent. War is about to become total and Europe will go up in flames. In that conflagration, the revolution and the real, the proletarian revolution this time, will break out again. This moment of truth is imminent ... 'This much is certain: the Holy Alliance will march this year ...'[11]

The apocalyptic tension of February reaches its climax in March. The Review for that month had to be held over to April for lack of space and only the section on England (composed in March) was printed.[12] This however drove expectation of an imminent revolution to the very threshold of tolerance. For England itself was now being drawn into the vortex. Already *The Times* had been provoked into furious slander of the triumphs of 'anarchy' in France after the radical by-election victories of 10 March (centrepiece of Chapter Three of the *Class Struggles*); it felt the blow in Paris in its own vitals.

For a sudden commercial crisis had broken upon the crisis in agriculture precipitated by the repeal of the Corn Laws. No country would be so hard hit in consequence as Germany, England's commercial alter ego. European and English crises would therefore intensify each other and in short order. 'The continental revolution will take on an unprecedently socialist character', and in England the Whigs would 'say farewell for ever to Downing Street'. The Tories would find every party ranged against them, led by the industrialists, and would be forced to carry through a parliamentary reform. This would 'open the doors of Parliament to the proletariat, place its demands on the agenda of the House of Commons and pitch England into the European revolution'.[13]

In an addendum written in April to accompany the actual publication of the Review, Marx was forced to concede that the English commercial crisis had abated, to the relief of the French bourgeoisie, but he dismissed this as the usual annual fluctuation and found salvation in a depression in America, even more important a fulcrum than Germany. His conviction did not slacken. The crisis would develop yet more rapidly ... 'daily forcing matters to a head ... *Que les destins s'accomplissent! Let destiny fulfil itself!* ...'[14]

In the same month as he wrote those words, the Central Committee of the Communist League joined Blanquists and revolutionaries among the Chartists to set up the secret and revolutionary World Society of Revolutionary Communists which 'dispenses with all national restrictions'. Article One of its constitution read … 'The aim of the association is the overthrow of all privileged classes and their subjugation to the dictatorship of the proletariat, which will carry through the permanent revolution until the realization of communism …'[15]

It was in the same month as he wrote Chapter Three of the *Class Struggles* and the Review which pitched England into the revolution that Marx, with Engels, composed the celebrated March Address of the Communist League which forcefully proclaimed the Permanent Revolution.[16] In a scathing self-criticism of their own practice during 1848-49 (characteristically addressed to un-named third persons), Marx and Engels asserted the imminent renewal of the revolution and made independent working-class organisation and action its central imperative. The Address is steeped in a profound suspicion of, and virulent hostility to, the petty-bourgeois democrats and republicans. The coming revolution would inevitably be led by such pitiable creatures in its early phases and workers would have to join them in the struggle against absolutism. But the moment that victory had been won, the proletariat had to press forward remorselessly from the overthrow of absolutism to the overthrow of capital itself. On no account, therefore, must it be ensnared in petty bourgeois offers of incorporation in a broad democratic alliance. Workers must maintain their own organisation, secret and open; at the moment of victory, they must force the petty bourgeoisie to 'carry out their terroristic phrases'. They must sustain every revolutionary enthusiasm; far from deploring 'excesses' as the democrats would do, they must not only tolerate but direct popular vengeance against hated individuals and symbolic public buildings. They must force demands and insist on guarantees that the petty bourgeoisie could not possibly concede. They must dictate conditions which would carry the seeds of the democrats' own self-destruction. To this end, they had to be armed in a proletarian guard, they had to create their own parallel anti-state in revolutionary councils and workers' governments. Although they would have to go through a 'protracted revolutionary process', this time, their march to communism must begin from the first hour ... 'Their battle-cry must be: The Permanent Revolution.'

And while the Address is directed to the League's members in Germany, it is written in hourly expectation of victory in France ... The revolution is imminent 'whether it is initiated by an independent rising of the French proletariat or by an invasion of the revolutionary Babel (France) by the Holy Alliance' ... This time, German workers 'can at least be certain that the first act of the approaching revolutionary drama will coincide with the direct victory of their own class in France ...'[17]

The Address is drenched in suspicion of petty-bourgeois democrats who in France are now calling themselves 'socialists'; organised hostility to, and preparation of the destruction of, them is its *raison d'être*. In any alliance with these wretches, it is absolutely essential to 'make as many inroads as possible', above all to force them to 'compromise themselves'. Nowhere is this obsession and its specific vocabulary reproduced more precisely than in the passage in Chapter Three of the *Class Struggles* where Marx describes the secret meeting between representatives of the Montagne and the clandestine workers' societies after the critical Assembly vote of 11 June 1849. The workers demanded an immediate revolt. The Montagne prevaricated and it was too strong to be challenged in the open ... 'The proletarian delegates did the only rational thing. They committed the Montagne to *compromise* itself, that is, to overstep the limits of the parliamentary struggle ... ' Throughout the farcical *journée* of 13 June, the proletariat 'maintained the same sceptically watchful position and waited for a serious, irrevocable clash between the democratic National Guard and the army in order to rush into the battle and to propel the revolution forward beyond the petty bourgeois aim set for it ...'[18]

And in the later phase of mobilisation after this defeat, so schematically but compellingly delineated in the *Class Struggles*, when just such a broad democratic alliance was forced into existence by the developing counter-revolution and when the fragmented forces of the petty bourgeoisie and even some of the bourgeoisie began to prate their rubbishy 'doctrinaire socialisms' and the social democracy of 'red republicans', it is the proletariat which Marx singles out as the heart and core, the veritable leader and driving force of the coalition, thrusting irresistibly forward to the supreme revolutionary climax of 10 March. This proletariat was rallying ever more around ... '*communism*, for which the bourgeoisie itself has invented the name of Blanqui. This socialism is the declaration of the *permanence of the revolution, the class dictatorship of the proletariat* ...'[19]

Neither the March Address nor Chapter Three of the *Class Struggles* was a model for the other. They were written simultaneously and within an identical perspective. Chapter Three is the dénouement of that Drama of Revolution which is Marx's theme. What the evocation of Marie Antoinette is to Edmund Burke's *Reflections on the Revolution in France*, the elections of 10 March 1850 are to Karl Marx's *The Class Struggles in France*.

Chapter Three begins with a full description of the abortive *journée* of 13 June 1849.[20] It is located squarely within the development of the European counter-revolution. Russians are marching on Hungary, Prussians on the German liberals, French on Rome; in France, the monarchists of the Party of Order are taking possession of the Republic. What confronts them? Ledru-Rollin, spokesman for the Montagne, the democratic republicans. He stands up in the Assembly to move his vote of censure on the Rome expedition in trenchantly revolutionary terms ... 'the eyes of all Europe were directed at Paris, and the eyes of Paris at the Legislative Assembly ...'

The petty bourgeois democrats, in their motion, attempted '*an insurrection within the limits of pure reason*, that is, a *purely parliamentary insurrection*', a perfect expression of the will of the democratic petty bourgeoisie which 'wished, as always, for nothing more fervently than to see the battle fought out above its head, in the clouds, between the departed spirits of parliament'. The defeat of their motion was followed by the shambles of their extra-parliamentary demonstration which was almost a caricature of the petty bourgeoisie in political action. Marx specifically contrasts the proletarian insurrection of June 1848 with that of the petty bourgeoisie of June 1849 ... 'each of these two insurrections the *classical* and *pure* expression of the class which had carried it out'.[21]

From this moment, the Assembly became nothing but the Committee of Public Safety of the Party of Order. A rolling tide of reaction breaks over France and royalists move openly towards a restoration of the monarchy. But the two months' prorogation of the Assembly reveals to Orleanists and Legitimists their fragmentation and lack of effective support, while Bonaparte, cherishing a dynastic *revanche* of his own, cultivates a demagogic stance in opposition. All this, needless to say, is paraded in caustic wit and brilliant if often oblique perception.

The serious business of the essay is resumed with the return of a chastened Party of Order and the final phase of the constitutional republic, its denial of its own legitimation in universal suffrage in its response to the by-elections of 10 March 1850. This is a hypnotic if highly schematic analysis of a remorseless process of polarisation which the continuing revolution enforces unwittingly, like some blind old mole.

Firstly, in the new Bonaparte ministry, the stock-exchange shark Fould becomes Minister of Finance. In a characteristically direct identification of an individual with a class or a fraction of a class, Marx says ... 'With Fould's appointment, the financial aristocracy announced its own restoration.' He explains how this power, against which the original revolution of 1848 had been directed, restored itself, displacing all other purposed restorations in the process. The analysis, while brief, is sharp and particular, inserted into his exposition of the relative backwardness of France in comparison with England.[22] There is, in consequence, a domino effect, with every class in French society having to fulfil the historic function of the class above it. The workers have been able only to proclaim their revolution not to make it. Now, however, there is a critical difference. The workers' revolution 'will not be accomplished within any national walls. The class war within French society will be transformed into a world war in which nation confronts nation' – that war of European liberation which Marx was at that moment announcing in his Reviews ... 'The worker's task will begin to be accomplished only when the world war carries the proletariat to the fore in the nation that dominates the world market, i.e. England' – an event which Marx in that same month was hailing as imminent.[23]

From Fould and his re-introduction of the hated tax on wine, Marx moves into the most breathtaking pages in the essay, on the revolutionising of the peasantry, the petty bourgeoisie and much of the middle class around the proletariat which assumes the leadership of a coalition. The wine tax opens a celebrated discussion of the peasantry which, in subtly but decisively mutated form, grew into the classic analysis of the *18 Brumaire*. Although he traces the ramifications of the wine trade throughout French society and identifies twelve million of its dependents, Marx treats the peasantry as a single undifferentiated bloc. They are subjected to precisely the same exploitation as the proletariat ... 'their exploitation differs only in *form* from that of the industrial proletariat. The exploiter is the same: *capital*'. The mystifying factor is their nominal ownership of private property. This is nullified by debt, mortgage and taxes. The peasant's enemy, in these oppressions, is the republic of the bourgeoisie. But the proletariat has also threatened their property, a menace skilfully exploited by the Party of Order which struck 'the true peasant tone with their crude exaggeration and brutal interpretation ... ' Hence Bonaparte as their man.

But the inexorable processes of revolution have unmasked the peasants' real enemies. The bourgeoisie in their Assembly crush them with taxes and now their own man betrays them with the wine tax ... '*Louis Bonaparte is like the others*'. Blow follows blow: gendarmes terrorise their villages, the law hunts schoolmasters ... 'those proletarians of the educated class ... the authorities, the spokesmen, the educators and interpreters of the peasant class' (an interesting prefiguration of the 'organic intellectuals' of Antonio Gramsci, born to a village 'intellectual') the education law condemns them to 'forcible stupefaction' at the hands of priests. Experience follows experience with revolutionary speed ... '*Revolutions are the locomotives of history*.'[24]

Citing several instances of radicalisation, which recent research has confirmed and amplified, Marx couples this baldly-defined peasant bloc with a sequence of equally bald assertions. Once the government deified taxes 'the peasant became godless and threw himself into the arms of the devil: *socialism*'. The most stationary class is being revolutionised, revolution has become 'a matter for peasants'. For the peasant, 'the *social democratic* or *red* republic is the dictatorship of his allies.'[25]

That republic takes shape daily.[26] In a brilliant and parallel passage, Marx detects group after group among the middle classes propelled into what they call socialism, for so their vital interests are described by the bourgeois dictatorship of the Assembly ... 'Abolition of the protective tariffs – socialism! For it strikes at the monopoly of the *industrial* fraction of the party of Order. Regulation of the state budget – socialism! For it strikes at the monopoly of the *financial* fraction of the party of Order ... Voltaireanism – socialism! ... ' – the catalogue lengthens.

In consequence, '*Resistance to bourgeois dictatorship, need for a change in society, retention of democratic republican institutions as the means to this end, regrouping around the proletariat as the decisive revolutionary force*': these are the common characteristics of the social republican or red party.[27]

Because of the objective centrality of the proletariat, all these classes and class fractions embrace 'socialism' and Marx analyses these variant socialisms with an irony which becomes overt and ferocious only in his *18 Brumaire*.[28] To Marx the 'communist' (a term from a far older tradition which he is revivifying) they are all 'doctrinaire' or utopian socialisms, the 'theoretical expression of the proletariat only as long as it had not developed further and become a free, autonomous, historical movement.' But in the pressure-cooker of the revolution, this transformation of the proletariat into an historically autonomous power was in fact happening. Its political expression comes in the by-elections held to replace the deputies purged after 13 June 1849.

These elections, in Marx's prose, become a moment of transfiguration. The red republic's election committee, '*completely under the influence of the workers*' (my italics)[29]

                    Gwyn A. Williams

chooses three candidates who, in the typical style of the *Class Struggles*,' represent the three allied classes'. Indeed they do not so much represent as personify them. De Flotte, a deported hero of June 1848, is the revolutionary proletariat, now the leader of the Left as finance capitalism is of the Right; Vidal is a 'doctrinaire' socialist, the petty bourgeoisie; Carnot (son of the Organiser of Victory in the great Committee of Public Safety of 1793) is the republican bourgeoisie, 'whose democratic formulas had gained a socialist significance in the struggle' since they 'had long since lost their own significance'.

This was a '*general coalition against the bourgeoisie and the government, as in February*' (1848). But this time 'the *proletariat was the head of the revolutionary league*'. And it won!

Marx greets the electoral victories of 10 March in the stentorian tones of a rabbi hailing the Messiah; it is the voice of a revolutionary Yahweh roaring over the waters ... '*The election of 10 March 1850 was the revocation of June 1848!*' – the bourgeois butchers of June 1848 enter the enemy Assembly trailing behind their former victims and mouthing the latter's principles. '*It was the revocation of 13 June 1849!*' – the Montagne re-enter the Assembly, no longer as the commanders of the revolution but merely as its advanced trumpeters. '*It was the revocation of 10 December!*' – Napoleon had been unmasked as a charlatan and a failure ... ' 10 March was a revolution. Behind the ballot slips lay the paving stones.' And that revolution would be the permanent revolution of the proletariat, whose programme Marx had outlined in the March Address.[30]

In response, its enemies panicked, rallied around the clown Bonaparte, called for a new Coblenz (the émigré invasion of the original French Revolution in the 1790s) which meant in effect a march on Paris by the Holy Alliance and, in a final confession of bankruptcy, demanded the *abolition of universal suffrage*.

'The basis of the Constitution is *universal suffrage. The destruction of universal suffrage* – this is the last word of the Party of Order, of the bourgeois dictatorship. Bourgeois rule as the product and result of universal suffrage, as the express act of sovereign will of the people – this is what bourgeois Constitution means. But does the Constitution still have any meaning the moment the content of this suffrage, the sovereign will, is no longer bourgeois rule?'[31] This seminal question which had echoed in Marx's thinking from his earliest writings and which echoes still through every parliamentary democracy grounded in capitalism, finds one of its classic analyses here and in the *18 Brumaire*. In those texts, the bourgeoisie, to preserve its own power, denies 'its own' ideology and destroys 'its own' specific form of parliamentary democracy. These essays in fact resume, in a wider and deeper context, the arguments which Marx deployed in his first political writings, on the Jewish question and on Hegel's Philosophy of Right in the early 1840s. In essentials, it is Robespierre and bourgeois democratic principles confronted with bourgeois democratic reality all over again.

In March 1850, according to Marx, all is stripped to a stark polarity. There is no hint here of any Bonapartist Third Way. The bourgeoisie in all its political expressions now stands irredeemably condemned ... 'Their republic had [note the past tense] only *one* merit; *it was the forcing house of the revolution.*' It had exhausted its historic mission. The moment of truth had come, the moment of the revolution which would be the permanent revolution of the proletariat ... '10 March 1850 bears the inscription: *Après moi le déluge!* After me, the deluge!'[32] ... *Que les destins s'accomplissent!*

The reader reels out of Chapter Three of *The Class Struggles in France* as, in my youth, I used to reel out of the Oddfellows' Hall Cinema in Dowlais, unwillingly ejected at the close of an episode of one of those riveting film serials which commandeered the Saturday mornings of a generation: hungrily willing away a week of my life in order to learn, in God's name, what happens next?

What happens next in 1850 is eight months of silence followed by a shattering anti-climax.

No further issue of the *NRZR* appeared until a double-number, which was its last, in November. In it, Marx's separate history of the French Revolution disappears into his final Review, covering May to October 1850.[33] This is a massive and meticulous examination of the general economic crisis, with its epicentre in England, which permitted the revolutions of 1848 to occur. No less massive an analysis follows of the return of prosperity, again focused on England, which exposed the ephemeral character of those revolutions. In consequence, 'the political activity of the last six months has been essentially different from that which preceded it. The revolutionary party has everywhere been driven from the field ...'[34]

France is treated in two sections of the Review, later combined into Chapter Four of the *Class Struggles* under the dramatic title, 'Abolition of Universal Suffrage in 1850'. This, too, is rooted in his novel economic analysis. And how the tone has changed! 'While this general prosperity lasts, enabling the productive forces of bourgeois society to develop to the full extent possible within the bourgeois system, there can be no question of a real revolution. Such a revolution is only possible at a time when *two forces* come into *conflict*: the *modern productive forces* and the *bourgeois forms of production ... A new revolution is only possible as a result of a new crisis; but it will come, just as the crisis itself ...*'[35]

Very sound, no doubt, but where now is the coalition of classes mobilising under the leadership of the proletariat? The peasantry, which had thrown itself into the arms of the devil of socialism and made revolution its business? ... Despite the general prosperity, twenty-five million peasants remain sunk in depression but 'the history of the last three years has sufficiently proved that this class is absolutely incapable of any revolutionary initiative'.[36]

And the abolition of universal suffrage in the teeth of the class alliance around the proletariat? The former retains its symbolic significance ... 'Universal suffrage had fulfilled its mission, the only function which it can have in a revolutionary period. The majority of the people had passed through the school of development it provided. It had to be abolished, by revolution or by reaction.'[37] It was achieved by the latter. The popular victory of 10 March was squandered in electoral frivolities such as multiple candidatures and the advancement of the diletantte Eugène Sue. The Party of Order regained confidence. It pressed ahead and the Montagne, though expressing a 'decent and educated humanism', contented itself with peaceful and ineffective protest, anxious not to give the proletariat its head.

In this reading, the petty bourgeois democrats completely dominate the Left; where now is the committee 'completely under the influence of the workers'? The Left goes down to defeat and, in explaining it, Marx deploys practically nothing of the class and structural analysis of Chapter Three. All is contingency, the cowardice of grocers, immediate political devices, which seem paltry and accidental in contrast to his previous power. The proletariat is not excluded from blame ... 'The victory which the people had won in alliance with the petty bourgeoisie in the election of 10 March was annulled by the people themselves ... ' For the rest, it is a matter of the play of surface political issues, but the surface they play over is that of economic recovery ... 'An army of 150,000 men in Paris, the long postponement of decision, the calls for restraint from the press, the pusillanimity of the Montagne and the newly elected representatives, the majestic calm of the petty bourgeoisie and, above all, the commercial and industrial prosperity: all these prevented any attempt at revolution on the part of the proletariat (a rare use of the latter term in Chapter Four, where it is largely replaced by 'the people'). Exit the grand coalition then – 'with the election law and the press law, the revolutionary party quits the official stage ...'[38]

O what a fall is there! This is bathos to equal that of the 13 June 1849 itself.

Between April and November 1850, of course, had fallen what David Fernbach justly calls the most important change in Marx's attitude during his entire political work as a communist.[39] In August 1850 he abandoned the permanent revolution. Aneurin Bevan, talking of his maiden speech in the Commons, said that he thought he had thrown a stone and found he had thrown a sponge. The British Museum had the same effect on the permanent revolution. Marx immersed himself in those economic studies which were ultimately to debouch in *Capital*. His thinking was radically transformed. The proletariat was still in its infancy; so was its parent, the mode of production of industrial capitalism. The revolution was postponed *sine die*.

He followed through with his customary rigour. He called on the Communist League to embrace his new perspective and ran into head-on collision with colleagues whom he denounced for making the revolution a voluntaristic act of will ... 'If you want to change conditions and make yourselves capable of government, you will have to undergo fifteen, twenty or fifty years of civil war ... '[40] In September, the League split and Marx and Engels withdrew into that isolation which had the latter writing a couple of months later ... 'And what have we ... to do with a "party", i.e. a herd of jackasses who swear by us because they think we're of the same kidney as they? Truly it is no loss if we are no longer held to be the "right and adequate expression" of the ignorant curs with whom we have been thrown together over the past few years ...'[41]

It was in this climate that Marx wrote the Review which became Chapter Four in the *Class Struggles*. In terms of what had gone before, the chapter was a total anti-climax. The essay's argument is fatally undermined. Chapter Four in fact destroys the *Class Struggles*.

It was over a year before Marx returned to this stricken field, a year of misery, suffering and isolation, of total immersion in all that 'shitty economic mess', with Engels constantly nagging him to produce 'a fat book'. Life abruptly returns in the December of 1851 when the clown Krapulinski, to the utter astonishment of intellectual Europe (including Marx and Engels) staged his coup to install a regime which, today, seems almost the prototype of so many of the political regimes of our own times. Within a day Engels in Manchester was dashing off letters bubbling with outrage and excitement in which the very words of Marx's most famous essay are precisely pre-figured ... 'The history of France has entered upon the stage of the most perfect comedy. Can one imagine anything more entertaining than this travesty of the 18th Brumaire ... ? ... it really seems as if old Hegel in his grave were controlling history as the world spirit and as if everything might be run twice with the greatest conscientiousness, once as a great tragedy and the second time as a rotten farce, Caussidière

Troops shooting the insurgents in Paris during the counter-revolution of 1851.

for Danton, L. Blanc for Robespierre ... we certainly seem to have arrived at the 18th Brumaire ... '[42] The commission from Weydemeyer followed and in the spring of 1852 Marx published his *18 Brumaire of Louis Bonaparte.*

In that seminal work, the anti-climax of Chapter Four of the *Class Struggles* is transcended. The themes of the latter are once more taken up; the analysis remains rooted in class structure and the fundamental Old Mole argument is the same. But the direct, one-to-one simplicities of the earlier text are abandoned, the relationship between a class and its politics is infinitely more nuanced, the autonomy of the political comes into its own and the whole discourse is lifted to a different plane. In no sense can the two pamphlets be read as a continuous text. They straddle an abyss and the later essay carries the reader into another world. It is the transition, rendered familiar by more recent experience, from a 'war of movement' to a 'war of position.'

The *18 Brumaire* is one of the finest texts in the Marxist political tradition.[43] It is Marx the historian at his most brilliant and challenging. Incomplete and ambiguous it certainly is; a European mountain of interpretation has been erected upon it. But the essay has echoed through generations and it will go on echoing. Lévi-Strauss the anthropologist, I have read, used to preface an arduous exercise in his craft with yet another immersion in the *18 Brumaire* as in a brisk, methodological cold shower. Clearly a man of taste and percipience; would that more professed Marxists followed his example.

In its basic purpose, in many of its assumptions and techniques, in some qualities of style and rhetoric, the *18 Brumaire* is a re-writing of the *Class Struggles.* Some sense of the autonomy of the political is certainly present in the latter, while the problems of the representation of a class by political groups and of the relationship of a state to modes of production dominates the former. In both, though in an infinitely richer manner in the *18 Brumaire*, every class in French society save one is subjected to minute and acute differential analysis. In the *18 Brumaire*, the *lumpenproletariat* is more effectively disengaged and related to a *bohemia* located elsewhere, if indeed at all, in a social structure – a practice which immediately poses the sharpest questions to Marxist historiography, questions which are impressionistically explored but never answered. In both texts, one class only remains immune to his analysis (more questions!) – Marx's own 'proletariat'.

Yet one has only to confront the two texts closely to realise the profound transformation which has occurred. In the *18 Brumaire*, gone is the direct connexion between a class and its political representatives, everything in the political arena is now mediation. Consider that remarkable definition, which has become a classic, of just how 'petty bourgeois' parliamentary deputies 'represent' street-corner grocers; it has become a seed-bed of creative thinking. Both books frequently cover the same ground. It is a fascinating and immensely rewarding experience to confront those passages in the two texts and to work through them in harness, line by line and metaphor by metaphor, to tease out the profound changes which textual variations reflect and express.[44] In so doing, you became aware that you are moving from one universe of discourse to another. The questions may be the same but the context in which they are posed has been transformed.

Engels, when he introduced the 1895 edition of the *Class Struggles*, wrote: 'History has proved us and all who thought like us, wrong. It has made clear that the state of economic development on the Continent at that time was not, by a long way, ripe for the elimination of capitalist production; it has proved this by the economic revolution which, since 1848, has seized the whole of the Continent … '[45] Indeed, he said that he and Marx had mistaken the birth pangs of capitalism for its death-throes!

Brood over that statement and the quite staggering adjustment which it implies. To call the passage from Chapter Three of the *Class Struggles* to the *18 Brumaire* a 'shift in perspective' is to call the passage from B.C. to A.D. a punctuation point.

Defeat has forced revaluations of similarly cosmic significance in more recent times. There is that moment which echoes still in Marxist thinking and practice, the European revolution which did not happen after 1917. Marxists invented whole structures of thought and action to confront that moment: an interpretation of the Bolshevik Revolution as a socialist success of world significance, the elaboration of a mode of discourse and practice precipitately labelled Leninism, the formation of the Comintern. Central to much of their thinking and their practice was Lenin's perception of imperialism as a 'moribund' form of capitalism, which underlay not only his pamphlet on the theme, his myriad tactical exhortations and the practice of the Comintern but that astonishingly successful text *'Left-wing' Communism: An Infantile Disorder?*

The experience of the 1920s, of the inter-war years and of the unparalleled success of imperialist capitalism after 1945 have forced a revaluation every whit as fundamental as that forced on Marx in 1850. It remains critically incomplete. Powerful and sophisticated analyses of imperialism we have in abundance; the analytical as opposed to the polemical scrutiny of the Comintern is in train. But there are so many lacunae. In particular, we lack a serious, systematic and instrumentally sympathetic analysis of those Marxists and communists, inside and outside the communist parties and not inconsiderable in number or quality, who formed a fragmented freemasonry far wider than that all-too-familiar Ultra-Left which dogma and neglect have turned into caricature; those men and women, unholy ghosts of history's communism, who were representative if often contradictory voices of an authentic European communism, whose analyses now seem more accurate and relevant than Lenin's and who were apparently expelled so easily from history by a single pamphlet. In consequence, we do not have an 18 Brumaire of the European-Revolution-that-never-was.

We are fortunate to possess one approximation to it, from a rather marginal corner of that failed Europe. Antonio Gramsci, together with his comrades and in succession to Marx, had to confront the shift from a 'war of movement' to a 'war of position'. His response grew into a major revaluation, an attempted translation into specific relevance of what, like his companions, he called Leninism. It is first visible, I believe, in that horrible Italian summer of 1920 when he was as isolated and as miserable as Marx had been in 1851; it acquires its characteristic physiognomy during his brief sojourn in the leadership of the Communist Party of Italy, particularly during 1926. In his Prison Notebooks, it broadens into a text as incomplete, baffling and ambiguous but as excruciatingly brilliant and as tantalisingly perceptive as Marx's own essay. This was Gramsci's 18 Brumaire of Benito Mussolini (and, indeed, in its final reduction, of Adolf Hitler).

It has rarely been in the celebration of victory but rather in the revaluation forced by defeat that Marxist political discourse has most enriched itself. This offers some consolation as we move towards what may prove to be the 18 Brumaire of Margaret Thatcher.

Notes

1. The standard reference for the two texts discussed here is Karl Marx and Frederick Engels, *Collected Works* (Vol. 10 for *The Class Struggles in France*, pp. 47-145, and Vol. 11 for *The Eighteenth Brumaire of Louis Bonaparte*, pp. 103-97), Lawrence and Wishart, 1978 and 1979 respectively; however for easy accessibility I have used the volumes in the Pelican Marx series, with introductions by David Fernbach which are excellent if very rigorous in the style called Marxism-Leninism. The relevant volumes are *The Revolutions of 1848* (1973; henceforth *Revolutions*) and *Surveys from Exile* (1973; henceforth *Surveys*). This passage is in *Surveys*, p. 35.
2. *Surveys*, pp. 236-37; as a founder member of the Antediluvian Left, I prefer the translation 'well grubbed' to 'well worked'.
3. *Revolutions*, pp. 265-81; the introductions by David Fernbach and the critical apparatus to both volumes in the Pelican Marx series effectively establish the context.
4. In no sense am I attempting an evaluation of Marx's historiographical practice in the style of, say, Gregor McLennan's excellent work in his *Marxism and the Methodologies of History* (New Left Books, Verso Editions, 1981). My aim is to establish the relationship between two texts by Marx produced in 1850-52; my comments on Marx's writing are therefore directed at the rhythm and pattern of his argument.
5. *Surveys*, pp. 111-112
6. *Surveys*, pp. 35-62 and 112.
7. *Surveys*, p. 71.

8. In general, *Surveys*, pp. 62-94.
9. *Surveys*, p. 72.
10. *Revolutions*, pp. 265-281.
11. *Revolutions*, p. 280.
12. In general, *Revolutions*, pp. 281-284.
13. *Revolutions*, p. 283.
14. *Revolutions*, p. 284.
15. David Fernbach, introduction, *Revolutions*, p. 57.
16. *Revolutions*, pp. 319-330.
17. *Revolutions*, pp. 321, 325.
18. *Surveys*, p. 97.
19. *Surveys*, p. 123.
20. In general, *Surveys*, pp. 94-128.
21. *Surveys*, pp. 94, 96, 100.
22. *Surveys*, pp. 109-111.
23. *Surveys*, p. 112.
24. *Surveys*, pp. 117-119.
25. *Surveys*, pp. 113, 117, 118.
26. *Surveys*, pp. 121-123.
27. *Surveys*, p. 121.
28. *Surveys*, pp. 188-190.
29. *Surveys*, p. 124.
30. *Surveys*, pp. 124-125.
31. *Surveys*, p. 127.
32. *Surveys*, p. 128.
33. The Review, minus the sections on France, is in *Revolutions*, pp. 284-318; the sections on France, forming chapter 4 of the *Class Struggles*, are in *Surveys*, pp. 128-142.
34. *Revolutions*, p. 284.
35. *Surveys*, p. 131.
36. *Surveys*, p. 130.
37. *Surveys*, p. 134.
38. *Surveys*, pp. 131-135.
39. David Fernach, introduction, *Revolutions*, p. 57.
40. From the Minutes of the Central Committee of the Communist League, 15 September in *Revolutions*, generally, pp. 339-344 and in particular, p. 341. September in *Revolutions*, generally, pp. 339-344 and in particular p. 341.
41. Engels to Marx, 13 February 1851, in *Collected Works*, Vol. 38, p. 290 (translated by Peter and Betty Ross), Lawrence and Wishart, 1982; also included in Fritz J. Raddatz (ed.), Ewald Osers (trans.), *The Marx-Engels Correspondence: the personal letters 1844-1877* (Weidenfeld and Nicolson, 1981), p. 25.
42. Engels-Marx, 3 December 1851, *ibid*, pp. 38-41.
43. *Surveys*, pp. 143-249.

44. I have in fact undertaken such an enterprise. It requires much more space than is available here, or perhaps anywhere, unfortunately (for me, that is, fortunately for you, since the result is probably unreadable). I made a start on it, in a totally different context, in a long essay for the Open University: *France 1848-51: interpretations of the French Revolution, Karl Marx and Alexis de Tocqueville*, Open University Course A231, Units 5-8 (mine is Unit 7) 1975.

45. Engels, introduction to the 1895 edition of *The Class Struggles in France*.

George Rudé

MARXISM AND HISTORY

Marxist historiography naturally begins with Marx and Engels; and in its making they played a dual role. In the first place, they formulated the main principles of what became known as 'historical materialism'; it was a long-drawn process stretching over nearly half a century from the jointly written *Holy Family* (1845-6) to Engel's *Socialism Utopian and Scientific* (1890). But long before its completion they had begun to apply these principles in practice to the writing of works of history. It is with these historical works that this essay is primarily concerned, and also with the work of half a dozen recent Marxist historians in France and Britain.

Here Engels was the first in the field and, when only twenty-four years old, quite independently of Marx, he published *The Condition of the Working Class in England*. It was the first major attempt by either writer to apply the Marxist theory of history, which was only then beginning to mature in their minds, to a major study in social and political history. The book also had the great merit to be the first great historical study of the Industrial Revolution in action at a time when the very notion of an industrial 'revolution' had only begun to exercise the minds and arouse the emotions of British writers and politicians. Its particular virtue perhaps was the author's capacity, after a short visit to England's industrial cities, to record clearly and comprehensively the industrial scene in Manchester, its slums and the lives and conditions of its working people, the first industrial proletariat in Europe. Engels also noted the doubtful benefits to the people of the rapid growth of cities that accompanied industrial advance: 'The brutal indifference [he wrote], the unfeeling isolation of each in his private interests becomes the more repellent and offensive, the more these individuals are crowded together.'

Other writers and chroniclers of the day – Disraeli, Kingsley and Mrs Gaskell – had also begun to describe and deplore the 'condition of the people' and to call on authority to lighten their burden. But Engels went much further. Not content with merely 'noting' and 'deploring' and calling on the government to intervene, he realized, three years before it became a central point in the *Communist Manifesto*, that the overcrowding and industrialization did not merely brutalize men and increase their sufferings but, having reduced them to 'machines pure and simple', also '(forced) them to think and demand a position worthy of men'. So a central feature of the *Condition of the Working Class* is the description of the beginning of workers' resistance to exploitation, of their growing consciousness and will to struggle and their capacity, by organization and numbers, to hit back at the all-powerful employing class; and he even forecasts, within a brief span of years, the outbreak of a 'revolution ... with which none hitherto known can be compared'.

Engels has, of course, been hammered by his critics for a tendency to idealize the 'golden days' of England's pre-industrial past and, even more, for his apparently rash and lightly undertaken prophesy of revolution: a revolution, as is well known, that never came about. And he himself came to realize his mistake and, in 1892, in his Preface to the first English edition (the book first appeared in German), wrote that his 'production bears the stamp of his youth, with its good and its faulty features, of neither of which he feels ashamed'. Among these 'faults' were his over-confidence in predicting a revolution; yet he very sensibly attributed this error to a number of factors, England's increasing industrial prosperity and the repeal of the Corn Laws among them.[1] He probably also had in mind the final passage in the book, in which he appears to be predicting that, in the last resort, avoidance of a bloody revolution would depend less on the objective social factors than on the possibility of reconciliation between the two contesting parties, that is, between 'the better elements of the bourgeoisie on the one hand and the more educated workers [having become Communists] on the other'.[2] It is hard to believe that such a conclusion would have been likely to commend itself to either Marx or Engels later; but, nonetheless, sandwiched between these lines is an important lesson in revolutionary strategy as valid today as when Engels penned it 150 years ago: that once the workers became organized and politically educated they would be less likely to engage in indiscriminate savagery and slaughter:

> In proportion as the proletariat absorbs socialistic and communistic elements will the revolution diminish in bloodshed, revenge and savagery.[3]

(It is curious that he puts the main emphasis on socialist ideas rather than on organization, or a combination of the two.)

Engels was also the author of the next historical work to be written by Marx or himself under the influence of the new ideas. It once more bore witness to his versatility as now, six years later, he was turning his hand to a subject that was a far cry from the industrial England of the 1840s: to the peasants of southern Germany in the late Middle Ages. *The German Peasant War*, like much of Marx's and his own historical work, appeared first as a series of articles for the press; written in 1850, they were not published as a book until 1870. Engels had by this time had some experience of peasant protest through his recent active participation in the battles fought in revolutionary Baden in 1849. Like other authors of the event, in writing of the Peasant War, Engels had three main problems to face. They were the extreme complexity of German society in this transitional period, with the delicate balance that had to be struck between the burgher-led Free Cities, the feudal Princes on their lordly domains, and the peasants of the countryside; the role played by religion in a pre-industrial peasant struggle; and the diversities in the character, ideas and party attachments of the two principal leaders in the War, Martin Luther and Thomas Münzer. From this jigsaw Engels was able to establish that while the peasant masses, stimulated by their own basic grievances against feudal lord and unreformed Church, provided the shock-troops of revolution, it was the burghers, centred on the Free Cities and propelled by their own grievances against the restriction of feudal authority combined with the crusading spirit and slogans of Luther's Reformed Church, that provided the money and machinery of organization. It was religion, however, both of the Reformed and radical-revolutionary kind, that provided the rebellious peasants and their 'plebeian' allies with an ideology of struggle.[4]

The author also showed considerable skill in presenting the character and behaviour of the two principal leaders and in describing how they reflected the composition and political attitudes of their respective parties. In this respect, he argued that Luther's 'indecision and fear of the movement' and 'his cowardly servility to the princes' faithfully mirrored 'the hesitant and ambiguous policy' of the burghers; and he contrasts this with Münzer's 'revolutionary energy and resolution', which in turn 'was reproduced among the most advanced section of the plebeians and peasants'. And he goes on to explain that whereas Luther 'confined himself to expressing the conceptions and wishes of the majority of his class', Münzer, the revolutionary, 'went far beyond the immediate ideas and demands of his peasant and plebeian supporters' and organized an 'elitist group of the existing revolutionary elements' which was never more than 'a small minority of the insurgent masses'. This was a comparatively early attempt to apply the Marxist principle of the primacy of man's 'material being' over his consciousness or, more specifically, to depict the behaviour and politics of leaders in terms of the struggle of contending social groups. However, as we shall see, this early attempt was soon far surpassed by Marx's more mature and more sophisticated portrayal of the Emperor Louis-Napoleon.

Both writers found themselves on more familiar ground when they wrote their articles (and subsequent books) on the revolutions of 1848 in France and Germany and on the Paris Commune of 1871. Their cooperation was so close at this time (in the early 1850s) that one might be excused for assigning a work to one writer when it should have been assigned to the other. Yet there were differences between them which are certainly more easily discernible today than they were to their contemporaries of the 1850s. Engels, for instance, appears to be more skilful in synthesis and in handling general history and in the narration of events (one might even say that he was the more accomplished historian of the two), whereas Marx is the great strategist of revolution and the master of satire and in handling the complex relations of classes and of political leaders and groups. But they were both faced by the problem of writing history almost as it passed before their eyes. The problem is really a two-fold one. One is the problem of changing perspectives determined by a sharp turn in events. An often quoted example is Marx's change of mind with regard to the seizure of power by the Commune. At first, as spokesman for the General Council of the First International meeting in London in September 1870, he warned the Parisians against 'the desperate folly' of attempting another uprising; but when the uprising took place six months later and the Commune was installed, Marx, responding to an entirely new situation, praised the Parisians for 'storming the heavens'. The other problem is that noted by Engels is his posthumous Introduction to Marx's earlier *Class Struggles in France* concerned with the French events of 1848-50, which he called 'Marx's first attempt, with the aid of his materialist conception, to explain a phase of contemporary history from the given economic situation'. But the problem, he noted (and he was writing forty years after the event), is that 'a clear survey of the economic history of a given period is never contemporaneous; it can only be gained subsequently after collecting and sifting of the material has taken place'.[5] He goes on to explain how far this affected Marx, who began his work at the end of 1849 and had completed his first three articles (or chapters) before he had occasion to appreciate the importance of the world trade crisis of 1847 as a precipitant of revolution in February and March 1848 and, later, of the renewed industrial prosperity of 1849-50 as a stimulus in turn to the revival of European reaction. So the forecast made late in 1848 of an imminent revival of revolutionary activity made in the first edition had to be discarded in the second.*

The *Eighteenth Brumaire of Louis Bonaparte*, which Marx began to write in the wake of the *coup d'état* of December 1851, had of course no such handicap as that mentioned above when it returned, briefly to the events of spring 1848 to Autumn 1850. But as the work is the subject of another study in this volume, I shall confine myself here to a brief word on Marx's famous portrait of Louis Napoleon and on his reappraisal of the role of the peasantry after December 1848. Napoleon is presented in the magnificent opening pages, among the other mock-heroes of 1848, as the phantom of the great Napoleon. 'From 1848 to 1851,' he writes, 'only the ghost of the old revolutionaries of 1789 walked about, from Marrast, the Republican in kid gloves, who disguised himself as the old Bailly, down to the adventurer who hides his commonplace repulsive features under the iron death mask of Napoleon.'[6] This is Marx's withering political satire at its best.

To the French peasants of 1848, still a subject of bitter debate among historians, Marx in this volume makes partial amends for his sweeping denunciation of their role in *Class Struggles in France*. The 'true peasant revolution' was then presented as the election of Louis Napoleon to the Presidency in December 1848, assured by a massive peasant vote. Now he conceded that, after the first *coup d'état*, a part of the peasantry were among the most vociferous to protest arms in hand against the outcome of their own vote of three years before. 'The school they had gone through since 1848,' he explains, 'sharpened their wits.' Nevertheless, he insists that the peasantry as a whole continued for some time to supply a solid background of support for the Bonapartist dynasty. Yet as the Presidency passed into the Empire, the peasant freeholders (writes Marx) began to become

* There is a further problem here raised by Engels's stated contention that Marx was attempting to explain a phase of history 'from a given economic situation'. It sounds as if Engels was slipping (or that the translator was at fault?) in choosing such a 'deterministic ' formula when we consider that it was only two years before that he had assured Bloch that 'the determining element is *ultimately* the production and reproduction in real life: more than this neither Marx nor I have ever asserted'.

persuaded that Louis Napoleon, for all his promises, was of no more use to them than the vote-seeking bourgeoisie. So, concludes Marx, 'the interests of the peasants ... are no longer, as under the first Napoleon, in accord with, but in opposition to, the interests of the bourgeoisie, or capital. Hence the peasants find their natural ally and leader in the *urban proletariat* whose task it is to overthrow the bourgeois order.'[7] While this belief in a close worker-peasant alliance proved, as the events of March-May 1871 would show, to be over-optimistic, Marx, having adroitly considered all the other political and social groups that Louis Napoleon would be able to dupe in turn, ends his book with the remarkably accurate prophecy that 'when the imperial mantle falls on the shoulders of Louis Bonaparte, the bronze statue of Napoleon will crash from the top of the Vendôme Column'.[8]

While Marx was writing the *Eighteenth Brumaire*, Engels resumed his own historical work by writing a dozen pieces for the *New York Daily Tribune* which, forty years later (in 1891), became a book entitled *Germany: Revolution and Counter-Revolution* (it was originally attributed to Marx). The value of some chapters, such as those relating to the rise and fall of the national-revolutionary or conservative-national movements of Magyars, Czechs and Slavs within the old Habsburg Empire, has probably proved ephemeral; but in handling the revolutions in Berlin and Vienna and peasant revolution in Austria he appears to have been on more familiar ground. His narrative and analysis of these events are of the highest quality throughout. His judgment on the peasant movement was that, in Austria at least, the peasants 'have been the real gainers by the Revolution'; their successes, Marx and Engels both believed, brought the Austrian peasants into line with the French who had won their liberation in 1789. Perhaps his most notable passage, however is the one where he describes, and explains, the disintegration of the alliance of forces that brought down Metternich in Vienna.

But [he writes] it is the fate of all revolutions that this union of different classes, which in some degree is always the necessary condition of any revolution, cannot subsist long. *No sooner is the victory gained against the common enemy than the victors become divided among themselves ... and turn their weapons against each other. It is this* rapid and passionate development of class antagonism which, in old and complicated organisms, makes a revolution such a powerful agent of social and political progress; it is this incessantly quick upshooting of new parties succeeding each other in power which, during these violent commotions, makes a nation pass in five years over more ground than it would have done in a century under ordinary circumstances.[9]

As historians and political scientists (for in their case it is not possible to keep the two categories apart), it is Marx that is generally the more subtle, 'philosophical' and speculative of the two: it is difficult to imagine Engels penning Marx's portrayal of Louis Napoleon, cited just now. This is another way of saying, too, that Marx was the greater polemicist. This is particularly evident in the last of Marx's historical works, put together from the long Addresses to the General Council of the International on the Paris Commune and a number of 'Fragments' and Appendices published in a single volume entitled *The Civil War in France* (1891). The book contains further pen-portraits in the *Eighteenth-Brumaire* manner, such as Ernest Picard, 'the Joe Miller of the Government of National Defence'; Jules Ferry, 'the penniless barrister' who, as Mayor of Paris during the siege, 'contrived to job a fortune out of famine'; and above all, there is the central villain of the piece, Thiers, 'that monstrous gnome' who, before he became a statesman, 'had already proved his lying powers as an historian'. But the satire is pushed aside in the magnificent final tribute:

Workingmen's Paris, with its Commune, will be for ever celebrated as the glorious harbinger of a new society. Its martyrs are enshrined in the great heart of the working class. Its exterminators history has already nailed to that eternal pillory from which all the prayers of their priests will not avail to redeem them.[10]

Engels, for his part, is the more 'political-theoretical' in that he is more inclined − sometimes to the indignation of present-day Marxist scholars or followers – to draw clearcut political conclusions regarding the need for authority in revolution. To take two examples, both concerning the Commune of 1871. One is the well-known, contentious, conclusion written twenty years after the event in his Introduction to Marx's *Civil War*. He is chiding the 'Social Democratic philistines' of the day for recoiling in horror at the mention of the term 'Dictatorship of the Proletariat'; and he adds: 'Well and good, gentlemen, do you want to know what this dictatorship looks like? Look at the Paris Commune; that is the Dictatorship of the Proletariat.' In a second passage, written in correspondence with an Italian socialist only eight months after the fall of the Commune, he is chiding rather than commending the Commune (as Marx did, too) for its 'want of centralization and authority that cost it its life'. And he adds (as if anticipating the views of some of the young 'revolutionaries' of our own time): 'When I hear people speak of authority and centralization as of two things deserving condemnation, I feel that those who say this either have no idea of what a revolution is or are revolutionaries only in name.'[11]

Later historians writing in the Marxist tradition have, of course, had the advantage (unless they have chosen to write of topical events) of not only learning important lessons from their forbears but also of seeing the whole history of which they are writing as *past* and not as 'contemporaneous' events. They have therefore not had the same excuse, except where new facts or new collections of documents have come to light, to change their minds on important matters of interpretation almost as the ink dried on their original draft, as Marx and Engels were occasionally obliged to do in writing of historical events that they had first witnessed as eyewitnesses or observers. Moreover, they have had the further advantage of access to new sources and to the new fields in the social sciences that have been opened up in the last eighty years and were unknown to Marx and Engels, whose historical writing was, as we have seen, mainly focused on the political and economic aspects of working-class movements and revolutions of the nineteenth century in Europe, the great exceptions being Engels's *Peasant War* and his sketch of man's pre-history (influenced by the American anthropologist, Lewis Morgan), the *Origin of the Family, Private Property and the State.*

But large regions of the world, such as Japan and the Pacific, Africa and Latin America (now being well trodden and explored by historians and anthropologists) were at that time virtually a closed book, as were the more recent vistas opened up by the behavioral sciences including modern social psychology. There were also other fields to which Marx and Engels made occasional reference, though they never had the opportunity to explore them adequately themselves; such were Marx's famous remark that religion was 'the opium of the people' and his tentative reference to popular collective ideology when (in his Introduction fo the *Critique of Hegel's Philosophy of Law*) he wrote that 'theory becomes a material force when it grips the masses'. Engels, too, in a letter to Joseph Bloch in 1890, allowed the ideological factor a part (though not 'the decisive one') in shaping man's history; he instances in particular 'the traditions which haunt men's minds'.[12] So it would be reasonable to suppose that both writers would have shown some sympathy for the work done in the past half-century by Marxist (or near-Marxist) scholars to explore these questions more fully. Moreover, it was Engels, who of the two lived long enough to have time to relax and reflect on such matters, who all but said so when he wrote to Conrad Schmidt, another correspondent, in August 1890:

> Our conception of history is above all a guide to history, not a lever for construction after the manner of the Hegelians. *All history must be studied afresh.*[13]

It would be foolish to imagine that it is only Western historians raised in a Marxist tradition that have learned to apply these lessons to the writing of history; but space will only allow mention of such 'fresh' thinking in the case of a half a dozen French and British historians who have been writing in the past fifty years. The first on my list is Georges Lefebvre, the great French historian of the Revolution of 1789; it was he who first called for a study of history 'from below'. His first important contribution was to 'discover' the peasants who, though constituting four-fifths of the French population at the time, had been largely neglected up till then. Though Lefebvre chose as his principle focus the peasants of the Department of the Nord, his book, *Les paysans du Nord*, first published in 1924, was so detailed and raised so many questions of a more general validity that his conclusions have been taken to apply to the country as a whole. One of these was that it was not true – as it had been supposed – that the revolution of 1789 was essentially an urban one and that the peasant rebellion, in spite of the longstanding grievances of the rural population, was an offshoot of the Paris events of July 1789. On the contrary, argued Lefebvre, the peasants had a revolution of their own which they started in their own time. To quote from a paper he read in December 1932:

> What I have tried to show is that there was a *peasant* revolution with its own autonomy as regards its origins, its direction, its crises. We say autonomous as to its origins because the peasant masses rebelled spontaneously under the impact of hunger and the hopes raised by the summoning of the Estates General; and, quite independently of the townspeople, the peasants conceived the notion of the 'aristocratic plot' without which the Great Fear [of 1789] would have been impossible to imagine.[14]

This 'Great Fear' was an important element in the peasant 'revolution' of that summer, and Lefebvre became its historian; his book, entitled *La Grande Peur*, was published in 1932 and was perhaps the most original of all his works. He showed how the countryside in a large part of northern and central France became gripped by an almost universal panic, fed by the rumour of soldiers disbanded after the Fall of the Bastille who (it was believed) eager to avenge their humiliations on the rebellious villages, were marching on the peasants' properties in the shape of marauding 'brigands'. Even when the 'brigands' turned out to be nothing more than hungry villagers seeking food and shelter in the farms and homesteads, the Fear continued, spreading from market to market and village to village along the river valleys; so (wrote Lefebvre) 'fear bred fear', and fear also gave a great stimulus to the revolution in the villages and market towns. And from all this bewildering confusion of myth and rumour, defensive reaction and both orderly and disorderly activity, Lefebvre drew the conclusion that the Great Fear was not just an interesting psychological phenomenon, underlying the idiocy and irrationality of human behaviour, but it had important positive historical consequences as well.[15] It was Lefebvre, too, who, in the same year, fired the first effective broadside at Gustave Lebon, the French fascist 'father' of crowd psychology, with his picture of the mindless mob responding blindly to the call of any ambitious 'leader'.[16]

If Lefebvre and his pupil, Albert Soboul, the Marxist historian of the Parisian 'small people' or *sans-culottes*, have been the greatest historians of revolution in France, in Britain that title should be given to Christopher Hill, the author of numerous volumes on the English revolution of the seventeenth century. In his earliest work, such as the tricentenary volume of 1940, Hill made an honest attempt to give the British reading public a Marxist synthesis of the revolution; but it was not distinguished by subtle argument or original thought (qualities that belonged rather to Maurice Dobb, the communist economist, whose chapters on the English seventeenth century in *Studies in the Development of British Capitalism* were written shortly after). But the difference was startling when Hill went on to deepen his study of Puritanism and became (with A.L. Morton) probably the first Marxist writer in the English language to explore some of those socio-political aspects of religion that Marx had touched on a century before. He carried the argument further when he went on, in *The World Turned Upside Down* (1972), to focus on the revolution 'from below' both in its political and religious-ideological aspects. There were, writes Hill in his Introduction,

> two revolutions in mid-seventeenth-century England. The one which succeeded established the sacred rights of property (abolition of feudal tenures, no arbitrary taxation), gave political power to the propertied (sovereignty of Parliament and common law, abolition of prerogative courts), and removed all impediments to the triumph of the ideology of the men of property – the protestant ethic. There

was, however, another revolution which never happened, though from time to time it threatened. This might have established communal property, a far wider democracy in political and legal institutions, and might have disestablished the state church and rejected the protestant ethic.[17]

A large part of the book is given over to the people who preached those radical ideas and those who received them; and the author has shown a unique ability to place the political and religious ideas of the common people side by side and to show how they merge in a common ideological context. On the one hand, there were the Levellers, apostles of a wider parliamentary democracy, and the Diggers who dug up the common land in search of a richer economic millennium with property held in common; and, on the other, there were the extreme religious sects, the Ranters, Seekers and socially radical Quakers, who preached free grace, denied sin and hell and preached sexual freedom and that 'all comes by nature'. But many men belonged to both: the Digger philosopher Winstanley was also close to the Ranters and Quakers; Milton, the Puritan poet and friend of Cromwell, has been called a 'precursor to the Ranters'; and the Ranters themselves, according to their historian A.L. Morton, probably drew support from 'migrating craftsmen' or 'masterless men'. Hill argues that all these ideas were radical, though he does not claim that all were equally dangerous to the establishment. (It is significant perhaps that the Ranters and Seekers only began to flourish after the Levellers had been virtually silenced at Burford in May 1649.) The Army radicals – at least the Levellers and Diggers – left a tradition that refused to lie down; and Hill quotes a conservative opponent as writing long after the revolution:

They have cast all the mysteries and secrets of government ... before the vulgar ... and have taught both the soldiery and people to look so into them as to ravel back all governments to first principles of nature ... They have made the people thereby so curious and so arrogant that they will never find humility enough to submit to a civil rule.[18]

Eric Hobsbawm and Edward Thompson have been the main pioneers of the 'new' labour history which began in England in the early 1960s. There were two books, in particular, that announced its arrival: Thompson's *Making of the English Working Class* (1963) and Hobsbawm's *Labouring Men* (1964). In his Preface Hobsbawm described the 'old' labour history, pioneered by the Webbs and G.D.H. Cole, as being a 'straightforward chronological or narrative history of labour movements' and claimed that hitherto 'there has been *comparatively little work about the working classes as such (as distinct from labour organizations and movements*) and about the economic and technical conditions which allowed labour movements to be effective, or prevented them from being effective.'[19]

The greater contribution to this 'new' history has no doubt been made by Edward Thompson, whose *The Making of the English Working Class* (first published in 1963) has probably been the most original and the most influential work in British labour and social history published since the last war. Thompson's concern for 'people' as against 'movements' or 'institutions' is implicit in his choice of title and also in the definition of 'class' that he gives in his preface: a 'historical relationship' which is neither 'structure' nor 'category' and which 'must always be embodied in real people in a real context'. Moreover, he sees it as a 'social and cultural formation', which can only be studied over a considerable span of time, in this instance over the half-century between 1780 and 1832, the time during which 'most English working people came to feel an identity against their rulers and employers'. As he is concerned with development and therefore with *pre-industrial* and *industrial society* (here completely at variance with the Webbs and Coles), he is bound – and he does so with zest – to challenge the received wisdom of a number of orthodoxies. He lists them as, first, the Fabian orthodoxy, in which 'the great majority of working people are seen as passive victims of *laissez-faire*'; secondly, the orthodoxy of the empirical economic historians, with their tendency to reduce workers to a 'labour force' or 'the raw material for statistical tables', and, finally, what he terms the

'Pilgrim's Progress' orthodoxy, 'in which the period is ransacked for forerunners – pioneers of the Welfare State, progenitors of a Socialist Commonwealth' and so on. His main quarrel with these orthodoxies is that they smother the workingman's own contribution to the 'making' of his history and that, by putting a premium on success, expose the 'losers' in the race – the Luddites, handloom weavers and their like – to 'the enormous condescension of posterity'.[20]

Hobsbawm has also paid attention to the 'losers', most spectacularly in his *Primitive Rebels* (1959) a treatment of recent archaic and millenarial movements in Spain, Italy and Latin America which, in spite of their proximity to developing centres of population and industry, remain largely untouched by the values and ethos of contemporary capitalism. But he is less scornful of 'movements' than Thompson and has cooperated with myself in writing *Captain Swing* (1969), a study of the English agricultural labourers' revolt of 1830 – a revolt that, though the labourers have been generally written off as 'losers', achieved some success in arresting the growth of threshing machines in England's southern counties.

Like Hill and unlike the earlier labour historians, all three of us have been concerned with the ideology of the common people as *history*, that is to attempt to trace the origins and development of the ideas that (in Marx's phrase) 'grip the masses'. Whereas the older labour historians ignored this element altogether or set its evolution in a narrow trade-union or 'labour' mould, Thompson was prompted, by the very nature of his subject, to construct a picture of the developing ideology of the working class in all its aspects, social, political and religious. Thus Methodism, for all its dubious benefits, is revealed as playing in some respect a positive role in stimulating the workers' political activities. The Swing rioters of 1830 were also stimulated by a medley of political and religious ideas in which tradition played a major part. At the same time the July Revolution in France roused hopes of an early political reform; several of the Hampshire men were already involved in the Reform movement at home; and some of the Wiltshire men, like the Dorset labourers of 1834, were Methodist activists or preachers. Again, there was the underlying sense of 'justice', probably more pervasive than the religious or political motivation that prompted the labourers to refuse to accept that machines, which robbed men of their 'natural right' to work and enjoy a living wage, should receive the protection of the law. On occasion, they invoked the authority of the magistrates or government, including the King himself, to justify their actions. And, in September 1832, a Norfolk rioter claimed that 'in destroying machinery, I am doing God a service'.[21]

In this respect – along the lines of Engels's 'traditions which haunt men's minds' – there is, of course, a great deal more to explore.

Notes

1. F. Engels, *The Condition of the Working Class in England*, Granada, 1981, p. 21. Moreover, to do Engels full justice, the 'prophecy' was hedged about from the start with a number of qualifications.
2. *ibid.*, p. 324.
3. *ibid.*, p. 321.
4. For an appreciation of Engels's history by modern historians of the event, both Marxist and non-Marxist, see the Special Issue of the *Journal of Peasant Studies* devoted to 'The German Peasant War of 1525', ed. Janos Bak, vol. 3, no. 1, Oct. 1975, pp. 89-135.
5. Engels, Introduction to Marx's *Class Struggles in France* (1895 edn) in Marx and Engels, *Selected Works in One Volume*, Lawrence & Wishart, 1968, pp. 641-58.
6. Marx, *Eighteenth Brumaire of Louis Bonaparte*, Moscow, 1977, pp. 10-12.
7. *ibid.*, pp. 107-10 (my italics).
8. *ibid.*, p. 116. In May 1871, the Vendôme Column, topped by a statue of Napoleon I, was destroyed by order of the Commune.
9. *Germany: Revolution and Counter-Revolution*, 1969, p. 141 (my italics).
10. Marx, *Civil War in France*, Martin Lawrence, 1933, pp. 23, 24, 63.
11. Draft of letter to Carlo Terzaghi, 14 Jan. 1872 (tr. from Italian), in *K. Marx and F. Engels on the Commune*, Moscow, 1971, p. 292.
12. Engels to Bloch, 21 Sept. 1890, in *Marx and Engels Correspondence 1846-1895*, Lawrence & Wishart, 1934, p. 476.
13. Engels to Schmidt, 5 Aug. 1890, ibid., p. 473 (my italics).

14. G. Lefebvre, 'La Révolution française et les paysans', *Etudes sur la Révolution française*, Paris, 1954, pp. 249-50.
15. *The Great Fear of 1789. Rural Panic in Revolutionary France*, NLB, 1973, pp. xi-xiii.
16. G. Lebon, *The Crowd* (London, 1904); Lefebvre, 'Foules révolutionnaires', in *Etudes sur la Rév. Fr.*, pp. 271-87.
17. C. Hill, *The World Turned Upside Down*, Temple Smith, 1972, p. 12.
18. *ibid.*, p. 58.
19. E.J. Hobsbawm, *Labouring Men. Studies in the History of Labour*, Weidenfeld, 1964, p. vii (my italics).
20. E.P. Thompson, *The Making of the English Working Class*, Gollancz 1963, pp. 9-13.
21. Hobsbawm and G. Rudé, *Captain Swing*, Lawrence & Wishart, 1969, p. 249.

Stuart Hall

The Problem of Ideology –
Marxism Without Guarantees

In the past two or three decades, Marxist theory has been going through a remarkable, but lop-sided and uneven revival. On the one hand, it has come once again to provide the principal pole of opposition to 'bourgeois' social thought. On the other hand, many young intellectuals have passed *through* the revival and, after a heady and rapid apprenticeship, gone right out the other side again. They have 'settled their accounts' with Marxism and moved on to fresh intellectual fields and pastures: but not quite. *Post*-Marxism remains one of our largest and most flourishing contemporary theoretical schools. The Post-Marxists use Marxist concepts while constantly demonstrating their inadequacy. They seem, in fact, to continue to stand on the shoulders of the very theories they have just definitely destroyed. Had Marxism not existed, 'Post-Marxism' would have had to invent it, so that 'deconstructing' it once more would give the 'deconstructionists' something further to do. All this gives Marxism a curious life after death quality. It is constantly being 'transcended' *and* 'preserved'. There is no more instructive site from which to observe this process than that of ideology itself.

I do not intend to trace through once again the precise twists and turns of these recent disputes, nor to try to follow the intricate theorizing which has attended them. Instead, I want to place the debates about ideology in the wider context of Marxist theory as a whole. I also want to pose it as a general *problem* – a problem of theory, because it is also a problem of politics and strategy. I want to identify the most telling weaknesses and limitations in the classical Marxist formulations about ideology;

and to assess what has been gained, what deserves to be lost, and what needs to be retained – and perhaps rethought – in the light of the critiques.

But first, why has the problem of ideology occupied so prominent a place within Marxist debate in recent years? Perry Anderson, in his magisterial sweep of the Western European Marxist intellectual scene (*Considerations on Western Marxism*, New Left Books, 1976) noted the intense preoccupation in these quarters with problems relating to philosophy, epistemology, ideology and the superstructures. He clearly regarded this as a deformation in the development of Marxist thought. The privileging of *these* questions in Marxism, he argued, reflected the general isolation of Western European Marxist intellectuals from the imperatives of mass political struggle and organisation; their divorce from the 'controlling tensions of a direct or active relationship to a proletarian audience'; their distance from 'popular practice' and their continuing subjection to the dominance of bourgeois thought. This had resulted, he argued, in a general disengagement from the classical themes and problems of the mature Marx and of Marxism. The over-preoccupation with the ideological could be taken as an eloquent sign of this.

There is much to this argument – as those who have survived the theoreticist deluge in 'Western Marxism' in recent years will testify. The emphases of 'Western Marxism' may well account for *the way* the problem of ideology was constructed, *how* the debate has been conducted and *the degree* to which it has been abstracted into the high realms of speculative theory. But I think we must reject any implication that, but for the distortions produced by 'Western Marxism', Marxist theory could have comfortably proceeded on its appointed path, following the established agenda: leaving the problem of ideology to its subordinate, second-order place. The rise to visibility of the problem of ideology has a more objective basis. First, the real developments which have taken place in the means by which mass consciousness is shaped and transformed – the massive growth of the 'cultural industries'. Second, the troubling questions of the 'consent' of the mass of the working class to the system in advanced capitalist societies in Europe and thus their partial stabilization, against all expectations. Of course, 'consent' is *not* maintained through the mechanisms of ideology alone. But the two cannot be divorced. It also reflects certain real theoretical weaknesses in the original Marxist formulations about ideology. And it throws light on some of the most critical issues in political strategy and the politics of the socialist movement in advanced capitalist societies.

In briefly reviewing some of these questions, I want to foreground, not so much the theory as the *problem* of ideology. The *problem* of ideology is to give an account, within a materialist theory, of how social ideas arise. We need to understand what their role is in a particular social formation, so as to inform the struggle to change society and open the road towards a socialist transformation of society. By ideology I mean the mental frameworks — the languages, the concepts, categories, imagery of thought, and the systems of representation — which different classes and social groups deploy in order to make sense of, define, figure out and render intelligible the way society works.

The problem of ideology, therefore, concerns the ways in which ideas of different kinds grip the minds of masses, and thereby become a 'material force'. In this, more politicized, perspective, the theory of ideology helps us to analyse how a particular set of ideas comes to dominate the social thinking of a historical bloc, in Gramsci's sense; and, thus, helps to unite such a bloc from the inside, and maintain its dominance and leadership over society as a whole. It has especially to do with the concepts and the languages of practical thought which stabilize a particular form of power and domination; or which reconcile and accomodate the mass of the people to their subordinate place in the social formation. It has also to do with the processes by which new forms of consciousness, new conceptions of the world, arise, which move the masses of the people into historical action against the prevailing system. These questions are at *stake* in a range of social struggles. It is to explain them, in order that we may better comprehend and master the terrain of ideological struggle, that we need not only a theory but a theory adequate to the complexities of what we are trying to explain.

No such theory exists, fully prepackaged, in Marx and Engels's works. Marx developed no general explanation of how social ideas worked, comparable to his historico-theoretical work on the economic forms and relations of the capitalist mode of production. His remarks in this area were never intended to have a 'law-like' status. And, mistaking them for statements of that more fully theorized kind, may well be where the problem of ideology for Marxism first began. In fact, his theorizing on this subject was much more *ad hoc*. There are consequently severe fluctuations in Marx's usage of the term. In our time – as you will see in the definition I offered above – the term 'ideology' has come to have a wider, more descriptive, less systematic reference, than it did in the classical Marxist texts. We *now* use it to refer to *all* organised forms of social thinking. This leaves open the degree and nature of its 'distortions'. It certainly refers to the domain of practical thinking and reasoning (the form, after all, in which most ideas are likely to grip the minds of the masses and draw them into action), rather than simply to well-elaborated and internally consistent 'systems of thought'. We mean the practical as well as the theoretical knowledges which enable people to 'figure out' society, and within whose categories and discourses we 'live out' and 'experience' our objective positioning in social relations.

Marx did, on many occasions, use the term 'ideology', practically, in this way. So its usage with this meaning *is* in fact sanctioned by his work.

Thus, for example, he spoke in a famous passage of the 'ideological forms in which men become conscious of ... conflict and fight it out'.[1] In *Capital* he frequently, in asides, addresses the 'everyday consciousness' of the capitalist entrepreneur; or the 'common sense of capitalism'. By this he means the forms of spontaneous thought within which the capitalist represents to himself the workings of the capitalist system and 'lives out' (i.e. genuinely experiences) his practical relations to it. Indeed, there are already clues there to the subsequent uses of the term which many, I suspect, do not believe could be warranted from Marx's own work. For example, the spontaneous forms of 'practical bourgeois consciousness' are real, but they cannot be *adequate* forms of thought, since there are aspects of the capitalist system – the generation of surplus value, for example – which simply cannot be 'thought' or explained, using those vulgar categories. On the other hand, they can't be *false* in any simple sense either, since these practical bourgeois men seem capable enough of making profit, working the system, sustaining its relations, exploiting labour, without benefit of a more sophisticated or 'truer' understanding of what they are involved in. To take another example, it is a fair deduction from what Marx said, that the *same* sets of relations – the capitalist circuit – can be represented in several *different ways* or (as the modern school would say) *represented within different systems of discourse.*

To name but three – there is the discourse of 'bourgeois common sense'; the sophisticated theories of the classical political economists, like Ricardo, from whom Marx learned so much; and, of course, Marx's own theoretical discourse – the discourse of *Capital* itself.

As soon as we divorce ourselves from a religious and doctrinal reading of Marx, therefore, the openings between many of the classical uses of the term, and its more recent elaborations, are not as closed as current theoreticist polemics would lead us to believe.

Nevertheless, the fact is that Marx most often used 'ideology' to refer specifically to the manifestations of bourgeois thought; and above all to its negative and distorted features. Also, he tended to employ it – in, for example, *The German Ideology*, the joint work of Marx and Engels – in contestation against what he thought were incorrect ideas: often, of a well-informed and systematic kind (what we would *now* call 'theoretical ideologies', or, following Gramsci, 'philosophies'; as opposed to the categories of practical consciousness, or what Gramsci called 'common sense'). Marx used the term as a critical weapon against the speculative mysteries of Hegelianism; against religion and the critique of religion; against idealist philosophy, and political economy of the vulgar and degenerated varieties. In *The German Ideology* and *The Poverty of Philosophy* Marx and

Engels were combatting bourgeois ideas. They were contesting the anti-materialist philosophy which underpinned the dominance of those ideas. In order to make their polemical point, they simplified many of their formulations. Our subsequent problems have arisen, in part, from treating these polemical inversions as the basis for a labour of *positive* general theorizing.

Within that broad framework of usage, Marx advances certain more fully elaborated theses, which have come to form the theoretical basis of the theory in its so-called classical form. First the materialist premiss: ideas arise from and reflect the material conditions and circumstances in which they are generated. They express social relations and their contradictions in thought. The notion that ideas provide the motor of history, or proceed independent of material relations and generate their own autonomous effects is, specifically, what is declared as speculative, and illusory about bourgeois ideology. Second, the thesis of determinateness: ideas are only the dependent effects of the ultimately determining level in the social formation – the economic in the last instance. So that transformations in the latter will show up, sooner or later, as corresponding modifications in the former. Thirdly, the fixed correspondences between dominance in the socio-economic sphere and the ideological: 'ruling ideas' are the ideas of the 'ruling class' – the class position of the latter providing the coupling and the guarantee of correspondence with the former.

The critique of the classical theory has been addressed precisely to these propositions. To say that ideas are 'mere reflexes' establishes their materialism but leaves them without specific effects; a realm of pure dependency. To say that ideas are determined 'in the last instance' by the economic is to set out along the economic reductionist road. Ultimately, ideas can be reduced to the essence of their truth – their economic content. The only stopping point before this ultimate reductionism arises through the attempt to delay it a little and preserve some space for manoeuvre by increasing the number of 'mediations'. To say that the 'ruling-ness' of a class is the guarantee of the dominance of certain ideas is to ascribe them as the exclusive property of that class, and to define particular forms of consciousness as class-specific.

It should be noted that, though these criticisms are directly addressed to formulations concerning the problem of ideology, they in effect recapitulate the substance of the more general and wide-ranging criticisms advanced against classical Marxism itself: its rigid structural determinacy, its reductionism of two varieties – class and economic; its way of conceptualising the social formation itself. Marx's model of ideology has been criticised because it did not conceptualise the social formation as a determinate complex formation, composed of different practices, but as a *simple* (or, as Althusser called it in *For Marx* and *Reading Capital*, an 'expressive') structure. By this Althusser meant that one practice – 'the economic' – determines in a direct manner all others, and each effect is simply and simultaneously reproduced correspondingly (i.e. 'expressed') on all the other levels.

Those who know the literature and the debates will easily identify the main lines of the more specific revisions advanced, from different sides, against these positions. They begin with the denial that any such simple correspondences exist, or that the 'superstructures' are totally devoid of their own specific effects, in Engels's gloss on 'what Marx thought' (especially in the later correspondence). The glosses by Engels are immensely fruitful, suggestive and generative. They provide, not the solution to the problem of ideology, but the starting point of all serious reflection on the problem. The simplifications developed, he argued, because Marx was in contestation with the speculative idealism of his day. They were one-sided distortions, the necessary exaggerations of polemic. The criticisms lead on through the richly tapestried efforts of Marxist theorists like Lukács to hold, polemically, to the strict orthodoxy of a particular 'Hegelian' reading of Marx, while in practice introducing a whole range of 'mediating and intermediary factors' which soften and displace the drive towards reductionism and economism implicit in some of Marx's original formulations. They include Gramsci – but from another direction – whose contribution will be discussed at a later place in the argument. They culminate in the highly sophisticated theoretical interventions of Althusser and the Althussereans: their contestation of economic and class reductionism and of the 'expressive totality' approach.

Althusser's revisions (in *For Marx* and, especially, in the 'Ideological State Apparatuses' chapter of *Lenin and Philosophy and Other Essays*) sponsored a decisive move away from the 'distorted ideas' and 'false consciousness' approach to ideology. It opened the gate to a more linguistic or 'discursive' conception of ideology. It put on the agenda the whole neglected issue of how ideology becomes internalized, how we come to speak 'spontaneously', within the limits of the categories of thought which exist outside us and which can more accurately be said to think us. (This is the so-called problem of the interpellation of subjects at the centre of ideological discourse. It led to the subsequent bringing into Marxism of the psychoanalytic interpretations of how individuals enter into the ideological categories of language at all). In insisting (e.g. in 'Ideological State Apparatuses') on the *function* of ideology in the reproduction of social relations of production and (in *Essays in Self-Criticism*) on the metaphorical utility of the base-superstructure metaphor, Althusser attempted some last-hour regrouping on the classical Marxist terrain.

But his first revision was too 'functionalist'. If the function of ideology is to 'reproduce' capitalist social relations according to the 'requirements' of the system, how does one account for subversive ideas or for ideological struggle? And the second was too 'orthodox'. It was Althusser who had displaced so thoroughly the 'base/superstructure' metaphor! In fact, the doors he opened provided precisely the exit points through which many abandoned the problematic of the classical Marxist theory of ideology altogether. They gave up, not only Marx's particular way in *The German Ideology* of coupling 'ruling class and ruling ideas', but the very preoccupations with the class structuring of ideology, and its role in the generation and maintenance of hegemony.

Discourse and psychoanalytic theories, originally conceived as theoretical supports to the critical work of theory revision and development, provided instead categories which substituted for those of the earlier paradigm. Thus, the very real gaps and lucunae in the 'objective' thrust of the Marxist theory, around the modalities of consciousness and the 'subjectification' of ideologies, which Althusser's use of the terms 'interpellation' (borrowed from Freud) and 'positioning' (borrowed from Lacan) were intended to address, became themselves the exclusive object of the exercise. The *only* problem about ideology was the problem of how ideological subjects were formed through the psychoanalytic processes. The theoretical tensions were then untied. This is the long descent of 'revisionist' work on ideology, which leads ultimately (in Foucault) to the abolition of the category of 'ideology' altogether. Yet its highly sophisticated theorists, for reasons quite obscure, continue to insist that their theories are 'really' materialist, political, historical, and so on: as if haunted by Marx's ghost still rattling around in the theoretical machine.

I have recapitulated this story in an immensely abbreviated form because I do not intend to engage in detail with its conjectures and refutations. Instead, I want to pick up their thread, acknowledging their force and cogency at least in modifying substantially the classical propositions about ideology, and, in the light of them, to reexamine some of the earlier formulations by Marx, and consider whether they can be refashioned and developed in the positive light of the criticisms advanced – as most good theories ought to be capable of – without losing some of the essential qualities and insights (what used to be called the 'rational core') which they originally possessed. Crudely speaking, that is because – as I hope to show – I acknowledge the immense force of many of the criticisms advanced. But I am not convinced that they wholly and entirely abolish every useful insight, every essential starting point, in a materialist theory of ideology. If, according to the fashionable canon, all that is left, in the light of the devastatingly advanced, clever and cogent critiques, is the labour of perpetual 'deconstruction', this essay is devoted to a little modest work of 'reconstruction' – without, I hope, being too defaced by ritual orthodoxy.

Take, for example, the extremely tricky ground of the 'distortions' of ideology, and the question of 'false consciousness'. Now it is not difficult to see why these kinds of formulations have brought Marx's critics bearing down on him. 'Distortions' opens immediately the question as to why some people — those living their relation to their conditions of existence through the categories of a distorted ideology – cannot recognise that it is distorted, while we, with our superior wisdom, or armed with properly formed concepts, can. Are the 'distortions' simply falsehoods? Are they deliberately sponsored falsifications? If so, by whom? Does ideology really function like conscious class propaganda? And if ideology is the product or function of 'the structure' rather than of a group of conspirators, how *does* an economic *structure* generate a guaranteed set of ideological effects? The terms are, clearly, unhelpful as they stand. They make both the masses and the capitalists look like judgemental dopes. They also entail a peculiar view of the formation of alternative forms of consciousness. Presumably, they arise as scales fall from peoples eyes or as they wake up, as if from a dream, and, all at once, see the light, glance directly through the transparency of things immediately to their essential truth, their concealed structural processes. This is an account of the development of working class consciousness founded on the rather surprising model of St Paul and the Damascus Road.

Let us undertake a little excavation work of our own. Marx did not assume that, because Hegel was the summit of speculative bourgeois thought, and because the 'Hegelians' vulgarized and etherealized his thought, that Hegel was therefore not a thinker to be reckoned with, a figure worth learning from. More so with classical political economy, from Smith to Ricardo, where again the distinctions between different levels of an ideological formation are important. There is classical political economy which Marx calls 'scientific'; its vulgarisers engaged in 'mere apologetics'; and the 'everyday consciousness' in which practical bourgeois entrepreneurs calculate their odds informed by, but utterly unconscious (until Thatcherism appeared) of, Ricardo's or Adam Smith's advanced thoughts on the subject. Even more instructive is Marx's insistence that (a) classical political economy *was* a powerful, substantial scientific body of work, which (b) *nevertheless*, contained an essential ideological limit, a distortion. This distortion was not, according to Marx, anything directly to do with technical errors or absences in their argument, but with a broader prohibition. Specifically, the distorted or ideological features arose from the fact that they *assumed* the categories of bourgeois political economy as the foundations of all economic calculation, refusing to see the historical determinacy of their starting-points and premises; and, at the other end, from the assumption that, with capitalist production, economic development had achieved, not simply its highest point to date (Marx agreed with that), but its final conclusion and apogee. There could be no new forms of economic relations after it. Its forms and relations would go on forever. The distortions, to be precise, within bourgeois theoretical ideology at its more 'scientific' were, nevertheless, real and substantial. They did not destroy many aspects of its scientific validity – hence it was not 'false' simply because it was confined within the limits and horizon of bourgeois thought. On the other hand, the distortions limited its scientific validity, its capacity to advance beyond certain points, its ability to resolve its own internal contradictions, its power to think outside the skin of the social relations reflected in it.

Now this relation between Marx and the classical political economists represents a far more complex way of posing the relation between 'truth' and 'falsehood' *inside* a so-called scientific mode of thought, than many of Marx's critics have assumed. Indeed, critical theorists, in their search for greater theoretical vigour, an absolute divide between 'science' and 'ideology' and a clean epistemological break between 'bourgeois' and 'non-bourgeois' ideas, have done much themselves to simplify the relations which Marx, not so much argued, as established in practice (i.e. in terms of how he actually used classical political economy as both a support and adversary). We can rename the specific 'distortions', of which Marx accused political economy, to remind us later of their general

                    Stuart Hall

applicability. Marx called them the *eternalization* of relations which are in fact historically specific; and the *naturalization* effect – treating what are the products of a specific historical development as if universally valid, and arising not through historical processes but, as it were, from Nature itself.

We can consider one of the most contested points – the 'falseness' or distortions of ideology, from another standpoint. It is well known that Marx attributed the spontaneous categories of vulgar bourgeois thought to its grounding in the 'surface forms' of the capitalist circuit. Specifically, Marx identified the importance of the market and market exchange, where things were sold and profits made. This approach, as Marx argued, left aside the critical domain – the 'hidden abode' – of capitalist production itself. Some of his most important formulations flow from this argument.

In summary, the argument is as follows. Market exchange is what appears to govern and regulate economic processes under capitalism. Market relations are sustained by a number of elements and these appear (are represented) in every discourse which tries to explain the capitalist circuit from this standpoint. The market brings together, under conditions of equal exchange, consumers and producers who do not – and need not, given the market's 'hidden hand' – know one another. Similarly, the *labour* market brings together those who have something to sell (labour power) and those who have something to buy with (wages): a 'fair price' is struck. Since the market works, as it were, by magic, harmonizing needs and their satisfaction 'blindly', there is no compulsion about it. We can 'choose' to buy and sell, or not (and presumably take the consequences: though this part is *not* so well represented in the discourses of the market, which are more elaborated on the *positive* side of market-choice than they are on its *negative* consequences). Buyer or seller need not be driven by goodwill, or love of his neighbour or fellow-feeling to succeed in the market game. In fact, the market works best if each party to the transaction consults only his or her self-interest directly. It is a system driven by the real and practical imperatives of self-interest. Yet it achieves satisfaction of a kind, all round. The capitalist hires his labour and makes his profit; the landlord lets his property and gets a rent; the worker gets her wages and thus can buy the goods she needs.

Now market-exchange also 'appears' in a rather different sense. It is the part of the capitalist circuit which everyone can plainly *see*, the bit we all experience daily. Without buying and selling, in a money economy, we would all physically and socially come to a halt very quickly. Unless we are deeply involved in other aspects of the capitalist process, we would not necessarily know much about the other parts of the circuit which are necessary if capital is to be valorized and if the whole process is to reproduce itself and expand. And yet, unless commodities are produced there is nothing to sell; and – Marx argued, at any rate – it is first in production itself that labour is exploited. Whereas the kind of 'exploitation' which a market-ideology is best able to see and grasp is 'profiteering' – taking too big a rake-off on the market price. So the market is the part of the system which is universally encountered and experienced. It is the obvious, the visible part: the part which constantly *appears*.

Now, if you extrapolate from this generative set of categories, based on market exchange, it is possible to extend it to other spheres of social life, and to see them as, also, constituted on a similar model. And this is precisely what Marx, in a justly famous passage, suggests happens:

This sphere that we are deserting, within whose boundaries the sale and purchase power of labour-power goes on, is in fact a very Eden of the innate rights of man. There alone rule Freedom, Equality, Property and Bentham. Freedom, because both buyer and seller of a commodity, say of labour-power, are constrained only by their own free will. They contract as free agents, and the agreement they come to, is but the form in which they give legal expression to their common will. Equality, because each enters into relation with the other, as with a simple owner of commodities, and they exchange equivalent for equivalent. Property, because each disposes only of what is his own. And Bentham, because each looks only to himself. The only force that brings them together and puts them in relation with each other, is the selfishness, the gain and the private interests of each.[2]

In short, our ideas of 'Freedom', 'Equality', 'Property' and 'Bentham' (i.e. Individualism') — the ruling ideological principles of the bourgeois lexicon, and the key political themes which, in our time, have made a powerful and compelling return to the ideological stage under the auspices of Mrs Thatcher and neo-liberalism — may derive from the categories we use in our practical, common sense thinking about the market economy. This is how there arises, out of daily, mundane experience the powerful categories of bourgeois legal, political, social and philosophical thought.

This is a critical *locus classicus* of the debate; from this Marx extrapolated several of the theses which have come to form the contested territory of the theory of ideology. First, he establishes as a *source* of 'ideas' a particular point or moment of the economic circuit of capital. Second, he demonstrates how the translation from the economic to ideological categories can be effected; from the 'market exchange of equivalents' to the bourgeois notions of 'Freedom' and 'Equality'; from the fact that each must possess the means of exchange to the legal categories of property rights. Third, he defines in a more precise manner what he means by 'distortion'. For this 'taking off' from the exchange point of the recircuit of capital is an ideological process. It 'obscures, hides, conceals' — the terms are all in the text — another set of relations: the relations, which do *not* appear on the surface but are concealed in the 'hidden abode' of production (where property, ownership, the exploitation of waged labour and the expropriation of surplus value all take place). The ideological categories 'hide' this underlying reality, and *substitute* for all that the 'truth' of market relations. In many ways, then, the passage contains all the so-called cardinal sins of the classical Marxist theory of ideology rolled into one: economic reductionism, a too simple correspondence between the economic and the political ideological; the true v. false, real v. distortion, 'true' consciousness v. false consciousness distinctions.

However, it also seems to me possible to 're-read' the passage from the standpoint of many contemporary critiques in such a way as (a) to retain many of the profound insights of the original, while (b) expanding it, using some of the theories of ideology developed in more recent times.

Capitalist production is defined in Marx's terms as a circuit. This circuit explains not only production and consumption, but *re*production – the ways in which the conditions for keeping the circuit moving are sustained. Each moment is vital to the generation and realization of value. Each establishes certain determinate conditions for the other – that is, each is dependent on or determinate for the other. Thus, if some part of what is realized through sale is not paid as wages to labour, labour cannot reproduce itself, physically and socially, to work and buy again another day. Thus 'production', too, is dependent on 'consumption'; even though in the analysis Marx tends to insist on the prior analytic value to be accorded to the relations of *production*. (This in itself has had serious consequences, since it has led Marxists not only to prioritize 'production' but to argue as if the moments of 'consumption and exchange' are of no value or importance to the theory – a fatal, one-side productivist reading).

Now this circuit can be construed, ideologically, in different ways. This is something which modern theorists of ideology insist on, as against the vulgar conception of ideology as arising from a fixed and unalterable relation between the economic relation and how it is 'expressed' or represented in ideas. Modern theorists have tended to arrive at this break with a simple notion of economic determinacy over ideology through their borrowing from recent work on the nature of language and discourse. Language is the medium *par excellence* through which things are 'represented' in thought and thus the medium in which ideology is generated and transformed. But in language, the same social relation can be *differently* represented and construed. And this is so, they would argue, because language by its nature is *not fixed* in a one-to-one relation to its referent but is 'multi-referential': it can construct different meanings around what is apparently the same social relation or phenomenon.

It may or may not be the case, that, in the passage under discussion, Marx is using a fixed, determinate and unalterable relationship between market exchange and how it is appropriated in thought. But you will see from what I have said that I do not believe this to be so. As I understand it, 'the market' means one thing in vulgar bourgeois political economy and the spontaneous consciousness of practical bourgeois men, and quite another thing in Marxist economic analysis. So my argument would be that, implicitly, Marx is saying that, in a world where markets exist and market exchange dominates economic life, it would be distinctly odd if there were no *category* allowing us to think, speak and act in relation to it. In *that* sense, all economic categories – bourgeois or Marxist – express existing social relations. But I think it *also* follows from the argument that market relations are not always represented by the same categories of thought.

There is no fixed and unalterable relation between what the market is, and how it is construed within an ideological or explanatory framework. We could even say that one of the purposes of *Capital* is precisely to *displace* the discourse of bourgeois political economy – the discourse in which the market is most usually and obviously understood – and to replace it with another discourse, that of the market as it fits into the Marxist schema. If the point is not pressed too literally, therefore, the two kinds of approaches to the understanding of ideology are not totally contradictory.

What, then, about the 'distortions' of bourgeois political economy as an ideology? One way of reading this is to think that, since Marx calls bourgeois political economy 'distorted', it must be *false*. Thus those who live their relation to economic life exclusively within its categories of thought and experience are, by definition, in 'false consciousness'. Again, we must be on our guard here about arguments too easily won. For one thing, Marx makes an important distinction between 'vulgar' versions of political economy and more advanced versions, like that of Ricardo, which he says clearly, 'has scientific value'. But, still, what can he mean by 'false' and 'distorted' in this context?

He cannot mean that 'the market' does not exist. In fact, it is *all too real*. It is the very life-blood of capitalism, from one viewpoint. Without it capitalism would never have broken through the framework of feudalism; and without its ceaseless continuation, the circuits of capital would come to a sudden and disastrous halt. I think we can only make sense of these terms if we think of giving an account of an economic circuit, which consists of several interconnected moments, from the vantage point of *one* of those moments alone. If, in our explanation, we privilege one moment only, and do not take account of the differentiated whole or 'ensemble' of which it is a part; or if we use categories of thought, appropriate to one such moment alone, to explain the whole process; then we are in danger of giving what Marx would have called (after Hegel) a 'one-sided' account.

One-sided explanations are always a distortion. Not in the sense that they are a lie about the system, but in the sense that a 'half-truth' cannot be the whole truth about anything. With those ideas, you will always represent a part of the whole. You will thereby produce an explanation which is only *partially* adequate – and in that sense, 'false'. Also, if you use only 'market categories and concepts' to understand the capitalist circuit as a whole, there are literally many aspects of it which you cannot see. In that sense, the categories of market exchange obscure and mystify our understanding of the capitalist process: that is they do not enable us to see or formulate questions about them, for they render other aspects invisible.

Is the worker who lives his or her relation to the circuits of capitalist production exclusively through the categories of a 'fair price' and a 'fair wage', in 'false consciousness'? Yes, if by that we mean there is something about her situation which she cannot grasp with the categories she is using; something about the process as a whole which is systematically hidden because the available concepts only give her a grasp of one of its many-sided moments. No, if by that we mean that she is utterly deluded about what goes on under capitalism.

The falseness therefore arises, not from the fact that the market is an illusion, a trick, a sleight-of-hand, but only in the sense that it is an *inadequate* explanation of a process. It has also substituted one part of the process for the whole – a procedure which, in linguistics, is known as 'metonymy' and in anthropology, psychoanalysis and (with special meaning) in Marx's work, as *fetishism*. The other 'lost' moments of the circuit are, however, unconscious, not in the Freudian sense, because they have been repressed from consciousness, but in the sense of being invisible, given the concepts and categories we are using.

This also helps to explain the otherwise extremely confusing terminology in *Capital*, concerning what 'appears on the surface' (which is sometimes said to be 'merely phenomenal': i.e. not very important, not the real thing); and what lies 'hidden beneath', and is embedded in the structure, not lying about the surface. It is crucial to see, however – as the market exchange/production example makes clear – that 'surface' and 'phenomenal' do not mean false or illusory, in the ordinary sense of the words. The market is no more or less 'real' than other aspects – production for example. In Marx's terms production is only where, analytically, we ought to start the analysis of the circuit: 'the act through which the whole process again runs its course'.[3] But production is not independent of the circuit, since profits made and labour hired in the market must flow back into production. So, 'real' expresses only some theoretical primacy which Marxist analysis gives to production. In any other sense, market exchange is as much a real process materially, and an absolutely 'real' requirement of the system – as any other part: they are all 'moments of one process'.[4]

There is also a problem about 'appearance' and 'surface' as terms. Appearances may connote something which is 'false': surface forms do not seem to run as deep as 'deep structures'. These linguistic connotations have the unfortunate effect of making us rank the different moments in terms of their being more/less real, more/less important. But from another viewpoint, what is on the surface, what constantly appears, is what we are always seeing, what we encounter daily, what we come to take for granted as the obvious and manifest form of the process. It is not surprising, then, that we come spontaneously to *think* of the capitalist system in terms of the bits of it which constantly engage us, and which so manifestly announce their presence. What chance does the extraction of 'surplus labour' have, as a concept, as against the hard fact of wages in the pocket, savings in the bank, pennies in the slot, money in the till. Even the nineteenth century economist, Nassau Senior, couldn't actually put his hand on the hour in the day when the worker worked for the surplus and not to replace his or her own subsistence.

In a world saturated by money exchange, and everywhere mediated by money, the 'market' experience is *the* most immediate, daily and universal experience of the economic system for everyone. It is therefore not surprising that we take the market for granted, do not question what makes it possible, what it is founded or premissed on. It should not surprise us if the mass of working people don't possess the concepts with which to cut into the process at another point, frame another set of questions, and bring to the surface or reveal what the overwhelming facticity of the market constantly renders invisible. It is clear why we should generate, out of these fundamental categories for which we have found everyday words, phrases and idiomatic expressions in practical consciousness, the *model* of other social and political relations. After all, they too belong to the same system and appear to work according to its protocols. Thus we see, in the 'free choice' of the market, the material symbol of the more abstract freedoms; or in the self-interest and intrinsic competitiveness of market advantage the 'representation' of something natural, normal and universal about human nature itself.

Let me now draw some tentative conclusions from the 're-reading' I have offered about the meaning of Marx's passage in the light of more recent critiques and the new theories advanced.

The analysis is no longer organized around the distinction between the 'real' and the 'false'. The obscuring or mystifying effects of ideology are no longer seen as the product of a trick or magical illusion. Nor are they simply attributed to false consciousness, in which our poor, benighted, untheoretical proletarians are forever immured. The relations in which people exist are the 'real relations' which the categories and concepts they use help them to grasp and articulate in thought. But – and here we may be on a route contrary to emphasis from that with which 'materialism' is usually associated – the economic relations themselves cannot prescribe a single, fixed and unalterable way of conceptualizing it. It can be 'expressed' within different ideological discourses. What's more, these discourses can employ the conceptual model and transpose it into other, more strictly 'ideological', domains. For example, it can develop a discourse – e.g. latter-day Monetarism – which deduces the grand value of 'Freedom' from the freedom from compulsion which brings men and women, once again, every working day, into the labour market. We have also by-passed the distinction 'true' and 'false', replacing them with other, more accurate terms: like 'partial' and 'adequate', or 'one-sided' and 'in its differentiated totality'. To say that a theoretical discourse allows us to grasp a concrete relation 'in thought' adequately means that the discourse provides us with a more complete grasp of all the different relations of which that relation is composed, and of the many determinations which form its conditions of existence. It means that our grasp is concrete and whole, rather than a thin, one-sided abstraction. One-sided explanations, which are partial, part-for-the-whole, types of explanation, and which allow us only to abstract one element out (the market, for example) and explain that are inadequate *precisely on those grounds*. For that reason alone, they may be considered 'false'. Though, strictly speaking, the term is misleading if what we have in mind is some simple, all-or-nothing distinction between the True and the False, or between Science and Ideology. Fortunately or unfortunately, social explanations rarely fall into such neat pigeonholes.

In our 're-reading', we have also attempted to take on board a number of secondary propositions, derived from the more recent theorizing about 'ideology' in an effort to see how incompatible they are with Marx's formulation. As we have seen, the explanation relates to concepts, ideas, terminology, categories, perhaps also images and symbols (money; the wage packet; freedom) which allow us to grasp some aspect of a social process *in thought*. These enable us to represent to ourselves and to others how the system works, why it functions as it does.

The same process – capitalist production and exchange – can

be expressed within a different ideological framework, by the use of different 'systems of representation'. There is the discourse of 'the market', the discourse of 'production', the discourse of 'the circuits': each produces a different definition of the system. Each also locates us differently – as worker, capitalist, wage worker, wage slave, producer, consumer, etc. Each thus *situates us* as social actors or as a member of a social group in a particular relation to the process and prescribes certain social identities for us. The ideological categories in use, in other words, *position us* in relation to the account of the process as depicted in the discourse. The worker who relates to his or her condition of existence in the capitalist process as 'consumer' – who enters the system, so to speak, through that gateway – participates in the process by way of a different practice from those who are inscribed in the system as 'skilled labourer' – or not inscribed in it at all, as 'housewife'. All these inscriptions have effects which are real. They make a material difference, since how we act in certain situations depends on what our definitions of the situation are.

I believe that a similar kind of 're-reading' can be made in relation to another set of propositions about ideology which has in recent years been vigorously contested: namely, the class-determination of ideas and the direct correspondences between 'ruling ideas' and 'ruling classes'. Laclau has demonstrated definitively (in *Politics and Ideology in Marxist Theory*, NLB, 1977) the untenable nature of the proposition that classes, as such, are the subjects of fixed and ascribed class ideologies. He has also dismantled the proposition that particular ideas and concepts 'belong' exclusively to one particular class. He demonstrates, with considerable effect, the failure of any social formation to correspond to this picture of ascribed class ideologies. He argues cogently why the notion of particular ideas being fixed permanently to a particular class is antithetical to what we now know about the very nature of language and discourse. Ideas and concepts do not occur, in language or thought, in that single, isolated, way with their content and reference irremovably fixed. Language in its widest sense is the vehicle of practical reasoning, calculation and consciousness, because of the ways by which certain meanings and references have been historically secured. But its cogency depends on the 'logics' which connect one proposition to another in a chain of connected meanings; where the social connotations and historical meaning are condensed and reverberate off one another. Moreover, these chains are never permanently secured, either in their internal systems of meanings, or in terms of the social classes and groups to which they 'belong'. Otherwise, the notion of ideological struggle and the transformations of consciousness – questions central to the politics of any Marxist project – would be an empty sham, the dance of dead rhetorical figures.

It is precisely because language, the medium of thought and ideological calculation, is 'multi-accentual', as Volosinov put it, that the field of the ideological is always a field of 'intersecting accents' and the 'intersecting of differently oriented social interests':

> Thus various different classes will use one and the same language. As a result differently orientated accents intersect in every ideological sign. Sign becomes the arena of the class struggle ... A sign that has been withdrawn from the pressures of the social struggle – which, so to speak, crosses beyond the pale of class struggle, inevitably loses force, degenerating into allegory and becoming the object not of live social intelligibility but of philological comprehension.[5]

This approach replaces the notion of fixed ideological meanings and class-ascribed ideologies with the concepts of ideological terrains of struggle and the task of ideological transformation. It is the general movement in this direction, away from an abstract general theory of ideology, and towards the more concrete analysis of how, in particular historical situations, ideas 'organise human masses, and create the terrain on which men move, acquire consciousness of their position, struggle, etc',[6] which makes the work of Gramsci (from whom that quotation is taken) a figure of seminal importance in the development of Marxist thinking in the domain of the ideological.

One of the consequences of this kind of revisionist work has often been to destroy altogether the *problem* of the class structuring of ideology and the ways in which ideology intervenes in social struggles. Often this approach replaces the inadequate notions of ideologies ascribed in blocks to classes with an equally unsatisfactory 'discursive' notion which implies total free floatingness of all ideological elements and discourses. The image of great, immovable class battalions heaving their ascribed ideological luggage about the field of struggle, with their ideological number-plates on their backs, as Poulantzas once put it, is replaced here by the infinity of subtle variations through which the elements of a discourse appears spontaneously to combine and recombine with each other, without material constraints of any kind other than that provided by the discursive operations themselves.

Now it is perfectly correct to suggest that the concept 'democracy' does not have a totally fixed meaning, which can be ascribed exclusively to the discourse of bourgeois forms of political representation. 'Democracy' in the discourse of the 'Free West' does not carry the same meaning as it does when we speak of 'popular-democratic' struggle or of deepening the democratic content of political life. We cannot allow the term to be wholly expropriated into the discourse of the Right. Instead, we need to develop a strategic contestation around the concept itself. Of course, this is no mere 'discursive' operation. Powerful symbols and slogans of that kind, with a powerfully positive political charge, do not swing about from side to side in language or ideological representation alone. The expropriation of the concept has to be contested through the development of a series of polemics, through the conduct of particular forms of ideological struggle: to detach one meaning of the concept from the domain of public consciousness and supplant it within the logic of another political discourse. Gramsci argued precisely that ideological struggle does not take place by displacing one whole, integral, class-mode of thought with another wholly-formed system of ideas:

what matters is the criticism to which such an ideological complex is subjected by the first representatives of the new historical phase. This criticism makes possible a process of differentiation and change in the relative weight that the elements of the old ideological used to possess. What was previously secondary and subordinate, or even incidental, is now taken to be primary – becomes the nucleus of a new ideological and theoretical complex. The old collective will dissolves into its contradictory elements since the subordinate ones develop socially, etc.[7]

In short, his is a 'war of position' conception of ideological struggle. It also means articulating the different conceptions of 'democracy' within a whole chain of associated ideas. And it means articulating this process of ideological de-construction and re-construction to a set of organised political positions, and to a particular set of social forces. Ideologies do not become effective as a material force because they emanate from the needs of fully-formed social classes. But the reverse is also true – though it puts the relationship between ideas and social forces the opposite way round. No ideological conception can ever become materially effective unless and until it *can be* articulated to the field of political and social forces and to the struggles between different forces at stake.

Certainly, it is not necessarily a form of vulgar materialism to say that, though we cannot ascribe ideas to class position in certain fixed combinations, ideas *do* arise from and *may reflect* the material conditions in which social groups and classes exist. In that sense – i.e. historically – there may well be certain *tendential alignments* – between, say, those who stand in a 'corner shop' relation to the processes of modern capitalist development, and the fact that they may therefore be predisposed to imagine that the whole advanced economy of capitalism can be conceptualized in this 'corner shop' way. I think this is what Marx meant in the *Eighteenth Brumaire* when he said that it was not necessary for people actually to make their living as members of the old petty bourgeoisie for them to be attracted to petty bourgeois ideas. Nevertheless, there was, he suggested, some relationship, or tendency, between the objective position of that class fraction, and the limits and horizons of thought to which they would be 'spontaneously' attracted. This was a judgement about the 'characteristic forms of thought' appropriate as an ideal-type to certain positions in the social structure. It was definitely not a simple equation in actual historical reality between class position and ideas. The point about 'tendential historical relations' is that there is nothing inevitable, necessary or fixed forever about them. The tendential lines of forces define only the *giveness* of the historical terrain.

They indicate how the terrain has been structured, historically. Thus it is perfectly possible for the idea of 'the nation' to be given a progressive meaning and connotation, embodying a national – popular collective will, as Gramsci argued. Nevertheless, in a society like Britain, the idea of 'nation' has been consistently articulated towards the right. Ideas of 'national identity' and 'national greatness' are intimately bound up with imperial supremacy, tinged with racist connotations, and underpinned by a four-century long history of colonisation, world market supremacy, imperial expansion and global destiny over native peoples. It is therefore much more difficult to give the notion of 'Britain' a socially radical or democratic reference. These associations are not given for all time. But they are difficult to break because the ideological terrain of this particular social formation has been so powerfully structured in that way by its previous history. These historical connections define the ways in which the ideological terrain of a particular society has been mapped out. They are the 'traces' which Gramsci mentioned: the 'stratified deposits in popular philosophy',[8] which no longer have an inventory, but which establish and define the fields along which ideological struggle is *likely* to move.

That terrain, Gramsci suggested, was above all the terrain of what he called 'common sense': a historical, not a natural or universal or spontaneous form of popular thinking, necessarily 'fragmentary, disjointed and episodic'. The 'subject' of common sense – is composed of very contradictory ideological formations – 'it contains Stone Age elements and principles of a more advanced science, prejudices from all past phases of history at the local level and intuitions of a future philosophy which will be that of a human race united the world over'.[9] And yet, because this network of pre-existing traces and common-sense elements constitutes the realm of practical thinking for the masses of the people, Gramsci insisted that it was precisely on this terrain that ideological struggle most frequently took place. 'Common sense' became one of the stakes over which ideological struggle is conducted. Ultimately, 'The relation between common sense and the upper level of philosophy is assured by "politics" ...'[10]

Ideas only become effective if they do, in the end, *connect* with a particular constellation of social forces. In that sense, ideological struggle is a part of the general social struggle for mastery and leadership – in short for hegemony. But 'hegemony' in Gramsci's sense requires, not the simple escalation of a whole class to power, with its fully formed 'philosophy', but the *process* by which a historical bloc of social forces is constructed and the ascendancy of that bloc secured. So the way we conceptualize the relationship between 'ruling ideas' and 'ruling classes' is best thought in terms of the processes of 'hegemonic domination'.

On the other hand, to abandon the question or problem of 'rule' – of hegemony, domination and authority – because the ways in which it was originally posed are unsatisfactory is to cast the baby out with the bath-water. Ruling ideas are not guaranteed their dominance by their already given coupling with ruling classes. Rather, the effective coupling of dominant ideas *to* the historical bloc which has acquired hegemonic power in a particular period is what the process of ideological struggle is *intended to secure*. It is the object of the exercise – not the playing out of an already written and concluded script.

It will be clear that, although the argument has been conducted in connection with the problem of ideology, it has much wider ramifications for the development of Marxist theory as a whole. The general question at issue is a particular conception of 'theory': theory as the working out of a set of guarantees. What is also at issue is a particular definition of 'determination'. It is clear from the 'reading' I offered earlier that the economic aspect of capitalist production processes has real limiting and constraining effects (i.e. determinancy), for the categories in which the circuits of production are *thought*, ideologically, and vice versa. The economic provides the repertoire of categories which will be used, in thought. What the economic cannot do is (a) to provide the *contents* of the particular thoughts of particular social classes or groups at any specific time; (b) to fix or guarantee for all time which ideas will be made use of by which classes. The determinancy of the economic for the ideological can, therefore, be only in terms of the former setting the limits for defining the terrain of operations, establishing the 'raw materials', of thought. Material circumstances are the net of constraints, the 'conditions of existence' for practical thought and calculation about society.

This is a different conception of 'determinancy' from that which is entailed by the normal sense of 'economic determinism', or by the expressive totality way of conceiving the relations between the different practices in a social formation. The relations between these different levels is, indeed, *determinate*: i.e. mutually determining. The structure of social practices – the ensemble – is therefore neither free floating or immaterial. But nor is it a transitive structure, in which its intelligibility lies exclusively in the one-way transmission of effects from base upwards. The economic *cannot* effect a final closure on the domain of ideology, in the strict sense of always guaranteeing a result. It cannot always secure a particular set of correspondences or always deliver particular modes of reasoning to particular classes according to their place within its system. This is precisely because (a) ideological categories are developed, generated and transformed according to their own laws of development and evolution; though, of course, they are generated *out* of given materials. It is also because (b) of the necessary 'openness' of historical development to practice and struggle. We have to acknowledge the real indeterminancy of the political – the level which condenses all the other levels of practice and secures their functioning in a particular system of power.

This relative openness or relative indeterminacy is necessary to Marxism itself as a theory. What is 'scientific' about the Marxist theory of politics is that it seeks to understand the limits to political action given by the terrain on which it operates. This terrain is defined, not by forces we can predict with the certainty of natural science, but by the existing balance of social forces, the specific nature of the concrete conjuncture. It is 'scientific' because it understands itself as determinate; and because it seeks to develop a practice which is theoretically informed. But it is *not* 'scientific' in the sense that political outcomes and the consequences of the conduct of political struggles are foreordained in the economic stars.

Understanding 'determinacy' in terms of setting of limits, the establishment of parameters, the defining of the space of operations, the concrete conditions of existence, the 'givenness' of social practices, rather than in terms of the absolute predictability of particular outcomes, is the only basis of a 'Marxism without final guarantees'. It establishes the *open horizon* of Marxist theorizing – determinacy without guaranteed closures. The paradigm of perfectly closed, perfectly predictable, systems of thought is religion or astrology, not science. It would be preferable, from this perspective, to think of the 'materialism' of Marxist theory in terms of 'determination by the economic in the *first* instance', since Marxism is surely correct, against all idealisms, to insist that no social practice or set of relations floats free of the determinate effects of the concrete relations in which they are located. However, 'determination in the last instance' has long been the repository of the lost dream or illusion of theoretical *certainty*. And this has been bought at considerable cost, since certainty stimulates orthodoxy, the frozen rituals and intonation of already witnessed truth, and all the other attributes of a theory that is incapable of fresh insights. It represents the end of the *process of theorizing*, of the development and refinement of new concepts and explanations which, alone, is the sign of a living body of thought, capable still of engaging and grasping something of the truth about new historical realities.

Notes

1. Marx, Preface to *A Contribution to the Critique of Political Economy*, Lawrence and Wishart, 1982, p. 21.
2. Marx, *Capital* Vol. 1., Lawrence and Wishart, p. 172.
3. Introduction to *Grundrisse*, Pelican 1973, p. 94.
4. *ibid.*, p. 94.
5. Volosinov, *Marxism and the Philosophy of Language*, Seminar Press, 1973, p. 23.
6. Antonio Gramsci, *Selections from The Prison Notebooks*, Lawrence and Wishart, p. 337.
7. *ibid.*, p. 195, quoted by Chantal Mouffe, in 'Hegemony and Ideology in Gramsci', *Gramsci and Marxist Theory*, ed. C. Mouffe, Routledge and Kegan Paul, 1979, p. 191.
8. Antonio Gramsci, *Selections from the Prison Notebooks*, Lawrence and Wishart, p. 324.
9. *ibid.*, p. 324.
10. *ibid.*, p. 331.

Alan Hunt

Marx – The Missing Dimension:
The Rise of Representative Democracy

I Introduction

The twentieth century, wracked by world wars, economic crisis, political and technological revolutions, has witnessed the significant persistence of representative democracy. It has provided the dominant political form for the most developed capitalist societies. Parliamentary or constitutional democracies have provided the basis of the political structure of, if not all, then the significant majority of the major Western powers.

The persistence of representative democracies has provided a challenge to Marxist socialists. The challenge is on two fronts: first to explain and understand the power of representative democracies and, second, to advance and implement political strategies for socialist advance which are founded upon and take account of this reality. It is my contention, that although important advances have been made, by and large Marxist socialists have not acquitted themselves well with respect to either of these challenges. Whilst each generation must accept the ultimate responsibility for its successes and failures, I want in this essay to argue that a significant element of that responsibility can and must be laid at the feet of Karl Marx himself.

It is important at the outset to be as clear as possible about the charges that are to be levelled against Marx. Marx, it is charged, failed to pay adequate attention to the emergence of the institutions and practices of representative democracies that were developing, particularly in Britain over the last two decades of his life. Whilst he successfully used British capitalism as the 'laboratory' for his economic theory and analysis of industrial capitalism, he failed to pay adequate attention to the corresponding *political forms* which were emerging.

The purpose that underlies the levelling of this charge against Marx is not to secure a conviction or record an acquittal but rather to stress the consequences for the subsequent history and development of Marxist political analysis. The line of this argument can be briefly sketched for later investigation. The failure of attention to the development of the state and political formations of industrial capitalism led directly to the seriously deficient analysis of the bourgeois state and to the politics advanced by Lenin. It is suggested that Lenin's text *The State and Revolution* has played a decisive part in the formation of and as a point of reference for Marxist political analysis. Lenin's text exhibits two central deficiencies: first, it fails adequately to emphasise the importance of variations in the political forms of twentieth-century capitalism; it eliminates or underplays the significance of representative democracy by lumping together all state and political forms as 'the dictatorship of the bourgeoisie', Second, Lenin further withdraws from analysis of the different political forms of modern capitalism by advancing the theory that in the era of monopoly capitalism, capitalism tends more and more towards authoritarian political forms.[1]

The result of the dominant weight of Lenin for orthodox Marxism has been a general failure to grapple with the reality of modern representative democracy. Much of the history of the variant developments within what has come to be called Western Marxism can be best understood as a series of attempts to come to grips with the real historical experience of the bourgeois democratic state. It is not my purpose to consider these more recent developments but to explore how it came about that the classical tradition of Marxist writings, especially of Marx and Engels, contributed so little to this task.

It may be objected that it is unreasonable to criticize Marx for failure to analyse an historical development (the rise of representative democracy) which was barely born during a period in which his health was failing and he was consumed by the struggle to complete *Capital*. Indeed one of the most detailed Marxist studies of the rise of bourgeois democracy lays great stress on its very *recent* emergence. Göran Therborn insists that the establishment of bourgeois democracy can be dated as occurring in 1928 in Britain (female franchise) and not until into the 1970s in the United States (black voting rights in the southern states). Indeed the 'earliest' bourgeois democracies, according to Therborn's classification were Australia and New Zealand in 1903 and 1907 respectively.[2]

If Therborn is right, any discussion of Marx's failure or omission becomes nonsensical or at best irrelevant. There is however a fundamental flaw in Therborn's procedure; his focus is on the *completion* of a political process. Yet a distinctive feature of Marx's own work was precisely the opposite emphasis, the insistence that what is new but uncompleted is the essence of the present and the harbinger of the future. The whole method and import of *Capital* rests on the analysis of the emergence of industrial capitalism, a process not 'completed' in Therborn's sense, during Marx's life. In other words, the deficiency (for our present purposes) of Therborn's analysis lies in its *formalism* and its consequent devaluation of major developmental tendencies. Therborn should properly be understood as making the entirely correct and valuable point that bourgeois democracy is not secured and completed through a single act of extending the franchise but is rather a long-run historical process. Yet he is wrong if he seeks to suggest that the major lines of development of bourgeois democracy are not seen to have irrevocably emerged by the last third of the nineteenth century.

If a central or critical turning point is to be identified it was, in Britain, the extension of the (adult male) franchise by the Reform Act of 1867 which signposts the emergence of representative democracy. At the risk of incurring feminist wrath I would go so far as to insist that, important though the securing of the (limited) adult female suffrage in 1928 was, it did not constitute the advent but only the completion of a process; the basic contours and consequences of representative democracy are to be seen in the extension of male franchise in 1867 and again in 1884.

It follows that if the emergence of representative democracy in Britain can be dated from 1867 and, perhaps of equal importance, from the political struggles of the Reform League that preceded the Reform Act, then we can quite properly evaluate what Marx and Engels said, or *did not* say, about this process.

II   *Marx and Engels on the Struggle for the Franchise*

The most striking feature of Marx's political writings is that their central preoccupation was with political developments in France and not with those in Britain. The three major texts, *The Class Struggles in France 1848-1850* (1850), *The Eighteenth Brumaire of Louis Bonaparte* (1851-52) and *The Civil War in France* (1871), embody the most sustained application of his theory and method to the analysis of contemporary political developments. In contrast Marx's writings on Britain during the same period are mere fragments; the majority are mere notes or comments on current events published in the *New-York Daily Tribune,* a venture which for Marx was as much commercial as political.[3] Marx's most significant writings on political developments in Britain were the sustained (and oft returned to) analyses of the factory legislation of the 1850s and 1860s; an important feature which links this treatment with the writings on France is its detailed attention to the role of political class struggle and the complex interaction of class alliances and class fractions.[4] Additionally we should note his detailed concern with foreign policy and British colonialism.

The failure of Marx to confront the emergence of representative democracy does not take the form of simple omission. It was not that Marx had nothing to say about the struggles for electoral reform. Rather it is the political evaluation, an evaluation that was explicit but undeveloped, that resulted in him 'missing' the longer term political significance of representative democracy. It will be further argued that the particular form of Marx's failure has direct continuity with

Lenin and with the modern history of orthodox Marxism.

As is well known, Marx – even before settling in London – formed a very positive estimate of the Chartist movement; it was for him both an expression of and a vehicle for the development of the British working class. It figures for Marx frequently as the forerunner of the mass political party of the working class. From the Chartist movement were drawn many of the more persistent and politically advanced British adherents of the International. The demand for universal franchise and the associated political conditions for its effective realisation (e.g. secret ballot, public election expenses, etc.) were the central demands of the People's Charter which survived beyond the Chartist movement itself. Marx was clearly enthusiastic in his support for these demands.

Indeed Marx goes further and unambiguously identifies the *revolutionary potential of universal suffrage.*

> Universal Suffrage is the equivalent for political power for the working class of England, where the proletariat forms the large majority of the population ... The carrying of Universal Suffrage in England would, therefore, be a far more socialistic measure than anything which has been honoured with that name on the Continent.
>
> Its inevitable result, here [in England] is the *political supremacy of the working class.*[5]

The central proposition which leads to the attribution of revolutionary significance to universal suffrage is that the working class constitutes the 'large majority' of the population. It should be noted that this line of argument continues to play to this day an important part in the political thinking of the British Labour Party. Put simply the view, generally of the left, has been that the Labour Party as the 'mass party of the working class' can realise socialist objectives if policy, programme and the working-class electors can be brought into alignment. Similarly, the majority place of the British working class has played a significant role in underpinning the Communist Party's strategy 'The British Road to Socialism'. It will be necessary to return to interrogate the implications of the size of the British working class.

The revolutionary significance of universal suffrage in Britain was also made in a more complex formulation contrasting France and Britain. Of universal suffrage Marx says:

> It is the Charter of the classes of the people and implies the assumption of political power as a means of meeting their social requirements ... There [France 1848] the immediate content of the revolution was universal suffrage; here, the immediate content of universal suffrage is the revolution.[6]

What is underlined here is that universal suffrage of itself has no necessary class or political character, but it is the historical context in which it exists that determines its class significance. As Marx had argued in *The Eighteenth Brumaire*, it was precisely the inability of the French peasantry, the overwhelming majority of the population, to enforce its class interests that resulted in universal suffrage electing Louis Bonaparte under an authoritarian democracy which proceeded to subordinate society to itself.

Marx was clear that parliamentary manoeuvres for a partial extension of the franchise were 'false pretences'. But at the same time there were elements of an analysis which pointed to the political conditions under which more fundamental reforms could occur, and he suggested that these would only come about under a Tory government.

When the popular struggle regained momentum, the demands of the Chartists were taken up by the Reform League. The successful mobilizations of May 1867 bore marked similarities with the earlier Chartist demonstrations. Marx had greeted the formation of the Reform League with great enthusiasm; he frequently claimed it as the result of the International's efforts.

> The great success of the International Association is this: The Reform League is our work.[7]

Marx's interest in the culmination of the struggle and the associated complex parliamentary processes resulting in the Reform Act of 1867 seems to have waned.[8] In fairness to Marx it should be noted that his health was deteriorating and that, as the biographies and his correspondence reveals, in 1867 he was much taken up with the final stages of the publication of the first volume of *Capital*.

For comment upon the significance of electoral reform and its immediate consequences we have to turn to Engels. We find Engels expressing very negative and pessimistic judgements about the immediate use to which the newly enfranchised working class actually put their votes. However, these immediate responses must be seen against an increasingly positive evaluation of the prospects of universal suffrage, culminating in his very controversial 1895 *Introduction* to Marx's *The Class Struggles in France*.[9]

Commenting on the 1868 elections in a letter to Marx, Engels is scathing.

> The proletariat has discredited itself terribly ... Everywhere the proletariat is the rag, tag and bobtail of the official parties, and if any party has gained strength from the new voters, it is the Tories.

His conclusion: 'a disastrous certificate of poverty for the English proletariat'. Engels, like Marx had often done, expressed the sanguine hope that the English working class, 'these thick-headed John Bulls' would learn from 'a really bloody encounter with those in power'.[10]

In his comments on the 1874 elections (this time with the further realisation of the Chartist demand, the secret ballot) which yielded a 'strong conservative majority'.

> And it is particularly the big industrial cities and factory districts where the workers are now absolutely in the majority, that send Conservatives to Parliament.[11]

He proceeds to examine how this state of affairs could come about. The analysis is not the clearest and is somewhat inconsistent. He sees the working class vote as both being a class conscious vote against 'the big barons of industry', as represented by the Liberal Party, but at the same time as a manifestation of the workers being 'duped' into playing the role of the left-wing of liberalism.

Additionally Engels refers to a number of loosely related factors. First that

> no separate political working-class party has existed in England since the downfall of the Chartist Party in the fifties.[12]

As a result only two workers, both from mining areas, were elected to Parliament. More generally the English working class had shared the crumbs of the industrial expansion of the previous decade and from imperial rule. The specific effect of which was the corruption of the Labour leaders. He denounces the collaboration of the leadership of the Reform League with the Liberal Party.[13] Additionally, he cites the perspicacity of the British ruling classes who

> have set themselves the task of carrying out, parallel with other concessions, one point of the Chartists' programme, the People's Charter, after another.[14]

Yet he concludes with some optimism for the future as a result of direct representation of workers in parliament, alongside a fresh upsurge of 'home rule' Irish representation.

In a letter to Kugelmann after the passage of the Reform Act 1867, Engels argues that English politics can never be the same again because the really positive consequence is that a revolutionary workers' party becomes possible which will build upon the general radicalisation of the politics of the working class which universal suffrage facilitates.[15]

We find that this theme of the importance of the formation of a worker's party becomes more and more pronounced in the later writings and correspondence of Engels. Thus in an article for *The Labour Standard* he presses the case for a new workers party in England; without it the English workers, despite their industrial organisation, can function politically only as the 'tail' of the Liberal Party. He re-emphasises the majority status of the working class:

> in England where the industrial and agricultural working class

forms the immense majority of the people, democracy means the domination of the working class, neither more nor less.[16]

He reports enthusiastically on the election of Keir Hardie to Parliament in 1892 as heralding 'an independent labour party is casting its shadow before'.[17]

He underlines very clearly the centrality of the formation of workers' parties:

> In our tactics one thing is thoroughly established for all modern countries and times: to bring the workers to the point of forming their own party, independent and opposed to all bourgeois parties.[18]

Yet one should note that Engels tends to exude an optimism which seems to have little contemporary justification. For example, in a letter to Plekhanov, noting that the thrust for political representation of the working class was coming from the trade-union movement, he argues

> as soon as a dozen branches of industry are represented class consciousness will arise of itself.[19]

He concludes his letter with a formulation which appears in a number of places and which has done much to give confidence to the socialist movement in Britain when it has been forced to recognize the slow growth of socialist aspiration.

> The 'practical' English will be the last to arrive, but when they do arrive their contribution will weigh quite heavy in the scales.[20]

At the same time Engels showed a detailed awareness of the political, legal and practical prerequisites for the full realisation of the potential of universal suffrage. Such practical barriers as the cost of acquiring copies of electoral registers, the cost of electioneering and the absence of salaries for members of parliament were all barriers impeding the emergence of an independent workers' party.

We may summarise the position with regard to representative

democracy taken by Marx and Engels as one of unqualified support for the struggle for universal franchise. The support has as its rationale the facilitative role of suffrage for the development and growth of independent workers' parties. It is precisely the same position taken by Lenin in favouring participation, even under very restrictive conditions, in electoral contests in Russia. Representative democracy is not itself seen as the objective, but as a means that facilitates the maturing of the working class and its party. For Marx and Engels this is especially the case in countries, like Britain, where there is a masssive and absolute growth in the size of the working class. There is, and this is the most important conclusion, little or no evidence of any change in their strategic conception of the nature of the struggle for socialism.

That is until we consider Engels's 1895 *Introduction* to Marx's *The Class Struggles in France*[21]; it was written in March 1895, (Engels died in August) and only incomplete versions were published at the time. Engels complained bitterly about the 'cuts' made by Wilhelm Liebknecht which tended to present Engels as an advocate of exclusively non-violent struggle.[22] Whilst his *Introduction* played an important part in German debates at the time, the absence, until much more recently, of the full authentic text seriously limited the attention given to its content. Indeed it is probably true that the controversy surrounding the form of its original publication has besmirched the text itself. Whilst in Germany it was treated as Engels's 'last testament', it has tended not to have been so regarded in Britain.

It is essential to emphasise the quite remarkable content of Engels's *Introduction*. It constitutes a major departure from the conception of socialist revolution advanced by Marx in *Class Struggles* and also, even more significantly, in *The Civil War in France*; more significant because it is there that Marx identifies the strategy of the Communards as laying down the general form of insurrectionary strategy and it is precisely this strategy which Lenin takes up and extends in *The State and Revolution*.

It is important to stress the extent to which the *Introduction* marks a departure from the earlier positions held by both Marx and Engels, but also to note that in important respects Engels does not follow through the implications of his own analysis and retains a different version of the 'insurrectionist' perspective. Alongside this he articulates more clearly than before what may be called an 'incrementalist' approach to the advance of worker's parties under universal suffrage.

Engels is at great pains to identify an error in the perspective held by Marx and himself.

> History has shown us to have been wrong, has revealed our point of view of that time to have been an illusion.[23]

> History has proved us [Marx and Engels], and all who thought like us, wrong.[24]

He leaves no doubt about the existence of error, but the text is not as clear as we might wish about the precise content of the error. What follows is an attempt to present both the elements to which Engels points and their interrelation.

First is an error concerning the trajectory of capitalist development. Following the defeats after the 1848 revolutions, Marx and Engels foresaw a lull: 'nothing was to be expected until the outbreak of new world economic crisis' (p. 123). The continental wide expansion of capitalism indicated that 'the Continent at that time was not, by a long way, ripe for the elimination of capitalist production' (p. 125). However, aside from this negative judgement, Engels offers no substantive analysis of capitalist development.

His attention is primarily focused on the *political* consequences. In general terms he insists that the period since 1848 had

> completely transformed the conditions under which the proletariat has to fight. The mode of struggle of 1848 is today obsolete in every respect (p. 123).

They had been 'under the spell of previous historical experience', particularly that of France.

> It was, therefore, natural and unavoidable that our conceptions of

the nature and the course of the 'social' revolution proclaimed in Paris in February 1848, of the revolution of the proletariat, should be strongly coloured by memories of the prototypes of 1789 and 1830 (p. 122).

The same objection applies also to the experience of the Paris Commune, so centrally placed in the historical lineage of the proletarian revolution by both Marx and Lenin. This experience also

> proved how impossible even then ... this rule of the working class still was (p. 127).

As argued earlier, Marx's 'model' of revolutionary struggle was that of France, and the lack of comparable forms in Britain led to, or at least facilitated, a blindness to the political forms of bourgeois rule developing under his nose in Britain. And the 'model of France' which Engels labels as 'obsolete' was that of the 'insurrection'.

The 'insurrectionary' revolution is presented as obsolete on two very different grounds. The first is premissed on the insistence, advanced in the *Communist Manifesto*, that the proletarian revolution distinguishes itself from all previous revolutions by being the revolution of the 'majority' against the exploiting minority. The French insurrections were however 'minority' actions and he insists upon the necessity in the socialist revolution for

> the masses themselves must also be in it, must themselves already have grasped what is at stake, what they are going in for, body and soul (p. 134).

There are real problems with the way in which Engels presents the question of minority and majority and the role of the masses. The present essay is not the occasion to pursue this matter in detail but it should be contended that it is not a question of insisting on the 'role of the masses' – all modern revolutions have insisted on this. What is central and not touched on by Engels is the form and content of the participation of the majority and in particular of the relationship between the 'leaders' or 'the Party' and the masses. It is a problem which equally confronts the modern mass civil wars, such as in China, and the mass electoral strategies for socialist transformation.

Engels's second reason is the transformation of military technology that produced 'a complete revolution in all warfare' and thereby relegated the barricades of urban insurrections to the museum.

The alternative to insurrectionary politics proposed by Engels was the utilisation of universal suffrage. The German Social Democrats rendered the great service to

> their comrades in all countries with a new weapon, and one of the sharpest, when they showed them how to make use of universal suffrage [which was] transformed by them from a means of deception which it was before, into an instrument of emancipation (p. 129).

> With this successful utilization of universal suffrage an entirely new method of proletarian struggle came into operation ... And so it happened that the bourgeoisie and the government came to be much more afraid of the legal than of the illegal action of the worker's party, of the results of elections than of the use of rebellion (p. 130).

It should be stressed that Engels is at pains to insist that street fighting may still play a role in the course of revolutionary events. And in general he insists on the 'right of revolution' and more specifically on the right to meet the violence of the ruling class with revolutionary defence and violence. (It was these passages which were cut by Liebknecht.)

Engels cites the details of the electoral advance of the German Social Democrats. Such is his enthusiasm for the movement of the 'swingometer' to the Socialists that he asserts that their

> growth proceeds as spontaneously, as steadily, as irresistibly, and at the same time as tranquilly as a natural process (p. 135).

Such historical inevitability of electoral advance must be rejected just as categorically as it is necessary to reject the historical inevitability of the collapse of capitalism or the inevitability of civil war.

But a more important issue is embedded in Engels's discussion. He imports a new version of the very insurrectionary perspective which he appears to distance himself from. Much of the manner in which socialist controversies over the last century have posed the question as opposition between 'peaceful' or 'violent', 'revolutionary' or 'electoral' socialist strategies. These oppositions are often less opposed than their protagonists have realised. It must be stressed that there is a more fundamental opposition between 'insurrectionary' and 'non-insurrectionary' socialist strategies, which Engels does much to initiate; but in a very important respect his position remains within the camp of insurrectionism. His advocacy of the utilisation of universal suffrage is still presented as a build-up to the 'decisive day' (p. 135), that is to the climax in which the transition from one social order to another is seen as a decisive historical moment, truncated and compressed into 'the revolutionary moment'. Such a position is, in essence, one of 'electoral insurrection', of the single moment in which an election victory marks the transition between one historical epoch and the next. Engels's strategy for European socialism is one of 'incrementalism', of the steady, patient advance, of keeping the powder dry, not risking provocation by the ruling class until the forces of socialism are ready for the decisive confrontation.

The problem is not simply an oversight on Engels's part. Certainly he stresses the necessity of 'long persistent work' and of 'slow propaganda work'. He goes further and recognises the possibility of temporary reverses. But the really difficult problem that the harnessing of universal suffrage puts on the agenda is one of abandoning any conception of a specific truncated moment of transition without at the same time lapsing into a purely pacific gradualism. The socialist movement is still a long way from being able clearly to distinguish between what, with deliberate contradiction, may be called 'revolutionary gradualism' and a naively gradualist or incrementalist view of socialism as the outcome of increments of social reform. This same problem is also captured by Colletti when he says that what Engels thought he was proposing was but a 'change in tactics' whereas to take the problems he raises seriously involves a 'change in strategy' which he fails to pursue but which is today the central problem confronting the socialist movement.[25]

III Conclusion

The above examination of the writings of Marx and Engels facilitates some preliminary conclusions. It is clear that both Marx and Engels evinced a definite political support for the struggle for electoral reform. It is equally clear that this exhibits itself more clearly and persistently in Engels than it does in Marx; but in Marx's case it may just have been contingent conditions of health and the effort to publish *Capital* that led to the apparent curtailment of his interest in the process of electoral reform just at the moment of the major changes in 1867.

The 'charge' which was set out in the introduction to this essay spoke of a 'failure to pay adequate attention'. Since it is not the case that Marx simply ignored the emergence of representative democracy, the issue must revolve around whether the attention paid was 'adequate'. The substantive conclusion to be argued is that the attention paid by Marx and Engels to the development of representative democracy was inadequate in that they failed to lay the basis for a developed analysis of the political formation of modern bourgeois democratic societies. For the present purpose it is intended to treat Marx and Engels as a unity since there is no divergence or inconsistency in what they wrote about electoral reform and its consequences.[26] Only the political conclusions drawn by Engels in the 1895 *Introduction*, discussed above, can be separated from their shared positions precisely because it is based upon the express attempt to correct the 'wrong' position earlier shared with Marx.

The general line of their treatment may be judged to be 'inadequate' in a number of related respects. Its inadequacy manifests itself in a myopic concern with electoral reform as facilitating the emergence of independent workers' parties; there is a complete absence of analysis of the consequences for such parties existing under the conditions of representative democracy. This failure has its roots in the unspoken theoretical assumption (albeit one that is made explicit elsewhere) that 'classes' are more or less directly expressed or represented by 'parties'; this involves the view that there is some *necessary* connection between class and party. Workers' parties will, according to this view, embody and express the class interests of the working class. This position is affected by a second, related, theoretical assumption which goes under the label of 'false consciousness'; when there is a non-correspondence between 'class interest' and the decisions of working-class electors (for example, to vote for other parties) this embodies and can be explained by reference to 'false consciousness' ('error' in identification of class interest or lack of maturity of consciousness).

Putting aside general problems raised by this theory of consciousness and of representation, it is apparent that both Marx and Engels treated the question of workers' parties operating under conditions of universal suffrage as involving what we can identify as a linear theory of class consciousness, that is one which sees the variation of consciousness as a movement from 'less' to 'more'. The index of this linear consciousness is, at the outset, the very existence of a workers' party and, later, the size of the vote which such a party attracts, the assumption being that increased electoral support signifies a higher level of class consciousness.

It is this linear view of class consciousness which allows us to understand the remarks by Engels, previously quoted, in drawing conclusions from election results in which he veers between optimism and pessimism in assessing their significance. Thus English workers handing electoral victory to the Tories after the 1867 reforms represents a low level of consciousness whereas the steady increase in the votes obtained by the German social democrats embodies an advancing class consciousness. The very limited character of the conclusions that can be derived from this theoretical starting point is apparent from any examination of the electoral successes and failures of major socialist parties in Europe; advances or declines in electoral support cannot simply be linked to increases or decreases in the class consciousness of the particular working class.

The most important deficiency in the treatment of representative democracy by Marx and Engels is the complete absence of discussion of its most distinctive feature. The very core of representative democracy is the fact of *political competition*. It is from the fact of 'political competition' that we can understand both the formation and development of political parties and can more generally come to grips with what 'politics' is actually about. It needs to be stressed that political competition between parties always takes place under definite conditions which influence both the forms of the competition itself and its outcome. There is no implication that competition necessarily takes place under conditions of equality or fairness, indeed it is frequently around the terms and conditions of political competition that political struggle occurs. Both Marx and Engels were conscious of the importance of some of the formal conditions of political competition and thus supported the Chartist demands for a secret ballot and for election expenses. But consideration of the wider ramifications of political competition for workers' parties and for the whole complex of parties, elections and parliamentary institutions, is a very distinctive and significant absence.

The heart of their omission is their failure to think through the general consequences of political competition. Whilst it is self-evident that electoral and parliamentary struggles are particular expressions of class struggle, it is of central importance to recognise that such struggles are not simply class struggles, and even more important to recognise that the particular form and framework that representative democracy imposes upon struggle has consequences for both the content and the result of that struggle. Thus, for example, the existence of parties under conditions of political competition imposes upon them the necessity to organise both internal and external alliances, to express and articulate interests which are not always mutually consistent, in such a way as to maximize their competitive advantage over other political parties by creating the maximum disorganization and disunity of their competitors.[27] The capacity to tackle such issues is greatly impeded by the limited or partial analysis of representative democracy and the inadequacies of the theory of consciousness and representation through which it is discussed;[28] to pursue the consequences of representative democracy more fully requires the discarding of such class reductionist theories. The essential point is to abandon ideas of consciousness which only have a hierarchical dimension, that is which only employ notions of 'more' or 'less' consciousness. The issue can be seen in a most interesting process of development in Gramsci's writings.

Gramsci identified quite distinct types or forms of consciousness. He was not entirely consistent in his terminology, but they include forms of consciousness which he called 'economic-corporate', 'national-popular collective will' and 'ethical-political hegemony'. It is, in any case, not the present intention to discuss the content of these categories. What is involved is the identification of a means of characterising the content of specific forms of consciousness. Yet it is also clear that Gramsci presents them as 'stages', that is, posits a movement from the lower (economic-corporate) to the higher (hegemonic). But he was most clearly aware that the problem of politics required the political party to be able to operate with a complex range of stages of consciousness, and is not reducible to the quest – which plays such a decisive part in Lenin's thought – of 'raising' the level of consciousness as a precondition of revolutionary action. Thus we find Gramsci speaking of the need to make 'sacrifices' of specific economic-corporatist interests of the organised working class in order to create and consolidate alliances of political forces.[29] One can go a stage further and insist that there is no automatic or necessary hierarchy of types of consciousness. The need to do so stems from a position which is here implicit, but which should be stated: that the working class has no necessary, let alone spontaneous, tendency towards the acquisition of a socialist consciousness. An alternative perspective insists that what politics is about is the construction and combination of quite different types of consciousness into the bases for viable political action for socialist objectives.

The insistence that political competition is a complex process, the analysis of which requires a more developed theory than that provided by Marx and Engels points towards two conclusions. The first is that the socialist movement has been handicapped in its understanding and capacity to conduct political struggle under conditions of political competition. The second is that there has been a general failure within the Marxist tradition to understand the specific contribution that representative democracy has made to the stability and persistence of capitalism in the twentieth century. An important ingredient is the capacity of non-socialist parties to attract and retain the support of working-class electors; this phenomenon is not explainable in terms of 'false consciousness', but it necessitates an analysis of the capacity of non-socialist parties to articulate immediate economic and social objectives alongside conceptions of the national interest. Very simply it must be understood that, for example, policies for reduction of direct taxation are no less capable of mobilizing working-class support, especially amongst the more highly paid and regularly employed, just because such policies bring greater benefit to higher income groups.

If we return for a moment to Engels's 1895 *Introduction*, the most specific 'error' which he identifies is Marx's very fundamental argument, which plays such a strong role in *Capital* itself, that industrial capitalism has reached its apex and that the historical scene was already set for socialist revolution. That Marx held this position goes a long way to explain the focus of Marx's *political* attention on France with its insurrectionary upheavals, and with the Paris Commune giving a brief glimpse of the working class in power. The general consequence of this line of thinking was and, to a very large degree, remains the failure of orthodox Marxism to come to grips with the persistence and stability of modern capitalism under conditions of representative democracy, despite the chronic economic crisis and vulnerability of many developed capitalist economies. It should be noted in passing that this political stability is in part a consequence of the failure of the socialism of Eastern Europe to come to grips with the problem of political competition and to create positive rather than repressive responses.

In a very profound sense there is *no Marxist theory of political democracy*. This is meant in the same sense that Althusser insisted that 'there does not really exist any "Marxist theory of the State" ';[30] what he was anxious to stress was that Marx was so intent on avoiding all bourgeois conceptions of the state that he ends up with a purely negative demarcation line producing what Althusser describes as 'the classical negative definition'. The history of Marxist discussion of representative democracy has been dogged by the same negativity; it has been constructed out of warnings against 'bourgeois illusions'.

For example, one extremely regrettable tendency has been to reduce the critique of bourgeois democracy to the exposure of the limitations of *formal* democracy to such an extent that 'bourgeois democracy' becomes reduced to this formalism alone; but such an analysis fails to discern the elements of representative democracy that underline the significant political stability of contemporary capitalism. And additionally the negative theory of democracy fails to identify the enduring principles inherent in representative democracy which will form essential and unnegotiable ingredients of socialist democracy. Thus such requirements as freedom of information and freedom of political association are necessary requirements of democracy and not just passing conditions of bourgeois democracy. Marxists in general and the Communist Parties in particular are still, in the main, a long way from understanding that until conditions of political democracy are secured and guaranteed in existing socialist societies, the overwhelming majority of the peoples of societies that have experienced representative democracy will continue to choose such a system, and, what is more important, that they are right to make such a choice.

The substance of this argument is that the failure to understand representative democracy is not just a result of the subsequent history of the Marxist movement (to be explained, for example, by reference to Stalinism as a political deformation or by the particular historical conditions after 1917). Rather it is argued that in important respects the precursors of that failure lie in the work of Marx and Engels themselves. Marx's emphasis upon the insurrectionary French model and his comparative neglect of the significance of representative democracy, emerging under his nose in Britain, has passed into the Marxist tradition, particularly through the influence of Lenin. The impact of Engels's major revision of socialist tactics in the 1895 *Introduction* was much restricted because of the way it was both distorted and taken-up by the 'revisionist' leadership of German social democracy; the result was that Engels's text itself became in a sense contaminated. I have argued that Engels's position is itself not without its deficiencies, but it deserves a much more central place in current discussions.

The more recent course of Marxist controversies has not helped serious discussion of the questions surrounding the problem of democracy. Engels himself introduces the distinction between the insurrectionary or 'violent' French model and the 'peaceful' possibilities of the utilization of universal suffrage. The counterposing of 'violent' versus 'peaceful' strategies has passed down to the present period. It became, for example, one of the central themes in the Chinese Maoist criticism of the Soviet Union and of the Western European Communist parties.[31] The counterposing of opposites which characterised these exchanges did nothing to concentrate the debate on the nature of the development of contemporary capitalism which placed on the agenda the need to consider a fundamental change in political strategy. It is precisely because of the central focus in Gramsci's thought on the production and mobilization of consent that his ideas came to have a much more powerful influence outside his native Italy. Yet it is important to stress that whilst Gramsci has provided the main thrust for contemporary Marxist thought he is only minimally concerned with the question of representative democracy; it was precisely the political backwardness of Italian society that focused Gramsci's attention on those processes which he came to identify as the struggle for hegemony whilst the electoral and parliamentary arena did not constitute anything like the central place realised in advanced capitalist societies and which Italy itself became after 1945.

This essay has sought to demonstrate that the impediments to the analysis of the role and significance of representative democracy have their roots in the work of Marx and Engels themselves. Marx's aphorism that 'the tradition of all dead generations weighs like a nightmare on the brain of the living' applies to the history of Marxism itself.[32]

Notes

1. It is important to insist on the presence of an important difficulty in the making of historical judgements about the responsibility of individuals. Lenin's analysis of the political trajectory of modern capitalism was made very specifically and concretely in the context of the 1914-18 War. He was clearly correct in stressing that despite variant political forms, the European states rushed into the inter-imperialist conflict of the First World War with equal enthusiasm and with the same scant regard for the consequences for the people of their own nations or for those of their enemies. The problem of historical assessment revolves around whether the responsibility for turning an empirically sustainable proposition into a general 'law' is to be attached to Lenin or to those who subsequently canonised his writings into the rigid orthodoxy of Marxism-Leninism. The difficulty involved in making such judgements in no way detracts from the major consequences that flow from this process.
2. Göran Therborn 'The Rule of Capital and the Rise of Democracy', *New Left Review*, 103 pp. 3-41 (1977); see also his important sequel on political development in Latin America, 'The Travail of Latin American Democracy' *New Left Review*, 113-114 pp. 71-109 (1979).
3. See the respective accounts in Franz Mehring *Karl Marx: The Story of His Life* (1936), pp. 227ff. and David McLellan *Karl Marx: His Life and Thought* (1973), pp. 265ff.
4. See in particular *Capital I*, Chapter 15.
5. 'The Chartists' (1852) in Marx and Engels, *Articles on Britain*, Moscow, 1971 p. 119; also Marx-Engels, *Collected Works*, Vol. 11, p. 335-6.
6. Marx 'The Association for Administrative Reform' (1855), Marx-Engels, *Collected Works*, Vol. 14, p. 243.
7. Marx 'Letter to Engels 1/5/1865' in Marx-Engels, *Selected Correspondence*, Moscow, 1975, p. 163.
8. This judgement is based on Marx's translated writings available at the time of writing; it is possible that the *Collected Works* volumes covering writings and correspondence for the period 1867 and 1868 may reveal more, but it is unlikely that any major or significant analysis not already published will be included.

9. Marx-Engels, *Selected Works*, Moscow, 1958, Vol. I, pp. 118-38, and Marx-Engels, *Selected Works in One Volume*, London, 1968, pp. 641-58.

10. Engels, 'Letter to Marx 18/11/1868', Marx and Engels, *On Britain*, Moscow, 1962 p. 545. This is a slightly different selection of texts, with the addition of letters, to that published as Marx and Engels, *Articles on Britain*, Moscow, 1971.

11. Engels, 'The English Elections' (1874), Marx and Engels, *Articles on Britain* p. 366.

12. *ibid.*, p. 368.

13. For a detailed discussion of the period see the very full account in Royden Harrison, *Before the Socialists*, London, 1965, Chapter 4.

14. *ibid.*, p. 368.

15. Engels, 'Letter to Kugelmann, 8 $ 20/11/1867', Marx-Engels, *Works*, Vol. 31 p. 568.

16. 'A Working Men's Party' (1881), Marx-Engels, *Articles on Britain* p. 381.

17. Engels, 'Letter to Bebel 5/7/1892', Marx and Engels, *On Britain* p. 573.

18. Engels, 'Letter to Kautsky 4/9/1892', *ibid.*, p. 575.

19. Engels, 'Letter to Plekhanov 21/5/1894, Marx and Engels *On Britain*, p. 583.

20 *ibid.*, p. 583.

21. Marx-Engels, *Selected Works* (1958), Vol. I, pp. 118-138. See the very important discussion by Lucio Colletti 'Bernstein and the Marxism of the Second International' in *From Rousseau to Lenin*, London, 1972.

22. See letters to Kautsky (1/4/1895) and Lafargue (3/4/1895), Marx-Engels *Selected Correspondence* (1975), p. 461.

23. Engels *Introduction* to Marx, *The Class Struggles in France* (1895), Marx-Engels, *Selected Works*, (1958), Vol. I p. 123.

24. *ibid.*, p. 125.

25. Colletti, 'Bernstein and the Marxism of the Second International' in *From Rousseau to Lenin*, London, 1972, p. 49.

26. Marx and Engels should, on this principle, only be treated separately where they exhibit marked contrasts in approach or where we know of significant differences that impinge upon the specific issue under consideration.

27. This general sketch of 'political competition' draws heavily upon Nicos Poulantzas, *Political Power and Social Classes*, London, 1975 and Ernesto Laclau, *Politics and Ideology in Marxist Theory*, London, 1977. Although implicit in their writing neither author places any specific emphasis upon the concept of political competition.

28. The point has been made by a number of commentators that whilst Marx advances a very simplistic theory of class consciousness in *The German Ideology*, in his more concrete historical writings – *The Eighteenth Brumaire* is perhaps the most important example – a much more complex and satisfactory analysis is presented.

29. Gramsci, *Prison Notebooks*, London, 1971, p. 161.
30. Althusser, 'The Crisis of Marxism', *Marxism Today*, July 1978, p. 219.
31. It is interesting to note that in the fullest and most theoretical reply to the Chinese from British communists, John Gollan, in an article entitled 'Which Road?' *Marxism Today*, July 1964, continued the debate in terms of 'peace' versus 'violence' and in doing so drew heavily on Engels's, 1895 *Introduction*.
32. Marx, *The Eighteenth Brumaire of Louis Bonaparte*, in Marx-Engels, *Selected Works* (1968), p. 96; *Collected Works*, Vol. 11, p. 103.

G.A. Cohen

Forces and Relations of Production

In Section I of this paper I present, in summary form, the interpretation of historical materialism offered in my book on *Karl Marx's Theory of History*.[1] I define and relate the concepts of forces and relations of production and I defend the thesis that the basic explanations of historical materialism are what have been called *functional* explanations. Section II places the idea that all history is the history of class struggle in the framework of the theory expounded in section I. Section III is a personal interlude, in which I explain how I came to write my book on historical materialism, and what happened to me after I had written it. The last section confronts ambiguities in the crucial notion of relations *fettering* forces of production, and proposes a revised version of the central formulations of historical materialism.[2]

I An Outline of Historical Materialism

My book says, and says Marx says, that history is, fundamentally, the growth of human productive power, and that forms of society rise and fall according as they enable and promote, or prevent and discourage, that growth.

The canonical text for this interpretation is the famous 1859 Preface to *A Contribution to the Critique of Political Economy*, some sentences of which we shall look at shortly. I argue (in section (3) of Chapter VI of *KMTH*) that the Preface makes explicit the standpoint on society and history to be found throughout Marx's mature writings, on any reasonable view of the date at which he attained theoretical maturity. In attending to the Preface, we are not looking at just one text among many, but at that text which gives the clearest statement of the theory of historical materialism.

The presentation of the theory in the Preface begins as follows:

> In the social production of their life men enter into definite relations that are indispensable and independent of their will, relations of production which *correspond* to a definite stage of development of their material productive forces. The sum total of these relations constitutes the economic structure of society, the real *basis, on which arises* a legal and political superstructure ...[3]

These sentences mention three ensembles, the productive forces, the relations of production, and the superstructure, among which certain explanatory connections (here indicated by italics) are asserted. I shall first say what I think the ensembles are, and I shall then describe the explanatory connections among them. (All of what follows is argued for in *KMTH*, but not all of the argument is given in what follows, which may therefore wrongly impress the reader as dogmatic).

The productive forces are those facilities and devices which are used in the process of production: means of production on the one hand, and labour power on the other. Means of production are physical productive resources: tools, machinery, raw materials, premises and so forth. Labour power includes not only the strength of producers, but also their skills, and the technical knowledge (which they need not understand) they apply when labouring. Marx says, and I agree, that this subjective dimension of the productive forces is more important than the objective or means of production dimension; and within the more important dimension the part most capable of development is knowledge. Hence, in its later stages, the development of the productive forces is largely a function of the development of productively useful science.

Note that Marx takes for granted in the Preface, what elsewhere he asserts outright, that 'there is a continual movement of growth in productive forces',[4] I argue (in section (6) of Chapter II of *KMTH*) that the relevant standard for measuring that growth in power is how much (or, rather, how little) labour must be spent with given forces to produce what is required to satisfy the inescapable physical needs of the immediate producers.[5] This criterion of social productivity is less equivocal than others which may come to mind, but the decisive reason for choosing it is not its relative clarity but its theoretical appropriateness: if relations of production correspond, as the theory says they do, to levels of development of productive power, then this way of measuring productive power makes the theory's correspondence thesis more plausible.[6]

I do not say that the only explanatory feature of productive power is how much there is of it: qualitative features of productive forces also help to explain the character of relations of production. My claim is that insofar as quantity of productive power is what matters, the key quantity is how much time it takes to (re)produce the producers, that is to say, to produce what they must consume to be able to continue working (as opposed to what they actually consume, which generally, and in contemporary capitalist society considerably, exceeds what they must consume). It is the amount of time available beyond, or surplus[7] to, that historically dwindling requirement that is so fateful for the form of the second ensemble we need to describe, the relations of production.

Relations of production are relations of economic power, of the economic power[8] people enjoy or lack over labour power and means of production. In a capitalist society relations of production include the economic power capitalists have over means of production, the economic power workers (unlike slaves) have over their own labour power, and the lack of economic power workers have over means of production. Immediate producers may have no economic power, some economic power, or total economic power over each of their own labour power and the means of production they use. If we permit ourselves a measure of idealization we can construct a table which rather neatly distinguishes the relations of production of historically important immediate producers:

                        G.A. Cohen

Amount of economic
power over

	His Labour Power	*The Means of Production He Uses*
SLAVE	None	None
SERF	Some	Some
PROLETARIAN	All	None
INDEPENDENT	All	All

The table gives three subordinate producers, and one independent. Since one may have no, some, or total economic power over each of one's labour power and means of production, there is a total of nine cases to consider. I think it is diagnostically valuable to inquire which of the remaining five cases are logically or otherwise possible, and which in turn of those are actual, but I shall not enter on that disccusion here.[9]

Now the sum total of relations of production in a given society is said to constitute the economic structure of that society, which is also called – in relation to the superstructure – the basis, or base, or foundation. The economic structure or base therefore consists of relations of production only: it does not include the productive forces. It is true that to exclude the productive forces from the economic structure runs against the usual construal of Marx,[10] but he actually said that the economic structure is constituted of relations of production, and he had systematic reasons for saying so.[11] People mistakenly suppose that the productive forces belong to the economic base because they wrongly think that the explanatory importance of the forces ensures their membership in it. But while the forces indeed possess that importance, they are not part of the economic base, since they are not economic phenomena.[12] To stay with the spatial metaphor, they are below the economic foundation, the ground on which it rests.[13]

The Preface describes the superstructure as legal and political. So it at any rate includes the legal and state institutions of society. It is customary to locate other institutions within it too, and it is controversial what its correct demarcation is: my own view is that there are strong textual and systematic reasons for supposing that the superstructure is a lot smaller than many commentators think it is.[14] It is certainly false that every non-economic social phenomenon is superstructural: artistic creation, for example, is demonstrably not, as such, superstructural for Marx. In these remarks I shall discuss the legal order only, which is uncontroversially a part of the superstructure.

So much for the identity of three ensembles mentioned in the Preface. Now relations of production are said to *correspond* to the level of development of the productive forces, and in turn to be a *foundation* on which a superstructure rises. I think these are ways of saying that the level of development of the productive forces explains the nature of the production relations, and that they in turn explain the character of the superstructure co-present with them. But what kind of explanation is ventured here? I argue that in each case what we have is a species of functional explanation.

What is functional explanation? Here are two examples of it: 'Birds have hollow bones because hollow bones facilitate flight', 'Shoe factories operate on a large scale because of the economies large scale brings'. In each case something (birds having hollow bones, shoe factories operating on a large scale) which has a certain effect (flight facilitation, economies of scale) is explained by the fact that it has that effect.

But now let me be somewhat more precise.[15] Suppose that e is a cause and f is its effect, and that we are offered a functional explanation of e in terms of its possession of that effect. Note first that the form of the explanation is not: e occurred because f occurred. If that were its form, functional explanation would be the exact opposite of ordinary causal explanation, and it would have the fatal defect that it represented a later occurrence as explaining an earlier one. Nor may we say that the form of the explanation is 'e occurred because it caused f'. Similar constraints on explanation and time order rule that candidate out: by the time e has caused f, e has occurred, so that the fact that it caused f could not explain its occurrence. The only remaining candidate, which I therefore elect, is: e occurred because it would cause f, or, less tersely but more properly: e occurred because the situation was such that an event like e would cause an event like f.

Now if this account of what functional explanations are is correct, then the main explanatory theses of historical materialism are functional explanations, for the following reason: Marx never denied, and sometimes asserted, that superstructures hold foundations together, and that relations of production control the development of the productive forces. Yet he held that the character of the superstructure is explained by the nature of the base, and that the latter is explained by the nature of the productive forces. If the intended explanations are functional ones, we have consistency between the effect of A on B and the explanation of A by B, *and I do not know any other way of rendering historical materialism consistent.*

I shall now expound in greater detail one of the two functional explanatory theses, that which concerns base and super-structure.

The base, it will be recalled, is the sum total of production relations, these being relations of economic power over labour power and means of production. The capitalist's control of means of production is an illustration. And the superstructure, we saw, has more than one part, exactly what its parts are being somewhat uncertain, but certainly one *bona fide* part of it is the legal system, which will occupy us here.

In a capitalist society capitalists have effective power over means of production. What confers that power on a given capitalist, say an owner of a factory? On what can he rely if others attempt to take control of the factory away from him? An important part of the answer is this: he can rely on the law of the land, which is enforced by the might of the state. It is his legal right which causes him to have his economic power. What he is effectively able to do depends on what he is legally entitled to do. And this is in general true in law-abiding society with respect to all economic powers and all economic agents. We can therefore say: in law-abiding society people have the economic powers they do because they have the legal rights they do.

That seems to refute the doctrine of base and superstructure, since here superstructural conditions – what legal rights people have – determine basic ones – what their economic powers are. But though it seems to refute the doctrine of base and superstructure, it cannot be denied. And it would not only seem to refute it, but actually would refute it, were it not possible, *and therefore mandatory* (for historical materialists), to present the doctrine of base and superstructure as an instance of functional explanation. For we can add, to the undeniable truth emphasized above, the thesis that the given capitalist enjoys the stated right because it belongs to a structure of rights, a structure which obtains because it sustains an analogous structure of economic power. The content of the legal system is explained by its function, which is to help sustain an economy of a particular kind. People do usually get their powers from their rights, but in a manner which is not only allowed but demanded by the way historical materialism explains superstructural rights by reference to basic powers. Hence the effect of the law of property on the economy is not, as is often supposed, an embarrassment to historical materialism. It is something which historical materialism is committed to emphasizing, because of the particular way it explains law in terms of economic conditions.

Legal structures rise and fall as they sustain or frustrate forms of economy which, I now add, advance the development of the productive forces. The addition implies an explanation why whatever economic structure obtains at a given time does obtain at that time. Once more the explanation is a functional one: the prevailing production relations prevail *because* they are relations which advance the development of the productive forces. The existing level of productive power determines what relations of production would raise its level, and relations of that type consequently obtain. In other words: if production relations of kind R obtain, then that is because R-type relations are suitable to the development of the forces, in virtue of their existing level of development: that is the canonical form of the explanation in the standard case. But I should also mention the transitional case, in which the relations are not suitable to the development of the forces but, on the contrary, fetter them. In transitional cases the prevailing relations obtain because they recently *were* suitable to the development of the forces, and the class they empower has managed to maintain control despite their no

                    G.A. Cohen

longer being so: it is because ruling classes have an interest in the maintenance of obsolete relations that their *immediate* replacement by freshly suitable relations is not to be expected. People do not rush towards the dustbin of history just as soon as they have played out their historical role.

Now since

(1)   the level of development of productive power determines what relations (that is, what sort of economic structure) would advance productive power,

and

(2)   relations which advance productive power obtain because they advance productive power,

it follows that

(3)   the level of development of productive power explains the nature of the economic structure.

(3)   assigns explanatory primacy to the productive forces. (2) does not by itself ensure that primacy, since it is consistent with, e.g.,

(4)   the dominant ideology determines what relations would advance productive power,

and if (4) is true, (3) is false.

I am greatly indebted to Philippe Van Parijs for his lucid insistence that the thesis of the primacy of the productive forces (i.e. (3)) requires that both (1) and (2) be true. He correctly points out[16] that certain formulations in *KMTH* (e.g. on p. 162) carry the false suggestion that (2) by itself ensures the explanatory primacy of the productive forces. Others (e.g. on p. 160) do affirm the conjunction required for an assertion of primacy, but it was Van Parys who brought the difference between the sound and the unsatisfactory formulations to my attention.

Now to say that *A* explains *B* is not necessarily to indicate *how A* explains *B*. The child who knows that the match burst into flame because it was struck may not know how the latter event explains the former, because he is ignorant of the relationship between friction and heat, the contribution of oxygen to combustion, and so on. In a widely favoured idiom, he may not know the *mechanism* linking cause and effect, or, as

I prefer to say, he may be unable to *elaborate* the explanation. In the relevant sense of 'how', we require an answer to the questions: *how does the fact that the economic structure promotes the development of the productive forces explain the character of the economic structure?* and *how does the fact that the superstructure protects the base explain the character of the superstructure?* Recall the functional explanation of the hollow bones of birds: to say, correctly, that birds have hollow bones because the feature is useful for flight is not to say how its usefulness accounts for its emergence and/or persistence. To that question Lamarck gave an unacceptable answer and Darwin an excellent one. To corresponding questions about explanations of large scale in terms of economies of scale one may answer by referring to conscious human purposes, or to an economic analogue of chance variation and natural selection, or to some mix of the two.[17] But no one has given good answers to the similar questions (italicized above) about historical materialism. I offer some not very satisfactory answers in Chapter X of *KMTH*. This seems to me an important area of future research for historical materialists, since the functional construal of their doctrine cannot be avoided.[18]

Let me now summarize my argument for the thesis that the chief explanatory claims of historical materialism are functional in form. Those claims are that

   (3)   the level of development of productive power explains the nature of the economic structure

and

   (5)   the economic structure explains the nature of the superstructure.

I take (3) and (5) to be functional explanations because I cannot otherwise reconcile them with two further Marxian theses, namely that

   (6)   the economic structure promotes the development of the productive forces

and

   (7)   the superstructure stabilizes the economic structure.

(6) and (7) entail that the economic structure is functional for the development of the productive forces, and that the

superstructure is functional for the stability of the economic structure. These claims do not by themselves entail that economic structures and superstructures are *explained* by the stated functions: *A* may be functional for *B* even though it is false that *A* exists *because* it is functional for *B*. But (6) and (7), *in conjunction with (3) and (5)*, do force us to treat historical materialist explanation as functional. No other treatment preserves consistency between the explanatory primacy of the productive forces over the economic structure and the massive control of the latter over the former, or between the explanatory primacy of the economic structure over the superstructure and the latter's regulation of the former.

I hold that the central explanations of historical materialism are functional explanations, and I defend functional explanation as an explanatory device, but I do not defend the sloppy functional explanatory theorizing in which so many Marxists engage.[19]

Many Marxist exercises in functional explanation fail to satisfy even the preliminary requirement of showing that A *is* functional for *B* (whether or not it is also *explained* by its function(s)). Take, for example, the claim that the contemporary capitalist state functions to protect and sustain the capitalist system. Legislation and policy in the direct interest of the capitalist class can reasonably be regarded as confirming it. But what about putative counter-examples, such as social welfare provision and legal immunities enjoyed by trade unions? These too might be functional for capitalism, in an indirect way, but that is something which needs to be argued with care, not just asserted. But those who propound the general claim about the state rarely trouble to say what sort of evidence would falsify or weaken it, and therefore every action of the state is treated as confirmatory, since there is always some way, legitimate or spurious, in which the action can be made to look functional.

Methodological indiscipline is then compounded when, having satisfied himself that state policy is functional, the theorist treats it, without further argument, as also functionally explained. He proceeds from '*A* is functional for *B*' to '*B* functionally explains *A*' without experiencing any need to justify the step, if, indeed, he notices that he has taken a step from one position to a distinct and stronger one.

II   *How Class Struggles Fits In*

'The history of all hitherto existing society,' says *The Communist Manifesto*, 'is the history of class struggles.'[20] Yet class struggle was hardly mentioned in the foregoing outline of historical materialism. Therefore, a critic might say, either Marx had more than one theory of history, or I have misrepresented his views.

One response would be to deflate the theoretical value of the quoted remark by emphasizing its political role as the first sentence of the main body of an insurrectionary text. But I prefer to leave the sentence intact and accommodate it. I do not want to deny that all history is the history of class struggle.

Why, then, did class struggle receive so little attention in section I of this paper? Because that section was devoted to the fundamental explanations of the course of history and the structure of society, not to the main events of that course and the surface relief of society, where class struggle looms large.

There are two ways of accepting the *Manifesto* sentence without sacrificing the theory of section I. The first, and less interesting, way is to take it as saying that *there is always a class struggle going on*. One may claim, in that spirit, that all history is the history of class struggle, without implying that that is all that history is, or even that that is what history most fundamentally is.

In the second way of taking the sentence all history is the history of class struggle in the more important sense that *major historical changes are brought about by class struggle*. Yet that is consistent with the doctrine of section I, since (so historical materialism says) if we want to know why class struggle effects this change rather than that, we must turn to the dialectic of forces and relations of production which governs class behaviour and is not explicable in terms of it, and which determines what the long-term outcome of class struggle will be.

Things other than forces and relations of production, such as the interactional structures studied by game theory,[21] help to explain the vicissitudes of class struggle and the strategies pursued in it, but they cannot give a Marxist answer to the question why class wars (as opposed to battles) are settled one way rather than another. *Marx finds the answer in the character of the productive forces*: 'The conditions under which definite productive forces can be applied are the conditions of the rule of a definite class of society'. The class which rules through a period, or emerges triumphant from epochal conflict, is the class best suited, most able and disposed, to preside over the development of the productive forces at the given time.[22] That answer may be untenable, but I cannot envisage an alternative to it which would qualify as historical materialist. It is, moreover, an answer which Marx did not merely give when generalizing about history, but which he applied to cases, as, for example, when he said that

> If the proletariat overthrows the political rule of the bourgeoisie, its victory will only be temporary ... as long as the material conditions have not yet been created which make necessary the abolition of the bourgeois mode of production.[23]

Note that Marx writes not 'make possible', but 'make necessary', a phrase which limits what can be independently decided by class struggle more than the former one would. *The Communist Manifesto* contains similar phrases,[24] and therefore cannot be recruited to the non-Marxist view that all history is, in the final analysis, *explained* by class struggle.

Prosecuting his contention that Marxism should abandon functional explanation and contract a liaison with game theory, Jon Elster remarks that 'game theory is invaluable to any analysis of the historical process that centres on exploitation, struggle, alliances and revolution'.[25] But for Marxian analysis those phenomena are not primary but, as it were, immediately secondary, on the periphery of the centre: they are among the 'forms in which men become conscious of the conflict [between forces and relations of production] and fight it out'.[26] To put the point differently, we may say that the items on Elster's list are the actions at the centre of the historical process, but for Marxism there are also items more basic than actions at its centre.

By 'revolution' Elster must mean the political phenomenon of transfer of state power, as opposed to the transformation of economic structure political revolution initiates or reflects. Many facts about political revolutions are accessible to game theoretical explanation, but not the world-historical facts that there was a bourgeois revolution and that there will be a proletarian one.

While realising that I insist on a 'fundamentalist' reading of historical materialism, Richard Miller notes that 'Cohen ... allows that political and ideological struggle may be essential to the destruction of the old social relations'.[27] Indeed, and I am prepared to go further. I do not wish to deny that class struggle is always essential for social transformation. My position does not prevent me from accepting Marx and Engels' statement that 'the class struggle is the immediate driving power of history'.[28] On the contrary: it is the doctrine expounded in Part I of this paper which illuminates the otherwise puzzling occurrence of the word 'immediate' in this important sentence. 'Immediate' is opposed to 'underlying'.

The reader might now agree that the following characterization of my views distorts them:

> Cohen ... seems committed to the view that the kind of human activity capable of effecting social change would have to be not consciously political activity but technical and scientific activity: the invention of new technology, having as its unconscious byproduct the emergence of new social relations.[29]

I do not see how one can wring out of my book a denial that consciously political activity effects social change. How could an explanation why politics effects this social change rather than that entail a denial that politics effects social change? Marx was not being untrue to what I claim was his theory when he called on workers, rather than scientists and technicians, to revolutionize society. In encouraging workers to bring about social change he was not asking them to bring about what would explain their doing so: the exhaustion of the progressive capacity of the capitalist order, and the availability of enough productive power to instal a socialist one.

I admitted on p. 119 that I do not have a good answer to the question how productive forces select economic structures which promote their development. To be sure, we can say that the adjustment of relations to forces occurs through class struggle. But that is not a fully satisfying answer to the question of p. 119, since it does not specify the filiation, or filiations, from contradiction between forces and relations of production to the class struggle supposed to resolve it. What activates the prospective new class? What ensures its victory? These are the questions that need attention, and not only for the sake of good theory.[30]

III Personal Interlude

This volume celebrates the continuing vigour of the Marxist tradition, and I am honoured that the editor has allowed me to discuss my interpretation of historical materialism in it. I should like to describe, very briefly, how my own allegiance to Marxism was formed.

My parents were Jewish factory workers in Montreal who met in the course of struggles to build unionism in the garment trade, in the face of (literally) brutal boss and police repression. When I was four years old they enrolled me in the Morris Winchewsky Jewish School, which was run by a communist Jewish organization. It was the only school I attended until I was eleven, when raids by the anti-subversive squad of the Province of Quebec police on the premises of the organization and on the school itself made it impossible for the school to continue. (This was in 1952, and the raids were part of the distinctive Québecois contribution to the Cold War Red Scare then in course in North America).

This background caused me to be familiar with rudimentary Marxist ideas pretty early on, and by the time I reached McGill University to embark on a B.A. I had read, with imperfect understanding, a number of what are sometimes called 'the classics'. I was certain, at seventeen, that Engels's *Anti-Dühring* contained all the philosophical truth there was. I came to see its limitations later, and I now regard the philosophical parts of it — as opposed to the social theory — as naïve. My commitment to historical materialism was more durable, and I long intended to expound and defend it as best I could, and that is how I came to write the book whose main lines are given in section I of this paper.

The book was a fairly strenuous labour since it had to be written in, so to speak, double harness: because it was a defence, and a defence of Marx, virtually every contention[31] had to be both plausibly attributable to Marx and plausible in its own right.

When I had finished the book, an unexpected thing happened. I came to feel, what I had not consciously anticipated when planning it or writing it, that I had written the book as repayment for what I had received. It reflected my gratitude to my parents, to the school which taught me, and to the communist community in which I grew up. It was my homage to the milieu in which I learned the plain Marxism defended in *KMTH*. But now that the book was written the debt was paid, and I no longer felt it necessary to adjust my thinking to that of Marx. I felt I could think fully for myself, for the first time. I do not mean that I forthwith stopped believing what I had believed when I embarked on the book, but I felt I did not *have* to believe it any more.

In the five years which have passed since *KMTH* was submitted to the publisher I have come to think more critically about historical materialism. I have not rejected it, but I have developed doubts about it.[32] I have also been involved, with many others, in investigations which seek to preserve what is good in it and eliminate what is bad. The tentative remarks which follow are a contribution to that collective process of revaluation.

IV Fettering

I found a good deal of ambiguity in traditional statements of historical materialism, and much of *KMTH* is an exercise in disambiguation. But I have become aware, partly because of the large amount of searching criticism I have received, that the book contains as much ambiguity as it dispels.

There is, for example, and as Richard Miller has noted,[33] a very important vacillation in it between contrasting conceptions of what it is for relations of production to *fetter* productive forces, conceptions which, following Miller, we can call those of *Absolute Stagnation* and *Relative Inferiority*. On the Absolute conception, fettering relations prevent all further improvement in productivity. On the Relative conception, they may or may not do so, and there is no reason to think that in general they do so, for on the Relative conception there is fettering when different feasible relations of production would develop the productive forces faster, and not just temporarily, but over a considerable period of time. On the Relative conception it suffices for fettering that existing relations are not optimal for the long run[34] development of the productive forces.

It is natural, at this point, to try to choose between the two conceptions, but, as we shall see, it is difficult to favour either. An adequate conception of fettering must meet two constraints, imposed by the 1859 Preface sentences in which fettering is described:

> At a certain stage of their development, the material productive forces of society come in conflict with the existing relations of production ... From forms of development of the productive forces these relations turn into their fetters. Then begins an epoch of social revolution.

The first two sentences lay down what may be called the *predictability constraint*: it must be plausible to suppose that, under continued development of the productive forces, relations do, sooner or later, become fetters. The *revolution constraint*, which comes from the third sentence, is that it must be plausible to suppose that when relations become fetters they are revolutionized.

Let me say what is meant by calling the foregoing *constraints* on an adequate conception of fettering. The constraint derives from what Marx said, together with the way the world is. To illustrate for the case of the revolution constraint: since Marx said fettering is followed by revolution, an adequate conception of fettering must make it plausible to say, *given how the world works*, that fettering would indeed be followed by revolution. The constraint is laid down by Marx, but how well it is met depends on the degree of fit between the concept we construct and the way the world is.

Now the reason why it is, as I said, hard to favour either the Absolute Stagnation or the Relative Inferiority conceptions of fettering is that neither seems able to meet both the predictability and the revolution constraints. The Absolute conception perhaps meets the revolution constraint, but it certainly does not meet the predictability constraint: there is no good reason to think, for example, that, were capitalism to last forever, then the development of the productive forces would grind to a halt, even if it makes sense to suppose that, were their development to stop, an epoch of revolution would ensue. (The more extreme devotees of the Law of the Tendency of the Rate of Profit to Fall think that not merely increases in productivity but production itself will stop, forever, if capitalism lasts. They have no difficulty espousing the Absolute conception of fettering, but non-communicants of their sect are less lucky).

The Relative Inferiority conception meets the predictability constraint better: it seems probable that all class bound relations of production are only finitely flexible, and that with continued development of productive power they become less good than other relations would be at facilitating further productive progress. But Relative Inferiority satisfies the revolution constraint less readily. For the costs and dangers of revolution, both to those initiating it and to those who follow them, make it unreasonable to expect a society to undergo revolution just because relations which are better at developing the productive forces are possible. Note that relations can be Relative fetters even when they are stimulating faster productive development than has ever before occurred. Is it plausible to suppose that revolution would be risked at a time of *accelerated* development of the productive forces, just because there would be still faster development under different relations? Would workers overthrow a capitalism which has reduced the length of each computer generation to one year because socialism promises to make it nine months?

My doubt that the Relative conception satisfies the revolution constraint is not based on the false proposition that people revolt only when it is in their selfish interest to do so: arguably, the structure of collective action is such that almost none would revolt, under any conditions, and on any conception of fettering, if that false proposition were true.[35] But one can affirm that unselfish inspiration is a necessary condition of revolutionary action and still believe that people are unlikely to embark on revolution when the *status quo* is not intolerable, the costs and dangers of insurgency are severe, and success is uncertain, and that is enough to generate doubt that the Relative conception satisfies the revolution constraint.

Neither Absolute Stagnation nor Relative Inferiority will do, and I am inclined to conclude that the notion that revolution follows on fettering of the *development* of the productive forces cannot be saved. I now think a quite different formulation of the Marxist theory of social change is required.

I think we shall reach the required formulation by exploring the idea that the fettering which provokes revolution is of the *use*, rather than of the *development*, of the productive forces. The development of the productive forces is growth in their productive power, or increase in how much *can be* (not *is being*) produced.[36] Fettering the development of the productive forces is, accordingly, restricting the growth of a capacity. It is, for example, reducing the rate of growth of productive capacity to zero, as in the Absolute Stagnation conception, or rendering that rate lower than it could be, as in the Relative Inferiority conception. But whether growth in productive capacity is in some way being impeded is a quite different issue from whether, and to what extent, productive capacity is being effectively used. And it now seems to me that the latter issue is the more important one from the point of view of the dynamics of social change.

I now attempt two illustrations of this point.

Early modern forms of division of labour in what Marx called 'manufacture' demanded the concentration in one place of large numbers of workers. Such concentration was variously forbidden and hampered by feudal and semi-feudal bonds and regulations, which tied producers to particular lords and masters in dispersed locations. Here, then, the relations of production fettered the use of the productive forces and, moreover, those relations came under pressure for that reason. Change occurred because of the gap between what *could* be achieved and what *was* being achieved, rather than because of the gap between how fast capacity was improving and how fast it could be improved: the second gap existed but it is hard to believe that it was comparably powerful as a precipitant of social change.

Another illustration. I would claim that capitalist relations of production impede optimally productive use of the high technology those relations are so good at creating. Under capitalism advances in computer and electronic engineering cause economic dislocation, unemployment, and the degradation of work sometimes called 'deskilling', whereas under different arrangements the same forces of production could be used to bring about a benign realignment of labour, leisure and education. I think, too, that there might be increasing recognition of the irrationality of the existing use of contemporary technological marvels and, as a result, socialist social change. If that happened, the change would occur not at all because capitalism does not replace a given generation of computers quickly enough, but because it does not make good use of any generation of computers. Once again, the operative discrepancy would be not between how fast what can be done improves and how fast it could improve, but between what is done and what could be done.

We can call the conception I have sketched Use Fettering, and we can think of Absolute Stagnation and Relative Inferiority as types of Development Fettering. Use Fettering seems to satisfy the predictability constraint better than Absolute Stagnation does. As I had occasion to remark earlier, all class bound economic systems are only finitely flexible, and they are therefore sooner or later unable to make optimal use of the developments in productive capacity which they induce or allow.[37] In addition, Use Fettering meets the revolution constraint better than Relative Inferiority does, since the discrepancy between capacity and use is more perceptible and is a more potent stimulant of unrest, protest and change than is the short-fall in rate of development implied by Relative Inferiority.

It might be said that I am exaggerating the size of the shift from Development Fettering to Use Fettering, since relations which make better use of existing productive capacity will tend also to be better at enhancing it. But I see no reason for believing that that is in general true. Many socialists would now concede that nothing can match capitalism as a stimulant to progress in productive power,[38] but they nevertheless favour socialism since they think somewhat slower productive progress is a reasonable price to pay for better use of productive power at every stage. Perhaps those socialists are being unduly pessimistic, but they are not wrong because of a law which connects the various virtues economic structures can have.

The move from Development to Use Fettering opens up (if I may be permitted the vulgarism) a whole new can of worms, and there are many difficulties in the foregoing sketch which the deadline for submission of this piece prevents me from confronting. Refinements will have to come later. For the time being let me indicate, perforce only grossly, how large a change in central formulations the recommended move demands. We now have to say, instead of what is said in the first sentence of Section I above, something like this: history is the growth of human productive power, and forms of society rise and fall according as they enable or discourage use of the productive capacity whose expansion that growth is. The connection between the dialectic of forces and relations of production on the one hand and class struggle on the other will also have to be rethought. I can do no more than mention these large problems here.

A critic sympathetic to Use Fettering might contend that what needs revision is what I created out of Marx, not Marx himself, who already preferred Use to Development Fettering. But I think we have reached the recommended new path by exploring ambiguities which Marx did not so much as glimpse, and he certainly did not have Use Fettering distinctly in mind when he wrote the crucial Preface sentence, 'From forms of development of the productive forces these relations turn into their fetters'. In the natural reading of this sentence, relations which have become fetters cannot also still be forms of development of the productive forces. But relations which fetter the use of the productive forces could still be forms of development of the productive forces. Hence Marx did not mean 'fetters on use of the productive forces' when he wrote 'fetters' in the above sentence.[39]

Notes

1. *Karl Marx's Theory of History: A Defence*, Oxford and Princeton, 1978; referred to hereafter as *KMTH*.
2. Sections I and II present a somewhat revised and expanded version of material which also appears in 'Functional Explanation, Consequence Explanation, and Marxism', *Inquiry*, Volume 25, 1982, pp. 28-35, and in 'Reply to Elster on "Marxism, Functionalism and Game Theory" ', *Theory and Society*, forthcoming. I am grateful to the editors of these journals for permission to use the relevant material here.
3. Preface to *A Contribution to the Critique of Political Economy*, 1859, many editions, italics added.
4. *The Poverty of Philosophy*, in Marx and Engels, *Collected Works*, Volume 6, London, 1976, p. 166.
5. As opposed, for example, to their socially developed needs, reference to which would be inappropriate here (though not, of course, everywhere).
6. For a set of correspondences of relations to forces of production, see *KMTH*, p. 198.
7. This is not the only important concept of surplus in Marxism, but I invoke it here because it is a concept of something purely material, and I conceive historical materialism as an attempt to explain the social by reference to the material: see *KMTH*, pp. 61, 98, and Chapter IV, *passim*, for defence of the distinction between material and social properties of society.
8. I call such power 'economic' in virtue of what it is power over, and irrespective of the means of gaining, sustaining or exercising the power, which need not be economic. See *KMTH*, pp. 223-4.
9. The discussion is pursued at pp. 66-69 of *KMTH*.

10. See *KMTH*, p. 29, footnote 2, for a list of authors who take for granted that productive forces belong to the economic structure.

11. See *KMTH*, pp. 28-9.

12. See *KMTH*, Chapter IV, section (1).

13. See *KMTH*, p. 30, for a distinction between the material and the economic bases of society: the productive forces belong to the former and are therefore not part of the latter.

14. I criticize the common practice of overpopulating the superstructure in a review of Melvin Rader's *Marx's Interpretation of History* (New York, 1979) in *Clio*, Volume X, No. 2, 1981, pp. 229-33.

15. But not as precise as in sections (4) and (7) of Chapter IX and section (2) of Chapter X of *KMTH*, where the structure of functional explanation is described in detail.

    For recent doubts about these matters, with which I did not want to complicate the present exposition, see 'Functional Explanation … ', op. cit., pp. 35-6.

16. In private communications and now in 'Marxism's Central Puzzle', in Terence Ball and James Farr (eds.), *After Marx*, Cambridge, 1983. (While I accept Van Parijs' criticism of my ambiguity and his proposal for eliminating it, I wholly reject the more substantive criticisms he attaches thereto. See my 'Reply to Critics', in *Analyse und Kritik*, forthcoming, which also contains a German translation of Van Parys' essay.)

17. See *KMTH*, pp. 287-9.

18. For recent valuable work on the problem of the mechanism in functional explanation, see Philippe Van Parijs, *Evolutionary Explanation in the Social Sciences*, Totowa, New Jersey, 1981.

19. For an impressive catalogue of methodologically lax uses of functional explanation, see Jon Elster on 'Marxism, Functionalism and Game Theory' in *Theory and Society*, forthcoming.

20. *The Communist Manifesto*, in Marx and Engels, *Collected Works*, Volume 6, op. cit., p. 482.

21. Jon Elster has persuaded me that game theory is supremely relevant to certain Marxist concerns, but I deny that it can replace, or even supplement, functional explanation at the very heart of historical materialism: see the *Theory and Society* symposium referred to in notes 2 and 19.

22. The quotation is from *The German Ideology*, New York, 1965, p. 85, and the sentences preceding and following it are from p. 149 of *KMTH*, which contains further discussion and more textual references.

23. *Moralising Criticism and Critical Morality*, in Marx and Engels, *Collected Works*, Volume 6, op. cit., p. 319, and see Allen Wood, *Karl Marx*, London, 1981, p. 250(41) for a list of texts which carry a similar message.

24. According to the *Manifesto*, the 'economic and political dominion of

the bourgeois class' was an outcome of the fact that feudal relations of production had become fetters on productive progress and therefore '*had* to be burst asunder' (ibid., p. 489).

25. Elster, *op. cit.*

26. Preface to *A contribution to the Critique of Political Economy*.

27. 'Productive Forces and the Forces of Change', *The Philosophical Review*, Volume XC, No.1 (January, 1981) p. 94. But Miller appears to think that this view of mine is an optional and rather arbitrarily added extra, 'readily detachable' from a theory assigning primacy to the development of the productive forces, since such a theory would 'suggest the effectiveness of an alternative to revolution, in which change is brought about by appeals to material desires common to all classes' ('Producing Change', in Ball and Farr (eds.), *op cit.*, p. 12 of typescript). This rather astonishingly presupposes that the material interest of humanity could not conflict with the material interest of ruling class persons. For my part, I expect no one under socialism to be as rich as Rockefeller, and I therefore expect Rockefeller to be hostile to the idea of socialism.

28. It comes from their letter of 17-18/9, 1879 to Bebel, Liebknecht and Bracke: see Marx and Engels, *Selected Correspondence*, Moscow, 1975, p. 307. (The word translated 'immediate' is '*nächste*'.)

29. From a review of *KMTH* by Richard Norman, in *The London Review of Books*, February 21, 1980, p. 6.

30. For good criticisms of my failure to deal well with these questions, see Jon Elster, 'Cohen on Marx's Theory of History', *Political Studies*, Volume XXVIII (March, 1980), p. 124; Andrew Levine and Erik Wright, 'Rationality and Class Struggle', *New Left Review*, No. 123 (Sept/Oct, 1980), pp. 58ff. Joshua Cohen, review of *KMTH* in *The Journal of Philosophy*, Volume LXXIX, (May, 1982), pp. 266ff.

31. The exceptions are noted in remarks at the end of the Foreword to the paperback edition.

32. See my 'Reconsidering Historical Materialism', in John Chapman and J. Roland Pennock (eds.), *Nomos*, Volume XXIV: *Marx and Legal Theory*, New York, 1983.

33. *Op. cit.*, pp. 96-7: Miller's reference to p. 175 of *KMTH* is particularly telling.

34. How long a run is that? It must be long enough to defeat the claim to superiority of relations which are merely ephemerally superior, but it need not be the longest conceivable run, which is all the way to the massive surplus associated with communism (see *KMTH*, p. 198): I fear I am not able at present to be more precise than that. It is logically possible that relations optimal in the relevantly long run are suboptimal, or even, logical possibility being what it is, disastrous, in still longer runs. But these logical possibilities are almost certainly not historical ones, so the conceptual embarrassment displayed in this footnote is almost certainly not damaging.

35. Purely selfish motivation tends to generate the game theoretical quandary known as 'Prisoner's Dilemma' in revolutionary situations, since, on selfish calculations, the marginal cost of participating in a revolution generally exceeds the maginal gain. The classic reference here is Mancur Olson, *The Logic of Collective Action*, Cambridge, Mass., 1965. See also Allen Buchanan, 'Revolutionary Motivation and Rationality', in M. Cohen *et alia* (eds), *Marx, Justice and History*, Princeton, 1980; William Shaw, 'Marxism, Revolution and Rationality', in Ball and Farr (eds), *op. cit.*, and my own 'Utopian and Scientific Socialism', forthcoming some day.

36. As I said on p. 56 of *KMTH*, the relevant 'concept of productivity differs from the one the economist uses when he compares the physical productivity of labour in different societies. Productivity in our sense is the maximum to which productivity in that sense could be raised, with existing means and knowledge ...'

37. 'Induce *or* allow' is of course, an all too pregnant disjunction. For a partial delivery of its meaning, see Chapter VI, section (7) of *KMTH*.

38. For a good discussion of this claim, see David Schweickart, *Capitalism or Worker Control?* New York, 1980, Chapters 3 and 4. For a vigorous rejection of it see the remarks from Jon Elster's unpublished 'Forces and Relations of Production' in section 12 of my 'Reconsidering Historical Materialism', *op. cit.* (I might add that Elster's work has so strongly influenced my views about forces and relations of production that I cannot tell which ideas in this final section of the present essay should be attributed to him).

39. I thank Arnold Zuboff for criticizing a draft of this piece with his customary care and insight, and I am particularly grateful for those of his objections and suggestions which provided the impetus to the shift from Development Fettering to Use Fettering. I also thank Steve Walt for his excellent criticisms of a preliminary version of the section on Fettering.

Gregor McLennan

Historical Materialism Today:
Some Variations and Problems

I

In his graveside tribute to Marx, Engels described his partner's chief intellectual discoveries as, first, the law of development of human history, and second, the motive principles of the capitalist mode of production. Marx's most systematic efforts went into the latter, and his enduring monument is unquestionably *Capital.* Yet it is the materialist conception of history (or historical materialism) which probably has been the more popular facet of Marxist teaching over the century since Engels's statement. The theory of value appears to have a technical basis that the theory of history lacks – certainly modern refutations of Marxian economics involve mathematical displays which are inappropriate to arguments for or against historical materialism. Moreover, historical materialism as a set of general principles does not strictly entail the *detail* of Marx's account of capitalist exploitation. So his two discoveries are in important respects separable.[1]

The very breadth of historical materialism has been one of its main strengths and sources of continued popularity: even the sharpest critics of Marxism appreciate Marx's bold strokes on the canvas of social history. However, the exact nature and content of historical materialism are not self-evident, and it seems worthwhile to take stock of the concept by reference to the competing interpretations in circulation, and to the quite taxing questions which can be raised about its definitions, historical scope, and its relevance to socialist politics. Of course, any such discussion will have its own preferred approach and guidelines, but one main aim of this essay is to leave open for digestion and further argument a number of problems or dilemmas which arise from my overall characterization of historical materialism.

This sort of analytical discussion perhaps requires a word of justification, since in its attention to conceptual rather than practical questions it exemplifies what many socialists take to be a peculiarly modern academic Marxism. The lessons of history, after all, should surely be practical rather than endlessly productive of intellectual tangles! No responsible Marxist student could fail to heed the real dangers signalled by that sort of criticism, or the deep social changes which fuel such well-meant warnings. But two things need to be said in defence of theory. First, it is seldom obvious – outside propaganda – what the lessons of history actually are. They depend very much on the questions asked of it and on agreement about the appropriate forms of analysis. So to demand that theory *directly* delivers politically usable lessons is to underrate the difficulties of research and generalisation; but it also plays down the primacy of strategic argument itself. Second, debates about the truth and scope of historical materialism are *not* merely the product of contemporary class-less Marxist philosophers. Marx himself left no absolute doctrines about history, and already in the 1880s socialist thinkers were busy constructing interpretations which relied on different aspects of Marx's legacy – interpretations which by and large are still with us. In the 1930s, Old Curiousity Shop in which political amateurs and literary dilettanti rummage around for decorative oddments'[2] – a sentiment which retains a certain resonance today. Yet Marxism has furnished a range of serious and spurious customers since its inauguration. And as an index of the longevity of 'academic' problems of definition, it should be pointed out that in his *Dialectics* (1936), Jackson himself spent around 100 pages defending historical materialism against his theoretical opponents without ever really presenting a clear and detailed exposition of the theory.[3]

II

One attractive way of forestalling disagreement within historical materialism is to see whether alternative interpretations or emphases can be located in the different phases of Marx's own theorizing. In a useful short introduction to the issues involved, Helmut Fleischer identifies three broad approaches in Marx.[4] The first is that of the 'early' Marx: here history is conceived as the process of human development and fulfillment. In that process, the alienation of man from man, and of individual from 'species-being' — intensified by class divided societies — is overcome in the self-identity of the socialist community. Fleischer is no anti-humanist, but he would agree with, for example, Althusser, that this view of the young Marx is excessively general and utopian. It seems to leave the details of historical change firmly relegated beneath a philosophical vision of the return of abstract, Promethean Man to 'himself'.

The second phase or approach is that of the 'pragmatic' or empirical Marx, exemplified in *The German Ideology* (1845-6). Marx and Engels firmly anchor the premises of ideas, social forms, and historical change in the production of material life. These facts and the connections they sustain are said to be empirically verifiable, containing no trace whatever of the philosophical speculation pedalled by the post-Hegelians — the 'putrescence of the absolute spirit'.[5]

The third conception of history in Marx is classically expressed in the 'Preface to the Critique of Political Economy' (1859). There, Marx asserts that the character of institutional superstructures and forms of consciousness is determined by the economic base, which consists of relations of production. These relations (forms of property and direct control of the means of production) in turn correspond to the level of the forces of production (technology, knowledge, labour skills, etc.). Entire systems of production relations are held to rise or fall insofar as they facilitate or fetter the growth of the productive forces. Marx also has it that there is a discernible and logical succession of these systems, the modes of production, from primitive communism through the asiatic, ancient, feudal, capitalist, and advanced communist modes. This is, for Marx, a progressive evolution.[6]

The first reason why historical materialism is disputed

territory is that these various approaches conflict at points, yet each has textual warrant in Marx's writings. In fact, it could be argued that Fleischer has too clearly separated the versions, and that this makes more difficult the task of arriving at 'what Marx really meant'. For example, while I'd agree with those who demote the 'early Marx', it is also clear that the 'philosophical' Marx has suffered some caricature recently. Most of the early writings, it is true, are not strictly historical. But they are, centrally, arguments against the illegitimate intrusion of idealist philosophy into questions which have a human and material foundation.[7] Similarly, the 'scientific' Marx of later years held on to some clearly 'philosophical' beliefs about historical necessity. Accordingly, Fleischer opts for the 'pragmatic' Marx. But in *The German Ideology* Marx lays down the first approximation to the necessary sequence outlined in the 1859 Preface – disliked by Fleischer because of its fatalism. In addition, the former book lays down elements of a *theory* of history, it is not itself a historical work, and so belongs to the early phase too. When we turn to Marx's 'genuinely' historical writings, like the *Eighteenth Brumaire* or parts of *Capital,* an amalgam of the various emphases mentioned can often be found. This fact indeed testifies to the richness of Marx's work, but it is difficult to find any direct 'confirmation' of general concepts, so specific is Marx's political and historical focus.[8] One recent commentator has added to this complex search for simple principles by arguing that it is in the Introduction to the *Grundrisse* (1857) where Marx's ideas about historical thinking are best (though not too clearly) laid down. Marx there is thought to maintain that historical logic is constructed from present concepts, and that 'the only reason in history is the reason in historical writing'.[9] This view, if true, would tend to undermine all three of Fleischer's Marx phases, and it is not implausible, given the tough formulations of the Introduction. But the sheer difficulty of 'returning to Marx' for explicit guidance about historical materialism is indicated when we consider that this construal (which denies the real existence of processes outside the theorist's conceptual apparatus) has been a fashionable position across a range of disciplinary interests in recent years. The point here is not that these exegetical issues cannot be settled, but that what we look for in Marx will be heavily governed by current preoccupations – to the stage where relatively little can be resolved about the nature and adequacy of the theory or method solely by reference to its author and origin.

III

By the 1890s, rather different reconstructions of historical materialism were already in play. In Perry Anderson's words, socialist theorists

> were concerned in different ways to *systematize* historical materialism as a comprehensive theory of man and nature, capable of replacing rival bourgeois disciplines and providing the workers' movement with a broad and coherent vision of the world that could be easily grasped by its militants. This task involved them, as it had done for Engels, in a two-fold commitment: to produce general philosophical statements of Marxism as a conception of history, and to extend it into domains that had not been directly touched by Marx. The similarity of the titles of some of their main expositions indicates their common preoccupations: *On Historical Materialism* (Mehring), *Essays on the Materialist Conception of History* (Labriola), *The Development of the Monist Conception of History* (Plekhanov), *The Materialist Conception of History* (Kautsky).[10]

Common preoccupations; but sharp exchanges too. Plekhanov defended a literally materialist view of history, highlighting the technical aspects of productive forces, and indeed the massive presence of physical geography, within a framework of economic determination. Labriola responded with the claim that Marxism was not a philosophy of history, and not a materialist determinism of any kind. In this he set a precedent for Gramsci's complaints against Bukharin thirty years later.[11] The emphasis within Italian Marxism then and now has been a concern to uphold Marxism as an empirical or historical method rather than an evolutionary pattern.

These two general perspectives – empirical-historical on the one hand, philosophical-evolutionary on the other – do not reduce to differences in 'national' or cultural context, and they remain one means of coming to terms with the options available within the Marxist tradition. Most writers would probably borrow from both angles of approach, and there is a spectrum of shifting emphases rather than a fixed polarity. But providing the 'abstract' and provisional nature of these contrasting emphases is marked, they serve to trace contemporary arguments between Marxists.

The idea that historical materialism is a method for empirical and provisional deployment seems to avoid the frequent anxieties expressed about historical determinism or dogmatic theorizing in Marxism. Engels and Lenin produced a number of telling criticisms of those Marxists who seemed to use the theory of history as a means of *avoiding* close contextual description. However, neither of those figureheads of the tradition thought of the materialist conception of history as being a method *distinct* from the theory of historical development as laid down in Marx's 1859 Preface. Today, there are at least two main versions of Marxism-as-method, and each has the merit of pointing to the empirical emcumbrances that 'technological' Marxists shoulder when faced with detailed historical questions.

The first current of Marxism-as-method rejects two key propositions of classical Marxism (at least in its appropriation by the official Communist movement this century): the primacy of the productive forces, and the distinction between base and superstructure. Social relations, it is claimed, are neither subordinate to the productive forces, nor restricted to a narrowly conceived 'economy'. On this view, Marxism definitely abolishes the splitting up of social and class relations into different 'factors', or spheres, or social 'levels'.[12] Productive forces themselves just *are* social relations, so have no independent causal or progressive presence outside the empirically open-ended character of social struggle and transformation.[13]

One objective of this sort of argument is to reinstate class struggle or political activism as the unpredictable heart of socialist analysis, be the struggle in the realm of production or culture. However the move from a concern to highlight empirical openness is not quite the same as giving 'an open-ended definition of the basic general concepts of historical materialism'.[14] This latter proposal in fact hides a substantial and certainly contestable alteration in Marxist (and Marx's) ideas about social causality. To say, for example, that productive forces are always embedded in social forms seems reasonable; to argue that this means forces *are* relations is idiosyncratic. When that proposal is combined with the rejection of the distinction between base and superstructure, then the very value of the term 'social relations' seems to come into question, since it must embrace a considerable range of different sorts of social interaction. Finally, Marxists who are fond of pointing to the 'bourgeois' or non-Marxist implications of a 'technological' theory of history must reckon with the fact that however impressive the terminology of struggle, 'activist' accounts of historical forces need not differ much from those of orthodox political science.[15]

Another strongly voiced current of opinion holds that Marxism is historical materialism and nothing more, where that term is identified with the detailed work of Marxist historians rather than philosophers or economists. Here, it is the closeness of Marx's methods of working to that of professional historians which confers merit upon his grander propositions. Pierre Vilar, for instance, takes pride in Marx's monumental and painstaking research procedures rather than the theses those labours served. If *Capital* is not quite a history book, he argues, it is certainly a historians' book.[16]

E.P. Thompson shares something of this attitude, though is inclined now to see *Capital* as problematical because it is not *enough* of a history book. Whilst philosophers such as Althusser defame Marx in the name of grotesque systems of pseudo-science, so Thompson's argument runs, it is also true that Marx himself was tainted by an unhelpful tendency to abstraction and speculation. Thompson therefore defends historical materialism in the empirical mode and according to the historians', not the philosophers', canon of proper explanation.[17]

These arguments appraise contributions to Marxism from an antecedent conception of historical writing and research. In fact, this is a very recent view. The claim made by Thompson that he is representing the *tradition* of historical materialism is surely an exaggeration. Whether it be Plekhanov or Christopher Hill, Porshnev or Dobb, Marxist historians have not generally disputed on narrow specialist grounds the close connections, within Marxism, of history, theory, and philosophy. Thompson's other major claim – that there is a distinct logic of explanation peculiar to historiography which must inevitably divide Marxists into historical materialists and idealists – is equally contentious.[18] It is doubtful if practising historians would, as a body, recognise or endorse that logic, whatever formulation it received. Moreover, the forms and labours of historical research are not of an entirely special kind; nor is it easy to split off the 'factual' or empirical basis of research methodology from wider political and theoretical organisation and argument within historiography. Indeed, it could be said that history, as a 'discipline', may be intrinsically *more* speculative than, say, sociology, due to the relative paucity of evidence and the need to organise it into a longer term analytic or narrative structure. So, like any other discipline, history has its research peculiarities, but what is important about its *explanations* is no less open to epistemological inquiry than any other knowledge-yielding activity. To present Marx himself as a technical historian as if that alone conferred greatness upon him, is a rather academic sense of specialism. And it is important to say that Thompson's arguments against philosophy and for empirical history – where that comes to be equated with Reason itself – are rather uneven, often relying on connotative or rhetorical connections rather than decisive analysis.[19]

IV

The other main perspective I have schematically highlighted is the idea that historical materialism must be a theory of history, and not merely an empirical methodology. As such, the formulations of the 1859 Preface are foundational. 'Old fashioned' historical materialism has made a come-back recently, its most precise and cogent form being articulated by G.A. Cohen.[20] The chief claims of this view are the 'primacy thesis' and the 'development thesis'. The first is that the level of development of the productive forces accounts for the rise or decline of particular sets of social relations of production. The second is that the forces tend inexorably to develop through history, thus providing the motor and goal of the historical process. The relation between the forces and relations of production is not necessarily deterministic, since both the specific character of the relations, and their ability substantially to react upon the forces, are not 'given' by the level of the forces. However, the relations come into existence because they serve to promote the forces' growth, and disappear when they cease to enhance the forces' development. This connection between forces and relations (and between base and superstructure) is said to be a functional one, and those writers who defend the new old-fashioned view regard it as an important part of their case to clarify functional explanation as against the unscientific, purposive connotations often detected in the idea of something 'serving the ends' of something else.

One achievement of this school of thought is to rescue a 'basic' historical materialism from charges of 'vulgar Marxism' – an all-purpose charge which is of no real use in advancing discussion. It has also helpfully argued that functional explanation is not the same as functional*ism*: the latter but not the former builds into its initial concepts the necessary 'fit' between cause and consequence. Finally, the proponents of the 'forces' perspective reintroduce the idea that in any Marxist outlook, the idea of history having a progressive direction cannot be wished away on either theoretical or moral grounds.

Two sets of difficulties confront even the best formulations of 'classical' historical materialism.[21] First, what exactly is a productive force and why should it be so important? No one denies that as a matter of historical existence, these two analytical aspects of production (the forces and relations) are intertwined. Consequently, their separation in theory leads to some odd empirical results. Cohen, for example, includes some sorts of clothing and food in the productive forces (those necessary to material production itself), but not others. In many cases this distinction must appear quite arbitrary, since it may not be possible to give a 'technical' ruling on what is strictly 'necessary' for a particular labour process. In addition, to separate the product of class and cultural struggle into 'material' and (presumably) 'leisure' components obscures how closely these elements are historically tied together. Similar difficulties of subdivision into material/technical and cultural/ideological categories affect discussions of the role of science, or the description of particular labour processes as a whole in versions of Marxism which do not shy away from its 'technological determinist' implications.[22] One overarching problem or fallacy is the tendency of proponents of the primacy thesis to attribute certain *needs* to the productive forces themselves which are then satisfied or temporarily unfulfilled by social relations. In fact this is a hypostatization of dubious use, since only people or societies have needs, which are met or thwarted by the level of available technology and by the state of popular control over production.

The second set of questions is to do with the capability of the primacy and development theses adequately to grasp historical processes. For example it is clear that, in at least some cases, new social relations emerge *before* new forces of production, and this seems to contradict the theses. Cohen and his followers respond by arguing that the outworn relations can fetter the very *potential* for growth in current forces, and so, perfectly in line with the theory, give way to new relations which *do* in fact facilitate that growth. However, this reply shows the flexibility of the primacy thesis only by revealing its massive generality: it becomes difficult to see what would not empirically confirm it. Certainly, Cohen and others are willing to say that, for example, in pre-capitalist modes of production the facilitation of the forces by the relations is *indirect* and not, as in capitalism, visible and strenuous. Some critics of historical materialism argue that its avoidance of empirical embarrassment only at the cost of excessive generality (especially concerning pre-capitalism) is the mark of the theory's failure, not its resilience.[23] Without going that far, it does seem clear that in the detail of the exposition, the centrality of social relations is conceded, since they are also allowed to govern the rate of growth in the forces — even to the point of regression or stagnation for long slices of historical time. The bold outlines of the theory may therefore be preserved, but its content remains fairly thin.[24]

The primacy thesis, then, applies principally to long-term processes, and refers to one main aspect of central historical transitions. One wary underwriter of this 'broad' interpretation of 'classical' historical materialism – Göran Therborn – can find only two central cases of its truth: when sufficient productivity allowed the emergence of class society; and when abundance will herald the onset of advanced communism. Yet history as we know it falls awkwardly and bulkily between those turning points![25]

V

The opposition between methodological Marxism and the so-called technological theory of history seems less sharp in the light of the discussion so far. In fact, as Croce pointed out in the 1890s, Marxism cannot literally be a method, since a technique of research is available to anyone, whereas a conceptual framework, however skeletal, demands allegiances of a different sort. Some theorists (for example Georg Lukács and G.D.H. Cole) misleadingly declared themselves for a 'methodological' Marxism when their own – very different – brands of Marxism clearly involved a substantive rather than 'open ended' interpretation of history.[26]

Correspondingly, productive forces Marxism is *less* directive and onerous than either its headline promise or its anxious opponents suggest. Cohen, for one, is keen to distinguish his indication of the broad features of historical change from a 'reading' of history.[27] One difference between these notions, I take it, is that a 'theory' but not a 'reading' requires and seeks empirical filling out and qualification. A theory in this sense is a framework of analysis rather than an irreversible attempt to *constitute* the meaning of history, a meaning which can be found pervading all its phenomenal forms and empirical appearances.

However encouraging this reconciliation between perspectives might appear, it is important to be aware of the variety and complexity of potential syntheses. Maurice Cornforth tried to combine a sense of the 'laws of history' (based on the primacy thesis) with an attachment to empirical openness in his primer *Historical Materialism*.[28] He offered an account of Henry VIII's dispute with the Pope in these terms, arguing that dissatisfaction with his wife was subject to no historical laws (a questionable deduction in the light of feminist analysis), but that Henry's confiscation of Church lands was perfectly explicable in terms of the 'contradictory' social relations of the period. No doubt this latter claim is right – but the status of the 'contradiction' is unclear, and anyway nothing is said of the factor which in such accounts is held to *ground* the historical 'laws', namely productive forces. Similar tensions between confident listings of concepts and laws on the one hand, and historical hesitation, contradiction, or simply non-correspondence, on the other, tend to show up in textbooks on historical materialism coming from the Soviet Union.[29]

The tension between a Marxist theory of history and a 'reading' of it is not obviously resolved either, and can take different forms. Lukács, for example, rejected the materialist and technical aspects of Marxism but produced an overly Hegelian philosophy of history in which class consciousness, empirical knowledge, and history itself formed an unbreakable unity at the conceptual level, thus making objections to that unity nothing more than deficiencies in understanding: a characteristic defence of a purely philosophical reading. But more empirical approaches to the necessity and essence of historical development can be given. Yuri Semenov, for example, has defended and extended the traditional Soviet viewpoint along these lines.[30] He reinstates the sequence of modes of production by criticising the commonly-held idea that each and every society must pass through the specified number of socio-economic formations. Instead, Semenov shows that sequence to belong to the *totality* of diverse social 'organisms'. Empirically, only small numbers of social organisms in any historical phase make the transition from one mode of production to another, and these tend *not* to be the previously advanced centres, but peripheral ones. However, it is only due to the historical experience and leading role of those advanced centres that the new social organisms can make the leap across the historical stages to become the next 'leaders' or carriers of historical progress. Semenov's empirical 'reading' is therefore novel in its theoretical and historical sensitivity, but retains the orthodox sequence of modes of production (in the course of which he reinstates the oft-discredited 'Asiatic' mode of production).

Semenov's theory must survive the scrutiny of historians versed in the particular transitions with which he deals. But, as Ernest Gellner points out, it is a philosophical argument in key respects.[31] It *assumes* the unity and unilinearity of history rather than displaying it from a relatively open-ended standpoint. Of course, it is true and important that in taking the 'essentialist' option, Semenov is no more or less justified than those who would protest about it on the grounds that history is intrinsically pluralist, or discontinuist: for that view too is a philosophical one, making many more assumptions than its advocates care to admit. Still, the idea that history is necessarily single, having a clear direction and essential structure needs more discussion and qualification than Semenov is prepared to allow. Moreover, the relation between his theory and Soviet global policy is one of sophisticated justification, and however sophisticated it may be, there is surely a great moral risk in talking of political strategy in terms of its conformity to historical necessity. From a theoretical point of view, Semenov's stress on the term 'socio-economic formation' reminds us of the subtle differences between this and 'mode of production' and the former's greater usefulness for historiography in its emphasis on societies rather than economies. Yet while Semenov supports the doctrine of the primacy of the productive forces, he does not show its real presence within, or connection to, explanations of empirical history in terms of successions of social formations.

In its own way, then, Semenov's approach confirms the discrepancies as well as the strengths of a synthesis between philosophical and empirical Marxisms. Here lies the scope for creativity in Marxism today, but also its 'crisis'; its distinctive corpus of concepts and concerns, but also the doubts about what, in real terms, that corpus delivers. In fact, contemporary Marxism is *defined* by this skeletal indispensibility of historical materialism. Successive 'western' Marxists have tried to systematize the 'basic' concepts in such a way as to preserve the long-standing claims to 'science' by Marxists, yet have worked to avoid the discrepancies and dogmatisms attaching to previous attempts to do a similar theoretical job. And in the course of that very enterprise of systematization, the striving after logical or historical guarantees of adequacy, Marxists can become starkly brought up against the limitations of any such 'basic' definitions. In spite of the persistence of the language of doctrinal purity, few people, whether long toothed militants, socialist teachers, or the new 'middle-strata' Marxists are free from the temptation either to lapse into 'self-criticism' and even disillusionment, or to search around for political and theoretical supplements to historical materialism, taken from rather different traditions.[32] Politically, Marxists have had to re-examine questions of democracy, of the state, and of the socialist future itself. Intellectually, Marxism has taken on a flurry of previously 'alien' influences, whether from semiotics, analytical philosophy, biology, or psychoanalysis.

In this context, it becomes difficult to say exactly what a 'basic' historical materialism consists in. My own view is to endorse Croce's statement that historical materialism is neither method nor theory, but a canon of historical interpretation. Over the long-term, concepts of the forces-relations contradiction and of modes of production remain defensible tools of analysis. In addition, the broad historical sequence outlined by Marx and extended by, amongst others, Semenov, continues to be a touchstone for revisions and elaborations in historiography.

As a social theory, Marxism relies for its distinctiveness on principles of the primacy of material production, and of the priority of 'base' over 'superstructure'. These ideas, it is true, rise and fall in significance according to the historical and intellectual force of idealism (which on the whole has drastically declined). Yet they *can* be endorsed on formal as well as heuristic grounds, forming a legitimate (if increasingly trespassed) boundary for what it is to be deemed a Marxist analysis.[33]

Thirdly, Marxism places social classes at the centre of its

political analysis. However, in the long term approach to historical materialism, human agency and class struggles are derivative, not primary. By contrast, 'empirical' Marxisms tend to give those agencies exaggerated powers of social intervention. Struggles seem to be readily found in every 'arena' and interstice of socio-cultural life. The fact that such struggles are termed 'class struggles' often only by analogy (and so can be politically misleading) is a point against the second perspective, whilst the general implications of passivity in the first perspective of human limitation before natural and technological imperatives does not obviously enhance Marxism's claim to *be* a weapon in struggle.

V

One conclusion of this survey is that historical materialism today consists in some combination of these three elements. To some, that result will seem disappointingly flat. Others have found that, together with the critique of capitalism, these Marxist ingredients still amount to 'a grand synthesis of human understanding'. In that respect, historical materiaiism has shown a remarkable continuity and resilience.[34]

What is perhaps new or changing is the acuteness of the relationship between crisis and creativity in Marxism. One sign of this is my argument that it is, if not impossible, then certainly unwise to declare that a single, definitive version of historical materialism can be laid down and other claimants expelled from the doctrinal domain. Moreover, the 'unity' of theory and history in Marxism remains a standing aspiration rather than a settled achievement. With the passage of time, the strengths which define those aspirations may become sources of contradiction, and Marxists are obliged to pose for themselves — conceptually or empirically — a series of questions traditionally lodged by non-Marxist theorists.

One general source of concern is the role and legitimacy of philosophy in the Marxist outlook. The first aspect of this issue is to do with the assumptions we make in speaking of Marxism as scientific knowledge. Historical materialism was for many taken to be the 'application' of a more general set of philosophico-scientific principles – dialectical materialism. In Engels's and Lenin's formulations, it is not altogether clear whether dialectical materialism is to be seen as the primary basis of scientific and political thinking, or as a secondary generalization from those activities. In modified form, 'diamat' is still supported today by some Communist Parties and professional philosophers, but its force has considerably diminished. Both the content of the doctrine, and its rather grandiose status as the 'foundation' of specialist knowledges are questionable. Its two component terms, moreover, are often in tension rather than in harmony. In its general deployment, 'dialectic' can become a catch-all category which evades as much as it answers. It has been used (dubiously) to suggest a higher form of logic, and it has been used (with some justification) to counter the mechanical forms of its partner, materialism. But of course materialism can be less than 'mechanical', and in its sense of 'objectivity' has served to cancel out the excesses of an overly idealist sense of the dialectic. These changeable, contrasting usages within the Marxist tradition have formed a polemical crust through which it is difficult to see whether Marxism offers a 'core' philosophy, or whether the swings and roundabouts of 'dialectical materialism' promotes or inhibits substantive analysis. In any event, the spirit of synthesis in 'diamat' has been retained even by its critics, and Marxist philosophers have persisted with the search for scientific credentials on behalf of historical materialism. The aim is to secure Marxism against charges of 'ideology' and falsehood, yet few would now confidently claim that Marxism can be the arbiter of debates within science or philosophy (however 'bourgeois' these practices are reckoned to be). Accordingly, Marxist philosophers have become embroiled in all the trends and complications of modern philosophy. Two recent lines of thinking seem worthy of summary mention.

The Althusserian current drew on structuralist theory, Spinoza, and modern 'conventionalist' philosophy of science in an attempt to portray Marxist philosophy as the 'theory of theoretical practice'. This served to highlight the autonomy, coherence, and freedom-from-ideology of scientific purity, and in its allowance to Marxist philosophy an excessive judgmental function, Althusser's system was in key respects idealist. Yet despite the novelty of his nomenclature, Althusser's efforts were directed towards a typically Marxist task of the justification of historical materialist ideas by means of a higher philosophical appeal. And in the aftermath of 'Althusserianism' it is clear that its critics have underestimated the relevance of structural Marxism to empirical research, as for example in anthropology and urban studies.

A number of Anglo-American writers have endorsed philosophical *realism* as the proper umbrella of natural and social science.[36] Realists hold that scientific concepts, when successful, are neither reducible to observable empirical forms (postivism), nor the product of the scientific community's theoretical constructs (conventionalism). Rather, they uncover or illuminate real 'generative' mechanisms and processes. Marxists inclined to realism argue that Marx's materialism contains at least the 'premises' of the modern realist treatment of the relation between concepts and the world. Theoretical importance is preserved, but empirical reality does not disappear (as it tends to in Althusser) into the purified ether of scientific concepts. Realism seems to advance on its predecessors within Marxism, because it need not claim any unique or privileged philosophical status for Marxism in order to point out the realist form of Marxist historiography, and the hints in Marx's work which seem to endorse that general epistemological standpoint.

Yet however persuasive particular epistemologies (or theories of science) appear at a given time, inevitably qualifications and reactions emerge – as indeed they have within modern 'realism'. This fact has led some writers sympathetic to Marxism to argue that all the talk about 'science' is a dead-end, since competing epistemologies draw guarantees around themselves such that the 'fit' between concept and reality is always exactly as the preferred epistemology states.[37] This refreshing critique encourages us to reject philosophy as a dogmatic, abstract form of debate, and to examine political and theoretical arguments as specific moral, ideological and cultural 'discourses'. This advice seems conducive to Marxist historians who understandably become weary with their philosophical comrades' relatively high level of abstraction. Yet those who challenge philosophy also appear to challenge 'rationality' as a serious criterion of discussion, promoting instead the view that discourses are not compared by examining the world outside discourse.[38] Rather, discourses *constitute* the worlds relevant to the problems addressed within discourse. Therefore, *any* Marxist account which posits an objective historical universe, or concepts which claim 'scientific' status are discredited by the 'discourse' theorists – and this must include positive claims by Marxist historians who may not be interested in the fine detail of philosophy.

The exact points of convergence and collision between these various positions are matters of ongoing debate. For example, realism seems committed, on materialist grounds, to denying the relativistic claims of 'discourse'. However, realists are not literal materialists, and the popularity of 'internal realism' – where our conceptual access to reality is indirect, not immediate – suggests that the two perspectives share something in common. The argument against philosophy or epistemology, in fact, is itself a familiar species of argument within the tradition of western philosophy of science.[39]

My own view is that there are indeed some common ideas between these apparent rivals, but that realism can fend off the relativistic challenge, thus preserving important (if not all-powerful) notions of science and historical objectivity. However, I am less concerned to make that case here than to point to a general paradox: that Marxist philosophy has become one aspect of a relatively autonomous discussion about truth and rationality, where once it seemed to offer clear militant solutions to such discussions. Arguably, only the misplaced pretensions of dialectical materialism in the past make this seem paradoxical. But the theoretical loosening-up of recent decades does indeed reduce the horizon of a specifically Marxist 'line' on a variety of abstract issues, and Marxist political perspectives as well as historiographical questions lose much of their apparent necessity when Marxism ceases to be regarded as 'applied' philosophy.

The second general philosophical problem is about whether

Marxism is a philosophy of history or an empirical theory of it. In our earlier discussion of this issue, it was perhaps insufficiently stressed that a great deal of Marxist historical research takes place at levels well 'below' the broad successions posited by historical materialism across history. How far, then, is the unity of history, and its progressive direction, a matter of inquiry, and how much a matter simply of political hope? This problem is certainly less dramatic now than when Karl Popper based his famous 'refutation' of Marxism on it, since today within scientific theory empirical counter-examples have considerably less force than Popper believed. Correspondingly, the presence of values, philosophical beliefs, and social goals looms larger in even the strictest logic of science.

However, one persistent difficulty with the philosophical form of historical materialism, in the 'productive forces' versions especially, is its evolutionary character. One strand of objections holds that historical materialism simply takes history as the story of humanity's growth into 'maturity', which is quite arbitarily equated with advanced communism. This 'ontogenesis' is simply wishful thinking couched in pseudo-scientific terms.[40] This protest is illuminating in resisting the moralistic and prophetic strands in Marxism which have always played a small but significant role. It does no disservice to the forward-looking morality of Marxists to insist that there is no necessary unity of moral and technical progress in history. The greater the opportunities for material progress, the greater the risk of regression and destruction. And as a form of social explanation, Marxism operates analytically and therefore principally with hindsight: it does not offer gratuitous predictions.

This conclusion is not to endorse the equation commonly made in the last decade between 'teleology' or misguided personifications of the 'ends' of the historical process, with the possibility of genuine evolutionary explanations at the social level. These sharp criticisms of Marxist evolutionism now seem exaggerated and sensationalist, and recent neo-Marxist defences of functional explanation and social evolution are important here, since they suggest that the broad lines of human development are, with due care, discernible and available to generalization at a level familiar to historical materialism.[41] There are of course Marxists who have illegitimately reduced historical struggles to no more than the necessary function of productive growth; and there are those who appear to see in every institution and reform the needs and logic of capital accumulation. However, the risks of functionalism attend every distinctive form of explanation and that risk does not mean that notions of growth, function, or logic are *intrinsically* bound to lead to reductionism or 'purposive' rhetoric.

The third general problem is the role of class struggle. 'Long term'historical materialists are concerned with the outcome of social conflict, whilst those who adopt an empirical approach try not to see beyond the contingencies of social forces. Or so, at least, my presentation would suggest. Yet it would be foolish to hope for an easy complementarity to be re-established, since in history or politics the balance is not easily arrived at. Those committed to such a balance, such as Therborn, have eloquently said that the theatre of class struggle consists of a stage set by long term processes, and a cast which must act out its own play. Yet nothing is said about whether the drama is rigorously scripted or merely improvised.[42] In any event, the sort of precise leadership given to strategy by theory, sometimes posited within historical materialism, is really unavailable, and this fact must cause some concern to those brought up in the tradition in which a discussion of historical materialism would conclude with explicit derivations for the political campaigns of the moment.

The problems I have been airing are also, therefore, dilemmas. The process of showing the considerable but skeletal strength of historical materialism also involves accepting its limitations. Critics of Marxism have also sharply posed this dilemma. Kolakowski, for example, considers Marxism's achievements as commonplace, and as outdated truisms.[43] This seems contentious, since important commonplace truths may be far from 'trivial' (Kolakowski's favourite term of dismissal). Indeed, the same point can be made as a *positive* characterization, as in the following statement from Isaiah Berlin's standard, but generally critical, introduction to Marx:

If to have turned into truisms what had previously been paradoxes is a mark of genius, Marx was richly endowed with it. His achievements in this sphere necessarily ignored in proportion as their effects have become part of the permanent background of civilised thought.[44]

One way of reconciling these apparently opposed evaluations is to regard historical materialism (in the terminology of the philosopher of science Imre Lakatos) as a research programme or research tradition.[45] The core principles of a research programme are said to be irrefutable, whilst their consequences, elaborations, and theoretical allies will tend to vary over time. According to this perspective, theoretical varieties and a range of political origins and influences are to be expected in any vibrant tradition; they are not the index of its incoherence. Yet Lakatos's apparatus does not really help in deciding whether and at what stage the 'core' principles themselves may be modified and whether, as a whole, a research tradition is in process of development or degeneration. With respect to Marxism (which Lakatos himself disparaged), the core principles of historical materialism can be defended and its defensible features and distinguished proponents put on display; yet it may nevertheless be the case that the *point* of such a defence, and the *force* of its classical propositions, are becoming relatively less urgent. There are good historical and theoretical reasons for this suspicion: the changes in social structure and political options requiring independent argument; the utilisation of Marxist insights by a range of non-Marxist scholars; the proliferations of specialisms and sub-theories in Marxism; the relative distance between philosophical and political directives in historical materialism; and so on.

Within historical work, these will become increasingly acute problems as sensitive Marxist historians come to terms with the empirical *weight* offered by, for example, concepts of gender and ethnicity, by notions of moral discipline and cultural identities, encompassing and possibly transcending those of class and production. This is to advise neither despair nor dogma: the deep-seated problems I have outlined are opportunities for historical materialism as well as the form of its theoretical crisis.

If today the materialist conception of history is to overcome any tendency to 'degeneracy', a creative combination of historical research and philosophical thoroughness will be necessary which both respects tradition and which rejects ideological stagnation. In that spirit, one of Marx's own permanent strengths will be reflected.

Notes

1. None of the essays in, for example, *The Value Controversy*, Verso/NLB, London 1981, whether for or against value-theory, imply that Marx's sociological perspective is directly dependent on it.
2. T.A. Jackson, *Dialectics*, Lawrence & Wishart, London 1936, p. 12.
3. One of Jackson's favourite terms of polemic was to describe critics of Marxism as 'lumpen-intelligentsia'. It is ironic that E.P. Thompson should – inadvertently – re-deploy this phrase against defenders of Marxist orthodoxy, since Thompson's views are very similar to those 'bourgeois' writers lambasted by Jackson. See Thompson, *Poverty of Theory*, Merlin, London, 1978, pp. 195, 385; Jackson, *Dialectics*, p. 154.
4. Helmut Fleischer, *Marxism and History*, Allen Lane, London, 1973.
5. Marx and Engels, *The German Ideology*, Lawrence & Wishart, London, 1970, p. 39.
6. Marx and Engels, *Selected Works*, Lawrence & Wishart, London, 1968, p. 182.
7. Marx, *Early Writings*, Pelican Marx Library, Harmondsworth, 1975.
8. I try to develop this line of thought in G. McLennan, *Marxism and the Methodologies of History*, Verso/NLB, London, 1981, Ch. 8. See also Richard Johnson, 'Reading for the Best Marx: history-writing and historical abstraction', cccs History Group, *Making Histories*, Hutchinson, London, 1982.
9. W.L. Adamson, 'Marx's Four Histories: an approach to his intellectual development', *History and Theory*, Beiheft 20: 'Studies in Marxist Historical Theory', 1981, p. 390.
10. Perry Anderson, *Considerations on Western Marxism*, NLB, London, 1976, p. 6.
11. N. Bukharin, *Historical Materialism*, Russell & Russell, New York, 1965. A. Gramsci, *Selections from the Prison Notebooks*, Lawrence & Wishart, 1971, Part III.2, p. 419ff.
12. Derek Sayer, *Marx's Method*, Harvester, 1979, p. 80; G. Williams, 'In

Defence of History', *History Workshop Journal* 7, 1978; S. Clarke 'Althusserian Marxism', in Clarke *et al*, *One-dimensional Marxism*, Allison & Busby, London, 1980.

13. D. Sayer, *Marx's Method*, pp. 80-88.
14. P. Corrigan, H. Ramsay, D. Sayer, *Socialist Construction and Marxist Theory*, Macmillan, London, 1978, p. 13.
15. Cf. Philippe Van Parijs, *Evolutionary Explanation in the Social Sciences*, Tavistock, London, 1981, p. 191.
16. P. Vilar, 'Marx and the Concept of History' in E.J. Hobsbawm (ed). *The History of Marxism*, Vol. 1., *Marxism in Marx's Day*, Harvester, Brighton, 1982, p. 78.
17. Thompson, *Poverty*, passim.
18. Thompson, *Poverty*, pp. 205-242. For a commentary, G. McLennan, 'The Historians' Craft', *Literature & History*, Vol. 5 No. 2, 1979.
19. This is of course a general feature of Thompson's distinctive style. For a general assessment, G. McLennan, 'E.P. Thompson and the Discipline of Historical Context', in CCCS History Group, *Making Histories*, Hutchinson, London, 1982.
20. G.A. Cohen, *Karl Marx's Theory of History: A Defence*, Oxford University Press, 1978.
21. One thing Cohen and his followers *do* provide is a welter of evidence to show that if this is a vulgar theory, then Marx himself wrote a good deal in support of it.
22. Cf. W. Shaw, *Marx's Theory of History*, Hutchinson, London, 1978, p. 5.
23. Cf. A. Giddens, *A Contemporary Critique of Historical Materialism*, Macmillan, London, 1981.
24. John MacMurtry holds that the primacy thesis applies only to the last 1000 years, and that a 'forfeit' (refutation) would have to apply 'permanently' (sic): *The Structure of Marx's World View*, New Jersey, 1978. William Shaw says that the forces are only really primary in capitalist society: *Karl Marx's Theory of History*, p. 157. And according to Allen Wood (*Karl Marx*, Routledge and Kegan Paul, London, 1981, p. 80) the theory is only an 'inevitable tendency' which cannot exclude serious productive retardation due to class struggle, natural catastrophe, or foreign influence.
25. G. Therborn, *Science, Class, and Society*, NLB, London, 1976, p. 364.
26. B. Croce, *Historical Materialism and the Economics of Karl Marx* (1896), Frank Cass, London, 1966; G.D.H. Cole, *The Meaning of Marxism*, London, 1948, p. 13; G. Lukács, *History and Class Consciousness*, Merlin, London, 1971, ppl, 46.
27. G.A. Cohen, *Karl Marx's Theory of History: A Defence*, Ch. 1.
28. Maurice Cornforth, *Historical Materialism*, revised edn, Lawrence and Wishart, London, 1962, pp. 21-22.
29. See for example, V. Kelle and M. Kovalson, *Historical Materialism*, Progress, Moscow, 1973.

30. V. Semenov, 'The Theory of Socio-economic Formations and World History', in *Soviet and Western Anthropology*, ed. E. Gellner, Duckworth, London, 1980.

31. E. Gellner, 'A Russian Marxist Philosophy of History', in *Soviet and Western Anthropology*.

32. The 'self-criticisms' of, for example, Althusser or Hindess and Hirst are well-known in intellectual Marxist circles, but Marxists of an earlier stamp have also thoroughly reconsidered some of their earlier tenets. cf. M. Cornforth, *Communism and Philosophy*, Lawrence and Wishart, London, 1981 or J. Lindsay, *The Crisis in Marxism*, Moonraker Press, London 1981; For a good example of innovative, wide-ranging elaborations of 'basic' historical materialism, J. Habermas, 'Toward a Reconstruction of Historical Materialism' in his *Communication and the Evolution of Society*, Heinemann, London, 1979.

33. G. Hellman, 'Historical Materialism' in J. Mepham and D.H. Ruben (eds), *Issues in Marxist Philosophy*, Vol. 2: *Materialism*, Harvester, Brighton, 1979.

34. R. Heilbroner, *Marxism: For and Against*, W.W. Norton, New York, 1980, p. 22.

35. L. Althusser and E. Balibar, *Reading Capital*, NLB. London, 1974.

36. R. Bhaskar, *The Possibility of Naturalism,* Harvester, Brighton, *1979;* T. Benton, *Philosophical Foundations of the Three Sociologies*, Routledge and Kegan Paul, London, 1977; R. Keat and J. Urry, *Social Theory as Science*, Routledge and Kegan Paul, London, 1976; G. McLennan, *Marxism and the Methodologies of History*, Verso/NLB, London, 1981; D.H. Ruben, *Marxism and Materialism*, Harvester, Brighton, 1979.

37. Cf. B. Hindness and P. Hirst, *Mode of Production and Social Formation.* Macmillan, London, 1977. A. Cutler, *et al, Marx's Capital and Capitalism Today*, Vol. I., Routledge and Kegan Paul, London, 1978. The latter critique remains the most forceful expression of the view that Marx's later work, substantive though it is, is riven with the contradictions inherent in an essentially philosophical or epistemological framework.

38. For a good example of the way this thesis can be used to reconstitute historical discourses, see K. Tribe, *Land, Labour and Economic Discourse*, Routledge and Kegan Paul, London, 1980. On the basis that 'the whole process of referring a discursive order to a non-discursive one for purposes of validation is misconceived', Tribe attempts a Foucault-influenced account of the parameters of classical political economy.

39. For a recent statement of non-Marxist internal realism, H. Putnam, *Reason, Truth and History*, Cambridge University Press, 1981.

40. S. Toulmin, 'Human Adaptation' in *The Philosophy of Evolution*, eds. U.J. Jensen and R. Harre, Harvester, Brighton, 1981, p. 186.

41. Parijs, *Evolutionary Explanation;* R. Bhaskar, 'The Consequences of Social-Evolutionary Concepts for Naturalism in Sociology' in *The*

Philosophy of Evolution; G.A. Cohen, *Karl Marx's Theory of History: A Defence.*

42. G. Therborn, *Science, Class, and Society*, pp. 360-1.
43. L. Kolakowski, *Main Currents of Marxism vol. 3: The Breakdown*, Oxford University Press, 1978, p. 524.
44. I. Berlin, *Karl Marx*, fourth edn, Oxford University Press, 1978, p. 116.
45. Cf. Howard R. Bernstein, 'Marxist Historiography and the Methodology of Research Programmes', *History and Theory*, Beiheft 20, 1981. William Shaw also considers Marxism in Lakatos's terms, citing the lack of a full replacement as the main reason for its continued importance. (*Marx's Theory of History*, p. 167).

Göran Therborn

Problems of Class Analysis*

The development of Marxist theory in the central regions of capitalism over the past hundred years may be divided into three major epochs, each characterized by a dominant language and a prevailing theoretical concern, each also predominantly borne by a particular type of intellectual. The first period was that of Classical Marxism, centering on the Critique of Political Economy. The combined effects of the October Revolution – the 'revolution against *Capital*' (Gramsci) – and the non-revolution in the West ushered in the era of Western Marxism, from Lukács to Althusser, when the Critique of Philosophy became the centre of theoretical discourse.[1] A third period seems to have begun in the late 1960s, which we might call Social Scientific Marxism, the main critical thrust of which has been the Critique of Sociology. Together with the capitalist state, class has so far been the most central substantive topic of the new Marxism — the conceptualization, the theorization, and the empirical investigation of classes in contemporary capitalism.

As is well known, Marx, when he began his work of historical materialism, disclaimed the discovery of either the existence of classes or of their struggle, their historical development and their 'economic anatomy'. What Marx, in his own opinion, had done was to show 'that the existence of classes is bound only to certain historical phases of development of production; 2. that the class struggle necessarily will lead to the dictatorship of the proletariat; 3. that this dictatorship itself only forms the

* This essay is based on my contribution to the *History of Marxism* (Einaudi/Harvester Press, forthcoming).

transition to the abolition of all classes and to a classless society'.[2]

That was said in 1852, but in his posthumous edition of *Capital*, Engels had to conclude the chapter on Classes, "Hier bricht das Manuskript ab', before Marx had entered into an exposition of his own class conception. Of course, Marx wrote much more on classes and class struggle, but it is important to remember that before the rise of social scientific Marxism in the 1960s, class analysis – its theory, methodology, and practice, – remained in roughly the same fragmented state as when Marx laid down his pen.[3]

Whereas Marxist class analysis hardly made much progress, in non-Marxist social and historical analysis after Ricardo and Guizot class had rather tended to disappear, to be marginalized, or to be turned upside down. The marginalist turn in economics had largely banned classes from economic analysis. Mainstream historiography had come to see history only marginally as a history of class struggle, at best. What was left of scholarly interest in class was largely concentrated into the new discipline of sociology. In the hands of leading sociologists, however, classes and class struggle had been subjected to a strange fate.

The American Sociology of Class and Stratification

By the late 1960s prevailing sociology offered two chief alternatives to Marxist class analysis. One was the theory and the study of 'stratification' the implicit conception of social dynamics of which is illustrated by the term's origin, in the earth sciences.[4] The theoretical line of it was developed by the functionalist theorists Talcott Parsons and Kingsley Davis.[5] The second, primarily represented by Seymour Martin Lipset, retained class and, to some extent, even class struggle as central concepts, but with a new, quite original twist.[6]

The condition of classes in the discipline of sociology at the time of the rise of student rebellions and of social scientific Marxism can be ascertained with some objectivity from two sources. One is a reader, *Class Status and Power. Social Stratification in A Comparative Perspective*, edited by S.M.

Lipset and R. Bendix. It had a great commercial success. The other, even more solemn source is the *International Encyclopedia of the Social Sciences* (New York, Macmillan, 1968).

A glimpse of the trajectory of sociological wisdom may be captured by relating this encyclopedia to its predecessor, the *Encyclopedia of the Social Sciences* (New York, Macmillan, 1930). In 1930 it was held appropriate, that an encyclopedia of the social sciences had entries on Class, Class Consciousness, and Class Struggle. By 1968, readers of canonized social science were instead referred to Social Stratification.

The dominant trend of sociology had thus been one from attention to problems of class, class consciousness, and, on special occasions even, class struggle, to social stratification, i.e. to differential ranking, according to this or that criteria, preferably many at the same time (a 'multidimensional' conception of stratification).[7] To functionalists Parsons and Davis, stratification – or more vulgarly put, inequality – was necessary, positive, and integrative.[8]

In the functionalist and the empiricist conceptions of stratification, class relations of exploitation, and domination, had been turned into a ladder of strata; the problematic of how class position determines class consciousness had been turned into one of how societal consciousness determines class or stratum by ranking social functions or occupations. Instead of viewing classes as manifesting themselves in class struggles, bearing upon the maintenance or the transformation of exploitation and domination, stratification was now looked upon as an aspect of societal integration, manifesting social consensus.

This complacent preoccupation with consensus and prestige was a significant sociological contribution to the 'Great American Celebration' of the 1940s and 1950s, a contribution rooted in a revamped import of European idealism married to the status concerns of prospering and upwardly mobile middle classes. But sociology also harboured, in central locations, another tendency of which Lipset at the time was the prime representative. This tendency was largely made up of liberal ex-

Marxist recruits to sociology, to which they carried over, and put to radically novel uses, certain aspects of their earlier formation.

Since the late fifties a number of European sociologists, Ralf Dahrendorf, David Lockwood, Stanislaw Ossowski[9] and others, had been submitting stratificationism to a series of critiques, drawing upon Marxian and Weberian notions.

Lipset, in his article, stated that 'the ideas generated by Marx and Weber remain the most fruitful sources of theory on social stratification'.[10] However, Lipset used Marx for his own variant of the American Celebration. Lipset's and Bendix's reader includes a chapter from Lipset's book *Political Man* (of 1960), entitled 'Elections: The Expression of the Democratic Class Struggle'. And for the *Encyclopedia* Lipset concludes that 'an unpolitical Marxist sociology would expect the social class relationships of the United States to present an image of the future of other societies that are moving in the same general economic direction'.[11] If anything would be left of the class struggle, then it would apparently look like the electoral contests of Democrats and Republicans.

The strange mixture of well-meaning eclecticism – sometimes muddle-headed confusion might be more apt – and blatant self-congratulation, illustrated by the stances on 'stratification', is part of the story about why sociology became an intellectual tempest zone in the late sixties. Sociology invited critics – of itself and of society – in its pre-paradigmatic all-embracing heterogenity, and it invited, and deservedly drew upon itself, frontal criticism in its provocatively complacent ideology. But when the dust settled after the battles of protest and reprisals, Marxism had acquired a certain, guarded right to exist in sociology, a space wider than in any other social science.

In fact, sociology was not Panglossian, corrupt or vicious all through, as it seemed to many rebels at the time. In spite of some people's strenuous efforts, sociology had never succeeded in forging strong links with the economic and political centers of power, and with its own internal divisions even in its core, sociology was the soft underbelly of bourgeois academia. More than that, outside its mainstream, but nevertheless in respected positions, pre-1968 sociology included figures clearly sympathetic to Marxism, in a non-emasculated sense (though one un-related to contemporary revolutionary politics). One remarkable representative of this scattered but significant tradition was the patrician Harvard Professor Barrington Moore Jr, who in an essay of 1958 on 'Strategy in Social Science' had listed Marx, Weber, and Parsons in a descending order of moral fibre and scholarly acumen in their treatment of social classes and affirmed the importance of considering 'the class struggle as the basic stuff of politics'.[12] In 1966 Moore published a major work of historical sociology, written in a clearly Marxian vein, *Social Origins of Dictatorship and Democracy* (Boston, Beacon Press). Ten years earlier, Thomas Bottomore, who was to become the President of the International Sociological Association in the mid-70s, had together with a French Marx scholar put together a selection of Marx's writings on 'sociology and social philosophy'.[13] In a little book of theoretical introduction and overview, *Classes in Modern Society* (London, George Allen & Unwin, 1965) Bottomore had himself taken a social scientific Marxist position and cautiously predicted a resurgence of working-class struggles.

There was also the radical-democratic tradition in American social thought, represented first of all by the widely inspiring work of C. Wright Mills. In his *The Power Elite* (1956) he had preferred a power elite approach to a Marxist class analysis,[14] for which he was taken to task not only by Paul Sweezy, the unswerving guardian of independent classical Marxism in the United States, but also by an older eminent sociologist out of the radical-democratic tradition, Robert Lynd.[15] But in 1962 Mills compiled, with clear sympathy, an anthology of Marxist selections, classical and contemporary, analytical and political, *The Marxists* (New York, Dell, 1962).

The Problematic Reality of Class

The meaning as well the relevance of class in the world of contemporary advanced capitalism were both ambiguous and controversial by the 1960s. The postwar boom in this part of the world had largely broken up or eroded old class communities and commonalities of class experience. Peasant villages and workers' neighbourhoods were being depopulated in migrations to new, historyless urban and suburban conglomerations. Memories and fears of unemployment faded away in the unprecedented boom. In the big and rapidly growing corporations the chain of hierarchy became vastly extended and complicated. The state apparatuses also expanded, both in functions and in size. On the basis of some parts of the fruits of the boom, novel patterns of mass consumption and of social relations emerged in the new, fragmented residential areas, seemingly sealed off from the punch of capital: the family life of the holy trinity of mass consumerist securalization, the family home, the family car, and the family TV. And surrounding each little family were not only the unclouded sunshine of the boom but also the net of public social security.

In the US the class crystallizations, however twisted, of the New Deal period, had been eroded or smashed. In Western European politics, this was the moment of Bad Godesberg, the programmatic abandonment of every trace of Marxist class politics by Social Democracy,[16] the protraction of the French left before the rise of Gaullism, the break-up of the Socialist-Communist alliance in Italy. And the first waves of a new oppositional politics hardly grew in a very direct manner out of the capital-labour nexus either – the campaigns, in Britain and in other northern European countries, against nuclear armament, and somewhat later the student movements from Berkeley to West Berlin.

What scholarly discourse there was about class, was mainly located within the sprawling academic aggregate called sociology, and within sociological discourse on class and stratification, confusion and controversy over basic principles were dominant features by the mid-1960s. From Marxists had come hardly a single major analysis of postwar advanced capitalism, till Paul Baran's and Paul Sweezy's *Monopoly Capital* (New York, Monthly Review Press, 1966), which provided a sort of living bridge but as it turned out, a subsidiary one, between classical Marxism and the new post-philosophical Marxism. But it was clear, that the class relations of contemporary capitalism had little of the apparent immediacy, either evolutionary or apocalyptic, of the classical periods of the Marxist labour movement.

This background of social complication, ideological denial, and of theoretical confusion will account for some characteristics of the new Marxist treatment of class. Its elaborate, often book-long efforts at the conceptualization of class,[17] its overriding concern with the determinants rather than the experience or 'consciousness' of class; its focus on mapping the whole class structure and not just the ruling class or the working class.

Four Empirical Class Analyses

The extensive and intricate statistical compilations and calculations by the West German Institute for Marxist Studies and Research (IMSF) and Project Class Analysis (PKA)[18] will constitute the most comprehensive quantitative sociography of any country. These heavy, table-packed tomes, clearly products of large *Autorenkollektive*, even appear rather awe-instilling. For all their length, the width of these studies is rather narrow, however. The PKA study is, by and large, a duplication of the slightly earlier and larger IMSF one, applying a different conceptualization of class but using largely the same kind of data and the same empirical approach. Both deal with the German Federal Republic 1950-1970, with certain backdrops into the earlier Germany. The focus is concentrated on population data, the macro-economics of national product, industry, and capital, employment, and, in the IMSF case, on education. Figures on wealth and income distribution and on social mobility are also reported. But there is nothing about how class relations are actually lived in the Federal Republic, about the functioning of class domination, about ideologies or about class struggles, only little (in the PKA) about organizations and institutions of class. Class is here, in both studies, used as a descriptive sociographic category.

The two other large-scale empirical Marxist class projects are much more analytically edged. None of them is completed at the time of this writing. But the information available about them makes it possible to comment on their outstanding importance. One is conducted by Adam Przeworski at the University of Chicago. It has an overriding explanatory objective, to explain the history of electoral strategies and electoral performance of workers' parties by the constraints of the class structure.[19]

The project of Erik Olin Wright, at the University of Wisconsin in Madison, cuts the most novel path in Marxist class analysis. Whereas almost all other Marxist researchers on class structure have started from the occupations listed in official statistics, trying to translate them, sometimes with the help of other pieces of statistical social historical information, into class categories, Wright is putting the sociological survey technique to use for getting first-hand information about class. Class location is tapped by asking interviewees questions about their control or not over investments, other employees, and over their own working conditions. A number of other questions, from kind of employer or business, income, sex and ethnicity to attitudes on social problems and political affiliation make possible a long series of analyses of the effects of class. It is also a comparative project, with representative national surveys conducted in the United States, Sweden, Finland, Australia, Norway, Canada, Italy and planned in Britain and Israel.[20]

If and when they are completed according to their design, the projects of Przeworski and Wright will certainly constitute landmarks of social scientific research as well as of Marxist scholarship.

The Sociological Impact

Theoretically, the new Marxist class analysis has brought about a shift in academic social science. The course of academic social vision from at least some recognition of the salience of class and class struggle to a focus on 'social stratification', as indicated by the entries of the 1930 and the 1968 encyclopedias of social science, has been turned left again, to a focus more on the centre of society so to speak after the previous rightwing twist.

Capitalism, capitalist property and wage labour are now regarded by non-Marxist sociological wisdom as central features of contemporary Western societies, without doubt overriding standard notions of pre-1968 sociology, such as 'industrial society' and its offspring 'post-industrial society', stratification of 'occupational status', manual/nonmanual categorizations. The best tribute to this is paid by prominent contemporary sociological critics of Marxism. Thus, e.g., Frank Parkin in a perceptive and serious but completely disrespectful critique of Marxist class theory takes his fellow bourgeois sociologists to task for having turned blind to property, forgetting that 'Weber was in full accord with Marx in asserting that "Property" and "lack of property" are the basic characteristics of all class situations'.[21] In the same vein Parkin also attacks Ralf Dahrendorf – the sociological theorist of authority relations instead of property as the basis of class domination and social conflict[22] – for not asking 'for what *purpose* is authority exercised and occasionally challenged?' Parkin supplies the answer: 'The command structure of a business enterprise is geared directly to the pursuit of profit, and those who staff the key posts are in effect the guardians of capital; they are not concerned with the enforcement of obedience as an end in itself.'[23]

Similarly, in another contemporary sociological critique of Marxism, not maliciously ironic but rather somewhat glibly pretentious in the draping of its often very thought-provoking and perceptive observations and arguments, Anthony Giddens puts capitalism and wage labour straight into the centre of his perspective on contemporary Western society. The distance travelled by mainstream sociological theory, of which Giddens must be regarded as a leading proponent among the younger generation, is indicated by the following verdict: 'There seems equally little doubt that Marx was right to locate this impetus [to economic growth and technical innovation] in the dynamic nature of production governed by price, profit and investment. If this appears something of a banality on the face of things, it becomes less so when in the light of the rival theory which for a long while dominated sociology the theory of 'industrial society'

... (and its latter-day affiliate, linked to a conception of a supposedly 'post-industrial' world) ...'[24] Certain Marxist themes are now regarded as self-evident to the extent that their lack of banality has to be explained by the weird ideas dominating sociology only a decade earlier.

Hard-nosed empirical sociologists have also got, by Erik Olin Wright, a demonstration on their own terrain – of operationalized concepts, representative quantitative data and explanation by regression equations – of the significance of class in the Marxist sense in accounting for income variations, in competition with rival theories of returns to occupational status or education.[25]

Problems of Class Analysis and Tasks for the Future

The empirical and the theoretical achievements indicated above bear witness to the vitality and the viability of social scientific Marxism, in stark contrast to the crisis of philosophico-political Marxism. However, the development of Marxist class analysis has yet hardly reached the state of a consolidated, cumulative enterprise of knowledge production, either theoretically or empirically. And Marxism would stagnate, if it grew complacent basking in the unreliable sun of non-Marxist sociological homage.

The unresolved problems cluster in two main areas. One of them may be said to relate primarily to *understanding the present* of class societies, the other to the understanding and to the *affecting* of *their future*. The former refers to issues of how to map the existing patterns of class relations and to find the processes making and sustaining them. The latter pertains to the political commitment of Marxist scientific analysis to contributing to the struggle for the abolition of exploitation and domination by providing knowledge about and for that struggle.

Four unresolved problems of contemporary Marxist class analysis

The difficulties may all be regarded as coming out of the

confluence of three sources, the fragmentary ambiguity of Marx's own treatment of class beyond a paradigmatic core, the vastly increased complexity of the social relations of capitalist societies since the time of *Capital* and thirdly, to some extent, also the still patchy structures experience of sustained serious international Marxist discussion, a legacy of Western Marxism and its break-up of the classical international Marxist discourse into self-contained philosophical schools mainly ignoring each other.[26] The amplitude of the problems involved here may be illustrated by the fact that the classes which correspond to the largest common denominator of definitional agreement among the major Marxist class analyses of the 1970's together make up one sixth of the Swedish population 18 years or older circa 1980. Put in other terms, all Marxists would unambiguously identify the class location of one sixth of the Swedish electorate. The proportion is unlikely to be substantially higher in any advanced capitalist country, and in some, such as the United States, it would most likely be not insignificantly lower. – The rockbottom agreement concerns manual wage-workers in the production, transport, and storage of goods, who work (or are looking for work) for capitalist enterprises, and, on the other side, owners-entrepreneurs-employers.[27]

a. The pertinence of Marxian economic theory

The largest common denominator of Marxist class analyses derives from Marx's most unambiguous formulations about the production and the appropriation of surplus value. The low figure coming out of it raises the question of the pertinence of Marxian economic theory to contemporary class analysis of advanced capitalism. The background of the new social scientific Marxism in critiques of certain philosophical traditions of Western Marxism (Poulantzas vis-a-vis Lukács) and of sociology rather than of political economy has resulted in some theoretical confusion.

Poulantzas argued very strongly, that 'it is mistaken to claim that ... relations of production are alone sufficient to define social classes'. Instead classes should be seen as 'an effect of the articulation of the [ideological and juridico-political as well as the economic] structures either of the mode of production or of the social formation'.[28] Here Poulantzas was primarily concerned with avoiding the counterposition of economic stasis and politico-ideological dynamics, class-in-itself as opposed to class-for-itself, of '(economic) class situation' on the one hand, and politico-ideological class position on the other.[29] That is a misleading way of putting the issue. The Marxian conception of regarding classes as the bearers (*Träger*) of the relations of production does *not* – in contrast to a strict definition in terms of property and non-property – denote a situation but a *process*. The classes are the bearers of the ongoing processes of the given mode of production. This constitutes the particular strength of Marxist class theory, that class denotes ensembles of men and women converging in wide-ranging conflictual relations and practices as they go on keeping a given kind of society going. While it is correct, as Poulantzas pointed out, that classes have necessary juridico-political and ideological *conditions of existence*, it does not follow from that, that classes have to be *defined* as the bearers of the overall social structure. The main reason why a class definition should not be extended in that direction is the loss of analytical edge resulting from such an operation. Historical materialism has identified the economic mode of production not simply as a structure but as structured system of processes with an inherent dynamics accessible to economic analysis. But neither Marx nor Poulantzas has defined any inherent dynamic in the state or in the system of ideology corresponding to that of capital accumulation.

Poulantzas's anti-economics led him to absurd conclusions about that major aspect of modern social complexity, the – deliberately using a banal commonsensical term – white collar strata. Poulantzas suggested that they and service and sales workers (non-producers of surplus value) should be regarded as a 'new petty bourgeoisie', thus a fraction of a class location in common with the traditional petty bourgeoisie of commodity producers and commercial middlemen not employing wage-labour. The argument was that, though economically differently located, the two were bearers of the same or similar ideology and politics.[30]

The absurdity resides in the cavalier manner with which this thesis is presented. Firstly, if it was true that distinctly different locations in the economic mode of production – one the product of developed capitalism, the other the social bearer of non-capitalist simple commodity production, an economic form preceding industrial capitalism, – produced the same kind of politics and ideology, then that should be considered a major flaw of historical materialism, requiring further questions into what extent the latter could still be held valid, if at all. But Poulantzas sees no problem at all. Secondly, the 'evidence' supplied for this far-reaching contention boils down to a few assertions simply meaning that neither fraction tends to have a revolutionary Socialist or Communist ideology.

Wright criticizes and rejects both Poulantzas's narrow definition of the working-class (including manual productive workers only) and his notion of the new petty-bourgeoisie. For the latter Wright substitutes the concept of 'contradictory class location', between the bourgeoisie and the working-class. The latter is defined much more broadly as all wage-workers having positions excluded from all control over money capital, physical capital and labour power.[31]

However, in spite of the references to 'capital', Wright, in fact, makes a consistent break with any dependence on capitalist economics for the analysis of class. The key criterion of class is *control* or no control, not location in the capitalist process of production. Therefore, bourgeoisie and working-class can be identified as easily in the state and in private non-profit organizations as in capitalist enterprise. 'In practice, these three levels [i.e. bourgeois, working-class, and contradictory] within the political and ideological apparatuses can be operationalized in much the same way that the social relations of production at the economic level were operationalized. That is, the working-class position in both cases involves exclusion from control over *resources, physical means* of production/administration, and labour power.'[32]

The rationale of this seems to be a substitution of an exclusive problematic of 'interest' – in preserving or in overthrowing the existing capitalist society – for the Marxian notion of class balances of force changing with changes in the capitalist mode of production. The quiet abandonment of Marxian economic analysis in the cited essay coexists unmediated, within the same book covers, with lengthy and insightful discussion of Marxist crisis theory.

In his ongoing research project Wright is revising his position. In a first data report, the bourgeoisie is now strictly confined to owners-employers with ten employees or more, and though state employment is still 'merged with capitalist production proper', Wright now holds that 'in many ways it may be more fruitful essentially to separate state production as a distinct form of production relation'.[33] In any case, as a well-designed empirical investigation, Wright's project and what can come out of it is largely independent of some questionable conceptualizations and theoretical assumptions. (Data on public employment, for instance, have been gathered and are reported).[34]

It would seem that the substitution of a critique of sociology for the one of political economy has not been without certain costs,[35] although, on the whole, it has proved a very fruitful road. And, as we shall see in a while, strict adherence to (a certain) analysis of economic form (as in the case of PKA) has not been without problematic effects either. The direction of the criticisms above have mainly been toward the need for clarifying the relationships between economic and sociological analyses. But my own conclusion from this need for more clarification is that class analysis would lose much from divorcing itself from analyses of the economic dynamics of capitalism, and from using basic Marxist approaches for such analyses.

The last point has to be specified, as it could mean at least two things. Either it may mean adherence to the Marxian theory of value with its concomitant foci on the production, appropriation, and redistribution of surplus value. Or, more modestly or 'revisionistically', it could mean focusing on capital accumulation and wage labour for capital, and on the conflictual relationship between capital-owners and wage-workers for capital. In the latter perspective, the Marxian conceptions of value and surplus value would be taken more as important pointers to crucial social relations, rather than as valid economic theory.

Something like the latter interpretation comes out as a conclusion of the perhaps most original of all recent Marxist theorizations about class, the Californian economist John Roemer's *A General Theory of Exploitation and Class* (Cambridge Mass., Harvard University Press, 1982). Roemer is out to give a precise meaning to exploitation under different economic conditions and to show how exploitation and class, defined in terms of property relations, are related. With regard to classical Marxian economic theory, the findings, demonstrated in the rigorous language of a mathematical economist (but argued in didactic prose as well), are mainly negative. A correspondence between exploitation and class presupposes, under general conditions of technology, that labour values depend upon equilibrium prices, rather than the other way around. Under the realistic assumption of different labour skills the surplus labour theory of exploitation ceases to give any socially meaningful results – because the relationship between wealth and the position of exploiter or exploited would be indeterminate. Rather than providing a scientific theory of the basis of class struggle under capitalism, the labour theory of value only makes sense as an economic model if one accepts the Marxist view of history that capitalist history is the history of class conflict between workers and capitalists. In a telling expression of the changed Marxist discourse, Roemer ends his book by abdicating, as an economist, from providing a theory of the basis of class struggle, instead calling for a 'sociology of moral beliefs or injustice'. The latter appears to be an important task. However, conflicts between capitalists and workers are hardly dependent upon conflicting moral beliefs between the two. Conflict follows rationally from the perspectives of capital accumulation and of consumption inherent in the two kinds of class positions. Marxian economics may then be read as an economics-based sociology of determinants of power relations in this class conflict as well as an economics-based normative theory of exploitation, and probably more fruitfully the former than the latter.

Whatever value may be attributed to value theory as an economic theory, it may, however, be said to possess certain heuristic sociological value pertinent to class analysis. Two examples. First, Neo-Marxist class analysts should not forget that the (by no means non-controversial) interpretation of Marxian value theory which leads to the definition of the working-class as manual workers in production, transport and storage can lean on, not only some passages of Marxian text, but also on a more solid block of socio-historical reality. That is, the actually existing working-class movement developed and grew among these workers, with the important assistance, in the beginning, of autonomous or semi-autonomous artisans. If one thinks of the working-class as made up of not only objects of exploitation and degradation but also of subjects of resistance with a counter-culture to capital, of knowledge, experience, solidarity, and organizational practices, this narrowly defined working-class and the boundaries between it and other workers and employees keep a significance also today, which should not be simply defined away.

Second, the notions of surplus-value production, appropriation, and redistribution may direct attention to an important assymetry in the possible sectoral location of working-class and capitalist bases of power resources. The working-class has always drawn its strength in the class struggle from its location in production, transport and storage, from workers' role as producers of surplus-value if you like. But the same does not hold for the bourgeoisie, the wealth and the power resources of which can have their immediate location in a variety of sectors, large-scale commerce, banking, real estate, etc., as well as production. And this may have very important consequences for the pattern of class relations and for the development of class conflict. Because, whatever the origin 'in the last instance' of mercantile, banking or real estate capital, classes and class struggles are situated in space. Other things being equal, the best situation for the working-class would be an economy – of a state, a region, a city – of large productive enterprises successfully operating under conditions of competition, employing a relatively homogenous workforce and having a weak capital base. At the other pole, the bourgeoisie would have a strong hand in an economy with its main centre in large concentrations of non-productive capital coming from ground-rent and windfall profits (oil deposits, fertile land, ore and attractive real estate), commerce, banking etc., facing a scattered, segemented workforce, in relatively small-scale productive units as well as in offices and service-shops. The working-class, according to the, between themselves different, criteria of IMSF, PKA, and Wright might be the same, but the conditions of working-class struggle would be vastly different. For future developments it seems that much is to be gained about the sociological reality of class struggle by putting the processes of capital accumulation and the different *regimes of accumulation* into the centre of class theorization and analysis. The latter concept – which is due to Michel Aglietta and other French Marxist economists, who so far have used it mainly for very broad, epochal characterizations[36] – holds considerable promise as a tool for grasping variations over time and space in patterns of capitalist class relations.

b. *The implications of the state*

One of the most immediate and simple consequences of linking class analysis with the processes of capital accumulation would obviously be a look at the actual range of wage-labour for capital accumulation. Certainly, the totality of a capitalist society depends upon, is crucially affected by capital, by the rate of profit and its use by capitalists. But, equally certain, it makes a significant difference to your social location whether you work for capital or not. Not necessarily always in your immediate working conditions but in your place in the class struggle.

The size of the *economically active* population which is not directly and immediately imbricated in the capital-wage labour nexus is quite considerable in contemporary advanced capitalist societies. In West Germany in 1970 those who were neither capitalists and capitalists executives nor employed by capital constituted at least 34% of the economically active population, which is an understatement since it excludes employees for cooperatives and of public capital.[37] In Sweden in 1972 only about 49-50% of the economically active population were employed by capitalist enterprises (private corporations or non-incorporated business enterprises having at least ten people or more occupied for a whole year). One third of the gainfully employed Swedish population in 1972 was not involved in any 'business-making' activity at all, i.e., in any production and circulation of commodities (other than their own labour-power).[38] For both countries, these figures of non-capitalist employment and non-commodity involvement will have increased significantly since 1970.[39]

The great majority of these between a third and a half or more of the economically active population of contemporary European advanced capitalist countries, who are not immediately involved in capitalist accumulation, are employed by the state. Some are self-employed, some work in petit-bourgeois enterprises, to which the personal work of the employer is crucial, others are employed by consumers' or producers' cooperatives, a few by private non-profit organizations. In Sweden in 1979 about 40% of the gainfully employed population (working at least 20 hours a week) were publicly employed, circa 37% if public enterprises are excluded.[40]

Marxist writers on the capitalist state, among whom Poulantzas was a modern pioneer, have, on the whole, paid scant attention to the massive growth of the state as employer.[41] Lacking are both any explanatory theory of this growth and any developed elucidation of its implications for the class relations of society. The state as an institution of power may well be characterized, *pace* Poulantzas, as a crystallization of the class relations of force in society, but public employment itself has become a heavy part of the class relations of advanced capitalism.

A look at the composition of this swollen public employment a striking novelty appears in comparison with the state at the time of Marx and, therefore, with the state in classical Marxian theory. A large part of public work – and the part which, above all, accounts for the growth of state employment – consists of what we might call work of *human reproduction*. Deliberately, the term reproduction of the labour power is avoided here, because a main point is that this work can hardly be said to be exclusively or even chiefly geared to commodity (re)production. Even though it certainly bears upon the latter, while itself, like almost everything else in a capitalist society being affected by capitalist commodity relations. It includes, care for the aged, who will never re-enter the labour force, social work directed towards the marginal population, child care, health care, the payment of social insurance to people who are not working, education, the provision of meals for schoolchildren and such like. In 1975 this kind of work made up 47% of Swedish public employment, 40% in 1965, 28% in 1950.[42] In West Germany the figure is lower, but still very high, around 35% in 1970, circa 30% in 1960.[43] Even the class analysis which has paid most attention and given weight to state employment, the PKA, has failed to grasp this feature other than negatively, as a form of public employment deriving exclusively neither from the 'bourgeois' nor from the 'societal' division of labour. To PKA, public employees, regardless of power and function, have the same, intermediary, class location as recipients of public revenue.

The reasons for this development, I would suggest, run deeper than the immediate politics of the welfare state. It turns out, that there are two major forms of work, which have never been more than marginally subjected to capitalist relations of production. One of them is human reproduction, in the immediate sense of which the word 'care' is a key denotation, the other is temperate agriculture. The latter has had, the former is having and will have very important effects upon the class relations of capitalist societies. To grasp this, however, we had better start from the third problem area of class theory, the *family*.

c. The effects and the legacy of the family

The articulation of the family with commodity relations of production has been little observed, understood, and theorized.[44] Rather, the general tendency both within Marxism and in non-Marxism social science has been to regard the family as simply outside commodity relations, either preceding commodity

                    Göran Therborn

production as a productive unit or as living its own life,
dependent upon what happens in the commodity sphere but with
little or no significant effects upon the latter. However, simple
commodity production has usually been linked with family
production, the petty-bourgeois *pater familias* being assisted by
his wife and his children. Nowhere has this been as important as
in the major branch of simple commodity production in modern
capitalism, in agriculture. To give a Swedish empirical
illustration again. In 1930, after sixty years of extraordinarily
rapid and successful capitalist industrialization, agriculture still
occupied almost half of the population active in the productive
sector. And within agriculture wage-labour supplied only 25%
of the labour force, the rest was provided by the farmers and
their family helpers.

This resilience of temperate climate agriculture to capitalist
penetration blocked the development of class polarization
predicted by Marx, as was noticed in German Social
Democracy already around the turn of the century. In recent
times the political problem has subsided with the rapid post-
World War II decline of the farming population in countries of
advanced capitalism. But this decline is *not* an effect of simple
agrarian commodity production being overtaken by capitalism.
Mainly it derives from the vastly increased productivity of non-
capitalist agriculture, which is now producing food surpluses
with a fraction of its former labour force. The total number of
farmers in Sweden in 1975 was a third of its number in 1950,
but those farmers who had at least one person employed
constituted only 15% of the employing farmers of 1950, and
20% of the total sum of farmers in 1975.[45]

Reproductive work too has never been more than marginally
subjected to capitalist organization. Classically, up to the most
recent times, it has been carried out in mainly two forms, as
unpaid family labour and as domestic labour, by servants paid
out of household revenue.[46] Then and today, reproductive work
is overwhelmingly female work. That part of the class structure
which consists of gainfully employed reproductive labour was
thus more directly regulated by tendencies in the rate of
marriage than by the rhythms of capital accumulation. In

Sweden paid reproductive work reached its first peak in 1930, with a trough in the marriage rate for the industrial era. Then the trend turned, from 11% of the economically active population in 1930 to 8% in 1950, the year when the proportion of women who are housewives to economically active men culminates for the whole century 1880-1980.

In recent times reproductive work has become increasingly public and regulated most immediately, on the one side by the development of public revenue, and on the other by the rate of labour force participation of married or cohabiting women. In Sweden the number of people employed in reproductive work overtook the number of housewives wedded to economically active men some time between 1975 and 1979.

Public non-commodity reproduction thus seems to take up the abdicated part of family commodity production in seriously complicating capitalist class relations. The tendency certainly takes different forms and force in other societies than the one used here for illustration. But clearly, the family and, more generally, gender relations should no longer be regarded as extrinsic and unimportant to class relations. The inner connections of these articulations of family and gender relations with non-capitalist forms of labour still have to be worked out. In the case of simple commodity production in temperate agriculture, the reason appears to be, as Harriet Friedman has suggested in a brilliant argument concerning the case of wheat that the productive forces of the kind of agriculture dominating the temperate zones have all the time remained correspondent to 'the demographic range' of the family, i.e. workable with little increased productivity returns to scale by members of a family, supplemented by a relatively small pool of agricultural labourers, some of whom younger sons of other farmers. Under such conditions simple family commodity production has a competitive advantage over capitalist production in its independence of maintaining the going rate of profit. In the case of reproductive work a theory is still lacking. Capitalist schools, hospitals, daycare centres, caring for the aged, domestic service agencies, etc., are not only conceivable, they exist. But why they have never been more than marginal still awaits cogent theorization. The issue is important not only to explain the intricacies of contemporary class structure. It seems to indicate a *structural limitation of capitalism*, and one taking on an increasing importance.

d. *The corporation and the prospects of the collective worker*

The complicating effects upon class relations of the development of the big business corporations with their large offices of employees separated from the shopfloor workers as well as from the board of directors and with their elaborate managerial chains were first signalled and hauled as a challenge to Marxists some 70 years ago by Emil Lederer.[47] It took some time for Marxists to take it up seriously, a relative neglect deriving its material sustenance from the obvious continuation of capital and wage-labour in constituting the decisive poles of class struggles. Here recent social scientific Marxism has made many important contributions. The two most perceptive analyses appear to be those of Carchedi and Wright. Both of them give due weight to complexity as well as to the off-centred character of the corporate hierarchy by focussing on the *contradictory* location of managerial personnel.[48]

They differ, however, in their definition of the basis of contradictority. Carchedi's discussion centers on two different functions in the production process, one deriving from the specific mode of production, the second from the technical division of labour. He identifies two global functions, the 'functions of capital', defined as the 'work of surveillance and control', and the 'function of the collective labourer', 'the work of coordination and unity of the labour process'.[49] The development of the corporation then means the growth of a 'new middle class' of employees hired by capital who have the task of simultaneously carrying out these two functions.

Wright questions the designation of the function of coordination as a technical relation and sees it as a power relation, with the result that participation 'in major decisions concerning the coordination and planning of production then becomes an aspect of … closeness to capital', even though it does not involve surveillance and control of workers.[50] To Wright, the contradictory location of the managerial strata derives instead from their having various degrees of partial control of power, over money capital, physical capital, and labour.

Future developments of class analysis would do well to try to combine the two perspectives, of function and of power. Because the development of power relations between the classes of capital and labour will depend upon what pole can appropriate for itself the function of the collective worker. The critical condition for capitalist power within the enterprise is that the cooperative production process of the enterprise, the function of planning and coordination, is an attribute of capital. Marx and Engels predicted a development of capitalism leading to this becoming an attribute of the collective workers, with capital and capitalists becoming increasingly externalized from the production process, retreating into the function of money capitalists only and thus becoming, in Engels' words, a 'superfluous' class.[51] Now, so far at least, that Marxian hypothesis has not come true. But the task for Marxist analysts is to find out exactly what has happened to the function of collective worker, and to its relationships with the poles of capital and wage labour, and why. Here neither Poulantzas's emphasis on the ideological demarcation of mental and manual labour, nor Harry Braverman's thesis[52] of a constant tendency towards degradation of work, clerical as well as manual, in the course of capitalist development, appear very satisfactory. It seems that over the last century there has been a tendency to the coming together of a 'collective worker', less internally divided and with a larger weight upon the prerogatives of capital. On the other hand, the scope of top managerial control has been vastly extended, as exemplified in the megacorporations, whose executives can control and coordinate the production processes spread across the five continents of the globe. It will seem that one of the most important aspects of the class relations determined by the rise of the big capitalist corporations to

                                   Göran Therborn

investigate, should be *the opposing tendencies of collective worker unification* and *expanding range of* possible *top managerial control.*

Another aspect of crucial importance appears to be the expanding size of markets in relation to the spatial organization of the non-capitalist classes and strata. Because in one sense, the conventional Marxist term for these big corporations, 'monopoly capital' is profoundly misleading. Though they certainly not have to take prices as simply given by the market as firms under perfect competition, these corporations operate under conditions of competition in worldwide markets. And this impersonal whip of the market is a crucial buttress to the increasingly anonymous power of capital in the big corporations.[53] Contrary to Marxian expectations, the biggest corporations have got a size and a capacity of economic coordination surpassing most current political units of the globe, and more adapted to the functioning of the world market than the territorial divisions of working class politics. Thus is being maintained an unexpected correspondence between a private character of the relations of production and the increasingly social character of the productive forces.

The Marxist class analyses of the 1970s have left a rich, complex heritage of analytical insights and elucidations and empirical knowledge. From there the tackling of further questions and problems can begin. Compared to that achievement, the mixed and sometimes bewildering bag of disagreements over definitional criteria, forms of conceptualization and boundary-drawing, also a part of the inheritance, is of secondary significance. What is important, however, is to develop further analytical approaches which are capable of grasping both the species of the capital-labour relation and the social complexity in which the latter is imbricated. Most immediately this means at least three things. Firstly, class analyses should never lose contact with economic analyses of capitalist dynamics. Secondly, class analyses should either start from or at least to take into account the totality of the adult population, and not only what, according to this or that criterion, is regarded as the economically active population.

Thirdly, whatever conceptualization is finally adopted, it is necessary to pay attention to the multiple determination of locations with regard to the relations of production. As Przeworski has stressed, the people directly involved in the capitalist production process is a minority of the total population, and the class struggle cannot be reduced to struggles between classes. It is also *struggles about class*, about the patterning of the field of social forces and conflicts in relation to the dynamic of capitalist societies, the process of capital accumulation and the social conflicts inherent therein.[54]

The Working Class and the Perspective of Marxist Politics

The fate of the working-class in the hands of social scientific Marxism so far is rather perplexing. If we look at the works of lasting theoretical and empirical achievements, beyond conjunctural polemics and stances now passed by, we find the working-class of contemporary advanced capitalism mainly in three locations. Firstly, in the elaborated works of class cartography we find the working-class as a structurally delimited take-off area for future revolutionary socialist politics, at some unspecified time, in unspecified forms, under unspecified conditions. Secondly, in some outstanding empirical works of the working-class condition the class is left stranded in the gloom of US 'monopoly capitalism'. Thirdly, when a major empirical study deals with the untemporary working-class and its politics in advanced capitalism and finds the Marxian thesis of the working-class as the agent of socialist transformation corroborated, this class then assumes the shape of existing Social Democracy, in particular Swedish Social Democracy.

Regardless of one's degree of despair of the United States or of one's belief in Swedish Social Democracy, it will be agreed that this is a rather lopsided set of conclusions. But let us first of all put on record the works on the American working-class and on Social Democracy.

The first major work on the American working-class was Harry Braverman's *Labor and Monopoly Capital* (New York, Monthly Review Press, 1974). In one sense it falls into the category of structural class analyses dominating Marxist class analyses in this period, focusing on 'the shape given to the working population by the accumulation process', analyzing working conditions, dissecting occupational statistics. In other respects it is very original. While mounting a critique of bourgeois sociology with great skill and verve, Braverman injects a rare non-academic freshness into Marxist analyses on the contemporary period, drawing upon his own variegated experiences as a craftsman and as a non-academic socialist intellectual. Its theme is given in the subtitle of the book, 'The Degradation of Work in the Twentieth Century'. This process is portrayed as a constantly onrolling juggernaut in the course of capitalist development, concentrating in the separation of conception and execution, investing the former increasingly, upwards in the managerial hierarchy while subjecting manual and clerical work alike to the execution of increasingly fragmented, pre-controlled tasks.

Less trail-blazing than Braverman's book but more brilliant in its analyses is Michael Burawoy's *Manufacturing Consent* (Chicago, University of Chicago Press, 1979). In format a monograph of industrial sociology, based on participant observation – and remarkable already from the fact that Burawoy, apparently by luck, discovered that he had chosen to study the same factory as another Chicago sociologist 30 years before – it branches out into a more general analysis of class relations as they are shaped by the organization of production. Burawoy did not find an intensification of the labour process or an increase of managerial control through separation of conception and execution compared to thirty years earlier. 'What we have observed is the expansion of the area of the "self-organization" of workers as they pursue their daily activities.'[55] On the other hand, this had consolidated the rule of capital even more. By constituting 'games' of limited choices, in which workers participated, games of affectable piece-rate systems, internal labour markets, and an 'internal state' of grievance procedures and collective bargaining, surplus value was simultaneously secured and obscured, and consent was manufactured by participation in the games on the shop floor offered by capital.

Though they might be said to have the character more of a synoptic overview than a full historical treatment, two long essays by Mike Davis on the socio-political history of the US working-class from its formation till the recent post-World War II period, should be noticed as probably the sharpest political analysis of the modern working-class of any advanced capitalist society.[56] Its running theme is neither any capitalist steamrolling, game-induced consent or any specific American values or institutions, but the class struggle, and, more precisely, 'the cumulative impact of the series of historic defeats suffered by the American working-class'.[57]

Walter Korpi's *The Working Class in Welfare Capitalism* (London, Routledge & Kegan Paul), by contrast, deals with the cumulative impact of a series of victories of the Swedish Social Democratic labour movement. According to Korpi the basic Marxian hypotheses about the tendency of the working-class to grow in unity and strength and to develop into the 'grave-diggers' of capitalism have been borne out, contrary to arguments by non-Marxist sociologists. The working-class and the reformist labour movement have not been 'incorporated' into capitalism, but gradual and decisive shifts of power are taking place in favour of labour and its strengthening organizations. The book ends by saying, refering to the unity call of the *Communist Manifesto* as well as to the Swedish union which organizes the great majority of all workers and employees: 'When the competition among the wage-earners ceases, the foundation of capitalism has eroded.'

Korpi's book is a remarkable Social Democratic *tour de force* both with respect to Marxism and to the sociology of industrial relations, from which the book originated. It is by no means a smug exhibition of Social Democractic self-congratulation, but rather an expression of the radicalization of the trade unionist wing of Swedish Social Democracy in the mid-70s – when it presented a proposal for the gradual collectivization of the major means of production – as well as an outstanding contribution to social scientific Marxism.[58] Whatever socialist hopes one may have in Swedish Social Democracy – and its mid-1970's proposals have at the time of this writing been watered down quite a number of times already – Korpi's analysis has at least one serious lacuna. It is almost completely centred on the labour movement, and therefore provides little analysis of what is being or is to be eroded, the 'foundation of capitalism'. What he has achieved, however, is in eroding much of the foundations of the various incorporationist theses.

Reformist trade unions, following the institutionalized rules of the game, and Social Democracy are the dominant forms of the working-class movement in advanced capitalist societies. There is no visible challenge to capitalist power in the United States. These are hard facts, which no Marxist can deny with his or her eyes open. But there is more to the history of the present than that. However, in the first 10-15 years of social scientific Marxism there has been a strong tendency to concentrate on the *structure* of the present, on its structured class boundaries for example, and to abdicate from seriously analysing the *history* of its class struggles.

The difficult relationship of the new Marxism to present working-class history is indicated by the works and the relation between them of Nicos Poulantzas, the most central figure in the emerging neo-Marxist theory of class and politics, and Edward Thompson, whose history of *The Making of the English Working Class* (1963) falls outside the set task of this essay, but which is without doubt the most monumental Marxist study of class in the period under review.

Two things are striking in Poulantzas's work in this respect. His *Political Power and Social Classes* comments on and relates to a considerable number of Anglo-Saxon sociologists and political scientists, but he does not say a word about Thompson's book. It is mentioned once, and then rather out of place, in a footnote of references about the capitalization of groundrent in the 1640 revolution.[59] Secondly, Poulantzas himself never even wrote a chapter about the working-class, his *Classes in Contemporary Capitalism* deals exclusively with the other classes of the contemporary world. Poulantzas's silence is more than a singular evasion. It covers a major theoretical problem never directly confronted, the problem of class agency.

The question which Thompson's work provides an elaborate and fascinating answer to, about the formation or making of a class, in the sense of class agency, is hardly even askable within the Althusser-Poulantzas problematic, where classes are always already formed or made.[60]

For his part, Thompson, though he has written proficiently on current affairs, has never written anything about modern working-class history. As a master craftsman Thompson also has an immense pride in his historian's craft — 'the Queen of the humanities'[61] with little more than utter contempt for the social sciences. And Thompson has his own particular way of evading the tricky but challenging problems of class agency, shortcutting the issue by defining class exclusively in terms of collective self-identification. This also had the remarkable consequences of allocating only a minor and marginal part to the formation of the world's first industrial proletariat in the vast drama of the 'making of the English working class'.[62]

In the relationship of Poulantzas, and many other Marxists of this period, to bourgeois sociology and political science there is also a remarkable gap. There is no discussion of, no reference to that part of political sociology which might seem most directly pertinent to a development of a Marxist theory of politics as class struggle, the works on 'political cleavages' and their social bases and historical origins by people like S.M. Lipset, Juan Linz, Stein Rokkan.[63] Instead, the references are to the most general and ahistorical works of academic political science and sociology.

Future developments will have to theorize and to analyse the historical articulation of patterns of capital accumulation and forms of class struggle with other, irreducibly different processes and forces, as well as forms of class organization and class struggle which do not correspond to classical canons.

Future Marxism will have to confront directly the problems of classes as historical actors of the present. This in turn will require the clarification of two crucial questions, which so far have received little serious theoretical attention. One concerns the meaning of *class agency*, the other the *relationship of class as a political* (and social) *subject to non-class subjects.*

Classes are not actors in the same sense as individuals, groups or organizations are, decision-making actors bringing about events or 'monuments', such as programmes, codes, etc. A class can never make a decision as a class. But nor is class agency, in the Marxist sense, a series of isolated actions, the indirect effects of which are gauged by the analyst in the form of a statistical measure of some sort, such as rates of economic growth, social mobility or electoral participation and the distribution of income or of votes. Class is a third kind of agency, of tendentially acting forces defined by their economic location, acting collectively, to an ever-varying but (virtually) never complete degree.

There is a Marxist tradition which has tended to treat class as an agency in the first sense, but this has meant little more than a metaphor or device for summing up some social process, referring to the bourgeoisie or the working-class thinking or doing this or that. In political sociology, on the other hand, class agency is usually conceived of in the second meaning, as an analytical construct for the ordering of individual acts, most often voting. But the intellectual, and political, challenge to social scientific Marxism will be to elucidate and to elaborate class agency as a specific, third kind of agency.

Classes act through the actions of individuals, groups, and organization. The operation of class agency may be seen in a commonality of concerns, in a parallelity of strivings, a similarity of the forms of actions and in interrelationships of mutual reinforcement between the actions of members of the same class. To what extent this commonality, etc., becomes conscious and manifested in processes of collective decision-making with a specific outcome is a set of empirical questions about class formation and class history.

Confrontations with the best of political sociology as well as with contemporary politics will make it necessary for Marxists to think about the relationship between class struggles and other forms of social conflict and of political cleavages, about the relationship between classes and other social and political subjects. This is something which will require not only ad hoc empirical attention but also, and first of all, systematic theorization. A first attempt has been made, by outlining 'the universe of ideologies' in the sense of the universe of forms of human subjectivity. There, class has been situated as one variant of one of four irreducible dimensions of human subjectivity, the historical-positional one. The other three being, an historical-inclusive one (illustrated by the nation), an existential-inclusive one (exemplifiable by religion), an existential-positional subjectivity (such as gender-subjectivity).[62] The tenability and the fruitfulness of this particular conceptualization still have to be demonstrated, but some such endeavour is needed. Class struggles are not only struggles between classes and about class unity, class boundaries, and class alliances. They are also about link-ups with non-class subjectivities and non-class struggles.

It is in the vacuum of serious Marxist theories and analyses of the social struggles of the present, that new anti-Marxist fads and utopias have begun to mushroom on the left, as substitutes for the abandoned extrapolations of the revolutionary Marxist faith of yesterday.

However, what some searchers of a new faith have come to regard as a God that failed is likely to be considered by more secularized Marxists as a stage of infancy and adolescence. And there is little reason to believe that social scientific Marxism will stop at this stage. Rather, it seems more probable, that after its political experiences of the 1970s, one of its future tendencies will be to drop its aloof silence about the actual history of the present and to develop a historical materialism of current social struggles and forces of stability, taking their intriguing complexity as an intellectual challenge. And such an open-ended, non-reductionist Marxism is likely to be of more use to socialist and other emancipatory politics than its more self-contained versions of the past.

Notes

1. Cf. P. Anderson, *Considerations on Western Marxism*, London, NLB, 1976.
2. Marx to J. Weydemyer, 5.3.1852, Marx-Engels, *Werke*, East Berlin, Dietz, Vol. 28, pp. 507-8.
3. This state refers to class analysis as a mode of comprehensive analyses of social structures and social processes.
4. B. Barber, 'Introduction', entry 'Stratification, Social', *International Encyclopedia of the Social Sciences*, New York, Macmillan, 1968, vol. 15, p. 289.
5. T. Parsons, 'An Analytical Approach to the Theory of Stratification', *American Journal of Sociology*, vol. 45 (1940), pp. 841-862; K. Davis, 'A Conceptual Analysis of Stratification', *American Sociological Review*, vol. 10 (1945), pp. 242-249.
6. The best of Lipset's class-conscious sociology of politics is best accessible via his collection of essays, *Political Man,* London, Heinemann, 1960. For Lipset's perspective on class and class struggle, see further below.
7. In a somewhat more sophisticated and roundabout way, Lipset in his *Encyclopedia* article finally comes down to a stratificationist position too: 'Highly developed societies ... are more likely to possess systems of social stratification – varied rakings – than social classes.' S.W. Lipset, Social Class, *International Encyclopedia of the Social Sciences*, op. cit., vol. 15, p. 314.
8. True, this was not swallowed by the whole sociological community. In fact, the Davis-Moore article referred to above triggered off a lengthy debate about the functionalist theory of stratification. Part of that debate is reprinted in the second edition of Bendix-Lipset, *Class, Status and Power* op. cit., pp. 47-72. Probably the most extensive analysis of the whole debate is G. Therborn, 'The Classes of the Disappeared Society. The Stratification Principles of Davis-Moore and Modern Sociology', published (in Swedish) in idem, *Klasser och ekonomiska system*, Staffanstorp, Cavefor, 1971.
9. R. Dahrendorf, *Class and Class Conflict in Industrial Society*, Standord, University Press, 1959; D. Lockwood, 'Social Integration

and System Integration', in G.K. Zollscham/W. Hirsch (eds.) *Explorations in Social Change*, London 1964, pp. 244-257; J. Goldthorpe/D. Lockwood, 'Affluence and the British Class Structure', *The Sociological Review* vol. 11 (1963) pp. 133-163. Lockwood also published a very important empirical work on class in this period, *The Blackcoated Worker,* London 1958; S. Ossowski, *Class Structure in the Social Consciousness*, London, Routledge & Kegan Paul, 1963.

10. Lipset, 'Social Class', op. cit., p. 305.

11. *ibid.*, p. 314.

12. B. Moore Jr., *Political Power and Social Theory*, New York, Humanities Press, 1958, pp. 116 (citation) and 123ff.

13. T.B. Bottomore/M. Rubel (eds), *Karl Marx. Selected Writings on Sociology and Social Philosophy*, London, Watts, 1956.

14. C.W. Mills, *The Power Elite*, New York, Galary Paperback edition, 1959, p. 277n.

15. P. Sweezy, 'Power Elite or Ruling Class?' and R. Lynd, 'Power in the United States', in: G.W. Domhoff/H.B. Ballart (eds.), *C. Wright Mills and the Power Elite*, Boston, Beacon Press, Paperback ed. 1969, pp. 115-132 esp. pp. 124ff and pp. 103-15, esp. pp. 111ff, respectively. – Domhoff has established himself as an important analyst of the American ruling class, in a series of works beginning with *Who Rules America?*, Englewood Cliffs N.J., Prentice Hall, 1967.

16. Austrian Social Democracy cut itself off from any programmatic link to Marxism in 1958, West German Social Democracy in 1959, and the Swedish one in 1960.

17. Typical was a two-volume pattern. Poulantzas's *Political Power and Social Classes* was wholly theoretical and methodological, whereas his next book, *Fascism and Dictatorship* (original French edition 1970) brought concepts of the first book to bear upon an analysis of the rise of Fascism and of the Comintern's relationship to it. *Classes in Contemporary Capitalism* (1974) had more empirical content in its theoretical argumentation, but the conceptualization of kinds of the bourgeoisies developed there were actually used in Poulantzas subsequent book (1975) on *The Crisis of Dictatorships*. The collective IMSF and PKA works on the West German class structure (op. cit.), started with one volume of extended theoretical exposition followed by one of the vast statistical data collection, of even in the case of IMSF of three empirical volumes. Erik Olin Wright's current empirical research project on comparative class structure has been preceded by several theoretical articles, the most extended one included in his book *Class, Crisis and the State* (London, NLB, 1978). Likewise, Adam Przeworski's big and, at the time of writing, unfinished empirical project has been preceded by an elaborate theoretical discussion of class conceptualization, 'Proletarians into a Class: The Process of Class Formation from Karl Kautsky's *The Class Struggle* to Recent

Controversies', *Politics and Society* (vol. 7 no. 4, 1977). Guglielmo Carchedi's also noteworthy volume *On the Economic Identification of Social Classes* (London, Routledge & Kegan Paul 1977), however, has no empirical companion in print.

18. Autorenkollektiv des IMSF, *Klassen- und Sozialstruktur der BRD 1950-1970*, 4 vols., Frankfurt/M, Verlag Marxistische Blätter, 1973 and 1975.
Projekt Klassenanalyse, *Materialien zur Klassenstruktur der BRD*, 2 vols., West Berlin, VSA, 1973 and 1974.

19. An idea of the project may be gained from Przeworski's article 'Social Democracy as a Historical Phenomenon', *New Left Review* no. 24 (1980) pp. 38ff.

20. E.O. Wright, 'The Comparative Project on Class Structure and Class Consciousness: An Overview', Unpublished MSS, Dept. of Sociology, Univ. of Wisconsin, Madison, Nov. 1981.

21. F. Parkin, *Marxism and Class Theory: A Bourgeois Critique*, New York, Columbia University Press, 1979, p. 48. Like much else in Parkin's book, the subtitle is meant ironically. Parkin's own perspective is rather that of a neo-Weberian Social Democrat.

22. R. Dahrendorf, *Class and Class Conflict in Industrial Society* op. cit.

23. Parkin op. cit., pp. 51-52.

24. A. Giddens, *A Contemporary Critique of Historical Materialism*, London, Macmillan 1981, p. 122. Giddens's own venture into class analysis, more theoretical than empirical, *The Class Structure of the Advanced Societies*, London, Hutchinson, 1973, is a mélange out of Marxisant and neo-Weberian elements.

25. E.O. Wright, *Class Structure and Income Determination*, New York, Academic Press, 1979. The data analysed are taken from a national American survey. A less methodologically rigorous but broader-ranging Marxist empirical study of property and inequality is J. Westergaard/H. Resler, *Class in A Capitalist Society. A study of Contemporary Britain*, London, Heinemann, 1975.

26. Cf. Anderson, *Considerations*) op. cit., p. 69. The new social scientific Marxism has certainly broken with the extreme parochialism of the schools of Western Marxism, but as yet it has hardly reached a stage of regular international communication and debate. Thus, Poulantzas never confronted his conception of class with that of Edward Thompson – more about this below; Heinz Jung, the director of the IMSF study, made references both to West German non-Marxist sociology – e.g. IMSF, op. cit., vol. 1, p. 186n – and to Soviet, GDR and PCF works, but he did not take issue with the work of Poulantzas; the PKA took up for critical discussion some West German works, Marxist and non-Marxist, and contemporary East and Western European Communist Party discussions, but likewise refrains from any confrontation with Marxist social science outside the Federal Republic

and of the orbit of the journal *Problems of Peace and Socialism*, PKA, op. cit., vol. 1, Part B. Przeworski and Wright, like the West Germans, discuss Marxist classics and non-Marxist sociology, but limit their discussion of contemporary Marxism to Anglo-Saxon works and to French works out of the Althuserian tradition, neither touching the West German endeavours, Przeworski, 'Proletarians into a Class ...', op. cit., Wright, 'Varieties of Conceptions of Marxist Class Structure', *Politics and Society*, vol. 9, no. 3 (1980), pp. 323-70.

27. Class figures are taken from my *Klasstrukturen i Sverige*, the main sources of which are censuses and official labour force surveys, and the size of the electorate from the official statistical publication *Allmänna valen 1979*, Stockholm 1980.

28. N. Poulantzas, *Political Power and Social Classes* London, NLB, 1973, p. 72.

29. N. Poulantzas, *Classes in Contemporary Capitalism*, London, Verso ed., 1978, p. 16. Cf. idem *Political Power* ..., op cit., pp. 60-61.

30. Idem, *Classes*, op. cit., pp. 205-6, 287ff.

31. Wright, *Class, Crisis and the State* op. cit., ch. 1.

32. *ibid.*, p. 96n. Emphasis added.

33. E.O. Wright et al., 'The American Class Structure', unpublished MSS, Dept. of Sociology, University of Wisconsin, Madison, Nov. 1981, p. 10.

34. The paper cited in the previous note contains a first, preliminary data report.

35. This statement includes self-criticism, in particular of the first two editions (of 1972 and 1973) of my work on Swedish class structure. But criticism may, of course, come from other directions too. One of Wright's associates in his ongoing international project makes an analysis of Sweden from Wright's point of view, and is therewith comparing the results of that with mine. A first outcome is G. Ahrne, 'Report on the Swedish Class Structure 1', Unpublished MSS, Dept. of Sociology, Uppsala University.

36. M. Aglietta, *A Theory of Capitalist Regulation*, London, NLB, 1979, pp. 68ff.

37. Calculated from PKA, op. cit., vol. 2, pp. 215 and 420. The figures include self-employed, state or non-business-employees 'Middle class' plus 'wage workers in non-capitalist commodity production'. The latter are workers in establishments with at most four employees (ibid. p. 156).

38. Calculations based on the Swedish 'Enterprise Census' (företags-räkning) of 1972, presented in: Therborn, *Klasstrukturen i Sverige*, pp. 100-101.

39. For Sweden see the text below. For West Germany, calculations from a new book by Joachim Bischoff and associates — *Jenseits der Klassen?*, Hamburg, VSA, 1982, a follow-up, a deepening of and a more

circumspect political rationale for the PKA study – yield a figure of 36% of the economically active population as either self-employed or non-capitalistically employed, pp. 88 and 96.

40. Therborn, *Klasstrukturen* ..., op. cit., pp. 115, 152-53. IMSF op. cit., vol. II, pp. 152-153 gives a corresponding West German figure for 1970 as 19.4% of the economically active population. The Swedish figure for 1965 was 21-22%, including employees of public capital.

41. The american economist James O'Connor is in this sense somewhat of an exception in paying significant attention to state employment through his trichotomization of the economy, into monopoly, competitive, and state sectors, *The Fiscal Crisis of the State*, New York, St Martin's Press, 1973.

42. Therborn, *Klasstrukturen* ..., op. cit., p. 116. Public employees here exclude employees of public corporations, who make up about 10% of all public employees.

43. Calculations from PKA, op. cit., vol. 2, pp. 309, 553 and 572-3, including what PKA class 'branch B' of public employment – which to them comprises a mixed bag of functions, deriving both out of the 'bourgeois' and the 'societal' division of labour – minus priests, clergymen and broadcasting personnel plus employees of public social insurance systems. The total number of public employees in West Germany in 1970 (inc. social insurance employees) would then be barely 16% – a figure reached in Sweden by 1950. IMSF gives a slightly higher figure, 18% (excluding employees of public corporations with an autonomous legal form), IMSF, op. cit., vol. II: 2, p. 321.

44. An important exception are the works of the American Marxist sociologist Harriet Friedmann on wheat production. See her article 'World Market, State, and Family Farm', *Comparative Studies in History and Society*, vol. 20 (1978) no. 4.

45. Therborn, op. cit., pp. 29, 83-83, 90. In West Germany owners and family helpers provided 80% of the agrarian labour force in 1950 and 88% in 1970, IMSF op. cit., vol. II: 1, pp. 184-85.

46. Domestic servants far outnumbered public employees in education and health care, in Sweden in 1930 by 2.5 to 1.

47. E. Lederer, *Die Privatangestellten in der modernen Wirtschafts-entwicklung*, Tübingen 1912.

48. G. Carchedi, *On the Economic Identification of Social Classes*, London, Routledge & Kegan Paul, 1977, ch. 1, esp. pp. 87ff. Wright discusses Carchedi's work in his 'Varieties of Marxist Conceptions of Class Structure' op. cit., pp. 356ff.

49. Carchedi op. cit., p. 65.

50. Wright, 'Varieties ...' op. cit., p. 363.

51. F. Engels, 'Necessary and Superfluous Social Classes', *Marx-Engels Werke*, East Berlin, Dietz, 1973, vol. 19, pp. 287-290. This kind of analysis is elaborated and discussed in my paper 'Enterprises, Markets

and States', Dept. of Sociology, Univ. of Toronto, Working Paper Series No. 9 (1979).

52. H. Braverman, *Labour and Monopoly Capital*, New York, Monthly Review Press, 1974. Braverman's chapter (15) on the degradation of clerical work and the inclusion in the working class of its performers appeared the same year as Poulantzas in his *Classes in Contemporary Capitalism* (in the original French edition by Seuil) and Baudelot et al. in their *La petite bourgeoisie en France*, op. cit., were arguing the crucial importance of the distinction between mental and manual labour, between office and shopfloor.

53. With their particular penchant for carrying arguments to their utmost conclusions, however absurd, the iconoclastic British Marxists Barry Hindess, Paul Hirst and their associates have characterized the class power configuration of temporary corporate capitalism thus: 'it is "capitals" which exist, not "capitalists" ', which managers are separated from the means of production like all other workers, A. Cutler et al., *Marx's Capital and Capitalism Today* 2 vols., London, Routledge & Kegan Paul, 1977, vol. 1, p. 312. Whatever one's taste for the authors' mode of argumentation, always arrogant and extreme in form while changing in content from one book to the next, and whatever one's degree of being convinced, this work is (also) in the best sense very thought-provoking.

54. Cf. Przeworski, 'Proletarians into A Class ...' op. cit., pp. 385ff.

55. Burawoy, op. cit. p. 72. Burawoy has also written a very profound theoretical critique of Braverman's mode of analysis, 'Toward a Marxist Theory of the Labour Process: Braverman and Beyond', *Politics and Society vol. 8* (1978), pp. 247-312.

56. M. Davis, 'Why the US Working Class Is Different', *New Left Review* no. 123 (1980), pp. 3-44; 'The Barren Marriage of American Labour and the Democratic Party', *NLR* no. 124 (1980) pp. 43-84.

57. Davis, 'Why the US Working Class ...' op. cit. p. 7, emphasis omitted.

58. Korpi is not alone among senior leftwing Social Democratic academics in turning towards a Marxist position. Another very interesting example is Ulf Himmelstrand, 1978-198? President of the International Sociological Association, and senior author of another significant work which posits the Swedish Social Democratic working class as an agent of Socialist transformation, U. Himmelstrand et al., *Beyond Welfare Capitalism*, London, Heinemann, 1981.

59. N. Poulantzas, *Political Power and Social Classes* op. cit., p. 169.

60. Poulantzas says, for instance: 'One reading of these texts (by Marx)' must be rejected from the start, for it is connected ultimately with the problematic of the 'social group' which has no place in Marx' analyses: this is the *historico-genetic* reading.' *Political Power* ... op. cit., p. 60.

61. E.P. Thompson, *The Poverty of Theory*, London, Merlin Press, 1978, p. 262. 'Bourgeois sociology' and 'Marxist structuralism' are just

'unhistorical shit' according to Thompson's conclusion, ibid., p. 300. For a sober and incisive reply to Thompson, see P. Anderson, *Arguments within English Marxism*, London, NLB and Verso, 1980.

62. Thompson chose to concentrate on the field labourers, the urban artisans and the hand-loom weavers 'because their experience seems most to colour the social consciousness of the working class in the first half of the (19th) century' (E.P. Thompson, *The Making of the English Working Class*, New York, Vintage Paperback ed., 1966, p. 212n.).

63. See, e.g., S.M. Lipset/S. Rokkan (eds.), *Party Systems and Voter Alignments*, New York, Free Press, 1967; S. Rokkan, *Citizens, Elections, Parties*, Oslo, Universitetsforlaget, 1970.

64. G. Therborn, *The Ideology of Power and the Power of Ideology*, London, Verso and NLB, 1980, pp. 22ff.

Michèle Barrett

Marxist-Feminism and the Work of Karl Marx

Any commemorative volume, let alone one whose subject is the greatest revolutionary thinker of modern history, tends to court the danger of hagiography. On the question of feminism, however, even the most committed Marxists now suspect that our idol has feet of clay. Many feminists, indeed, see this weakness as one which vitiates the whole of Marx's work. Gone are the days when 'the woman question' could be answered from the writings of Marx; his treatment of the issue is now widely regarded as scattered, scanty and unsatisfactory. The situation is scarcely improved by the fact that much of what is attributed to Marx, particularly in relation to a programme for the emancipation of women, was in fact the work of Engels. It is not entirely clear how far Marx himself accepted arguments such as those eventually set out in Engels's *The Origin of the Family, Private Property and the State* (1884).

The fact that Engels took such an interest in questions about the family and the oppression of women makes it difficult to take a charitable view of Marx's own failings in this area. He cannot be 'let off the hook' by saying that gender inequality had yet to be discovered at the time he lived and wrote. In any case such an argument does Marx a disservice that borders on insult. Marx's ability to penetrate the appearance of social relations and expose their underlying exploitative character is the basis of the explanatory value of Marxism. We can see this ability applied to a broad enough range of phenomena to be conscious of its *not* being applied to questions of gender. To exonerate Marx by an appeal to a supposedly 'pre-feminist' culture is both to underestimate the currency of feminist ideas in the nineteenth century and to underestimate the usual level of perception of Marx.

In order to consider the place of Marx's thought in the tradition of socialist feminism we shall need to look at several different types of question, ranging from general philosophical orientation to specific formulations and analyses.

I Egalitarianism and Humanism

Many people see a 'natural' sympathy between all struggles against oppression. Class struggle, anti-racist struggle, feminist struggle are all self-evidently directed against inequality and towards human liberation and hence may be expected to enjoy relationships of mutual support. The history of these struggles is less the history of easy alliances, however, than it is a history of distance and division. Alliances have to be built in a mood of conscious solidarity and are not naturally given by the simple fact of oppression.

The vocabulary of 'inequality' comes from liberalism rather than Marxism and there is considerable evidence that Marx is misrepresented when he is portrayed as a gladiator of egalitarianism. In fact, Marx regarded the notion of 'equality' as not merely an idea that historically coincided with bourgeois rule but as a *bourgeois idea*. This is the point he makes in the well-known discussion of 'ruling class and ruling ideas':

> If now in considering the course of history we detach the ideas of the ruling class from the ruling class itself and attribute to them an independent existence, if we confine ourselves to saying that these or those ideas were dominant at a given time, without bothering ourselves about the conditions of production and the producers of these ideas, if we thus ignore the individuals and world conditions which are the source of the ideas, we can say, for instance, that during the time that the aristocracy was dominant, the concepts honour, loyalty, etc. were dominant, during the dominance of the bourgeoisie the concepts freedom, equality, etc. The ruling class itself on the whole imagines this to be so.[1]

Equality, justice and rights are not embraced in the abstract by Marxism. Engels's lengthy polemic against Dühring makes it very clear that what might be called 'ethical socialism' — socialism based upon truth and justice as goals – differs sharply from the Marxist view of socialism as the historically given mission of the proletariat.[2] Marx and Engels both display an antipathy to the doctrine of egalitarianism which they identify as part of the political arsenal of the ascendent bourgeoisie. As Allen Wood puts it: 'On the basis of the texts, I think we must regard Marx as an opponent of the ideal of equality, despite the fact that he is also and not any the less an opponent of all forms of social privilege and oppression'.[3]

Wood inclines to the view that it would be in keeping with 'the spirit of Marxism' to regard movements based on the concept of equality – such as feminism or anti-racism – as progressive. This, in a sense, is the view generally held on the left today. We cannot be too confident, though, that Marx would have agreed with it. The nineteenth century saw several manifestations of the call for women's suffrage. Marx, however, having plenty of opportunities to identify himself with this movement, failed to do so. Just as he was happy to leave the theorization of 'the woman question' to Engels, so he left its political profile to others such as his daughter Eleanor. The implication must obviously be that, to say the least, he regarded such issues as marginal.

Neither Marx nor Engels saw fit to attempt to rebut the classic statements in favour of women's rights. Wollstonecraft and Mill remain unanswered where similarly egalitarian and liberal arguments on other topics are despatched with vigour. It is not perhaps surprising that, although Marx and Engels might be ready enough to approve the organization of *women workers*, they did not see that the cause of socialism had much in common with that of women's rights. Engels noted in the early eighteen-nineties that 'The foremost English champions of the formal rights of women ... are in a large measure directly or indirectly interested in the capitalist exploitation of both sexes.'[4] It is no coincidence that this last reference is from Yvonne Kapp's biography of Eleanor Marx, for – such is the paucity of research on the attitudes of Marx and Engels to feminist issues –

it is an invaluable source of information on Marx and Engels too.

It can be argued that feminism as a modern political doctrine is based principally on a philosophy of egalitarianism.[5] Underlying many feminist political positions is the variant of humanism that demands equal rights for all individuals. Historically, feminism has arisen as part of bourgeois liberal ideology, though undoubtedly most feminists today would resist Marx's implication that this renders feminism a bourgeois notion *tout court*. One way of posing a philosophical distance between feminist thought and that of Marx, is in terms of egalitarianism. The dominant traditions of feminism are couched in terms of morality, justice or equal rights, and attempts to draw up a model of male dominance with an explanatory value to match that of Marxism's historical materialism have been, so far, problematic. The claim of Marxism, of course, is to provide a scientific account of the exploitation we experience, with a view to over-throwing it; it is precisely this claim to a scientific status that differentiates Marxism from 'ethical' or egalitarian political doctrines.

In so far as egalitarianism is a source of conflict and disagreement between feminism and Marx, it might be thought that humanism would be a point of philosophical agreement. Attempts to develop rigorously non-humanist versions of feminism and Marxism have proved extremely difficult. On the Marxist side there is considerable scope for movement since the later Marx is patently more amenable to an anti-humanist reading than the early Marx. My own view would be that both feminism and the approach of Marx himself are essentially humanist in orientation. This would not necessarily make them compatible, however, since there could be substantial differences of emphasis. Feminism could be said to rest, ultimately, on an appeal to justice within the category of humanity. It relies on a notion of the self-evident fairness of distributing rights and opportunities equally among humans. The case is the same for anti-racist philosophy. The humanism in Marx's thought, notwithstanding the disavowals of egalitarianism, is in some respects similar. The theory of alienation (to be discussed in more detail later) is the obvious example to take. It argues that certain categories of people (labourers under a capitalist labour process for instance) are deprived of what belongs to them by virtue of their humanity.

Marx's writings are shot through with various aspects of humanist philosophy. One elementary example is the sharp distinction Marx draws between humanity on the one hand and the animal kingdom on the other. Humans have the ability to transform nature through labour, they can plan and execute their projects and are not limited by patterns of instinctual behaviour. This insistence on the distinctive abilities of humans gives rise, as Timpanaro's work suggests, to a certain 'triumphalism' in Marxism.[6] There are difficulties with this variant of humanism in that it partakes of a typically bourgeois complacency and conceit over the superiority of humanity. Raymond Williams is critical of Marx's use of 'man's conquest of nature':

> ... in both its moderate and its extreme forms, the notion of the 'conquest of nature' belongs not simply to Marxism but to a whole period of bourgeois thought. Indeed it became an almost inevitable generalization from the extraordinary achievements in material transformation of the industrial revolution and of advances in the physical sciences ... But it can now be clearly seen that this triumphalist version is, in an exceptionally close correspondence, the specific ideology of imperialism and capitalism, whose basic concepts – limitless and conquering expansion; reduction of the labour process to the appropriation and transformation of raw materials – it exactly repeats.[7]

It is significant that this version of humanism is predicated upon the centrality of *labour*. Although in principle human labour is exactly that – neither male nor female – there is a tendency in Marx's more specific analyses to imply that labour power is generally male. Many anthropologists would now insist, as indeed Engels did, that women played a dominant part in the transformation of nature in societies where survival depended less on the construction of iron bridges and more on maintaining adequate food supplies. In the analysis of capitalism, however, we tend to find (a point to be dealt with in more detail later) an assumption that the wage labourer is a man. The 'triumphalist' element of Marx's humanism is one that has lent itself, in its application to specific societies, to a marked gender imbalance.

A rather more complex issue arises if we consider another aspect of Marx's humanism — the one classically thought of when humanism is identified with atheism or secularism. Marx was implacably opposed to religion in any version. Those who speak of 'Christian Marxism', for instance, are invoking a Marxism that Marx himself would not recognize. So central to his philosophy was Marx's demystification of religion that he claimed that ' ... the criticism of religion is the presupposition of all criticism'.[8] Marx saw religion as necessarily involving the impoverishment of humanity, as necessarily alienating. Although it could be argued that philosophical anti-Christianity is not historically a feature of feminism — indeed the reverse would be true if we look to the nineteenth century development of evangelical influences on feminism[9] — certain problems do arise in the relationship between Marx's anti-religious humanism and the equal-rights humanism more characteristic of feminism.

Feminist humanism tends to be based on notions of justice and equality within the human species. Marx's humanism is in the main directed towards a future human liberation or emancipation. Marx argues that this is why the proletariat has the transcending purpose that he ascribes to it. The proletariat, as the utterly exploited class has literally nothing to lose — it is the *universal* class and is hence capable of bringing about a revolution that, in liberating itself, must liberate everyone.[10] Only then is it possible to speak of *human* emancipation. Marx's critique of religion is an important prerequisite of his theory of human emancipation, since religion (here Marx follows Feuerbach) provides a prime case of the alienation from humanity of all that is conceived of as good. The creation of Gods must be at the expense of humanity.

The relationship between religion, alienation and emancipation is explored in Marx's analysis of 'the Jewish question' and his discussion there is of particular relevance to feminism. Essentially Marx argues that the call for emancipation of the Jews is a call for merely 'political' emancipation: it would not amount to human emancipation. He writes:

> So we do not say to the Jews, as Bauer does: you cannot be emancipated politically without emancipating yourselves radically from Judaism. Rather we say to them: because you can be politically emancipated without completely and consistently abandoning Judaism, this means that political emancipation itself is not human emancipation. If you Jews wish to achieve political emancipation without achieving human emancipation, then the incompleteness and contradiction does not only lie in you, it lies in the nature and category of political emancipation. If you are imprisoned within this category, then you are sharing in something common to everyone.'[11]

The underlying problem is — to put it another way — human alienation: if all religion is dehumanizing then Judaism is no different from Christianity. As Karl Löwith puts it: 'What is needed for a genuine emancipation of the Jews, as of the Christians, is not freedom of religion decreed by the state, but human freedom from religion as such.'[12]

The key point in all this for a consideration of feminism is Marx's distinction between *political emancipation* and human emancipation. The goal of 'equality' is directed towards political emancipation and, as we have seen, Marx considered this not merely a limited category but a mystificatory one. He analyses the bourgeois liberal state as resting on the very inequalities — he cites 'birth, class, education and profession'[13] as examples — that it denies to be salient political differences. There can be little doubt that the categories of race and gender would — had Marx considered them in this context — form two further distinctions of civil society and its systems of rank. Marx's general position on the political emancipation of the Jews is to regard it as at best a limited project pending more fundamental human emancipation. At worst, he implies, such mere political emancipation distracts our attention from the degree to which we are all 'imprisoned' together: emphasis on sectional political emancipation blinds us to more fundamental shared, *human*, emancipation.

It must be noted that Marx's position on the Jewish question

 Michèle Barrett

would be regarded as somewhat reductionist today. He would have had little sympathy for our efforts to engage with anti-semitism as an autonomous political ideology. On the basis of his own arguments it would be difficult to see – *pace* the spirit of human emancipation – how he would have supported a political movement aimed solely at abolishing the particular and specific oppressions of gender. My reading of Marx suggests that the feminist movement would undoubtedly fall within the circumscribed, if not illusory, gains to be obtained from 'mere' political emancipation.

Unless, of course, we adopt an extremely devout adherence to Marx's texts, this does not necessarily resolve our difficulties. We need to consider further whether Marx was right to be so critical of political emancipation or whether we might wish to conceive it as more progressive than he did. Secondly we might want to question the exclusively class-based orientation he has towards human liberation.

On the merits of egalitarian political emancipation versus the revolutionary potential of immiseration, readers no doubt have their own views. Decades of labourism and welfarism and feeble attempts to provide 'equality of opportunity' have tended to bear out Marx's gloomy predictions on the value of abolishing inequalities of earning, occupation, political rights and so on. Who, however, would care to argue against a systematic political project of eliminating racism and sexism from the working class on the grounds that such inequalities were not of prime significance? Marx's arguments on the place of 'political emancipation' need to be considered over his whole lifetime and changing views, and in the light of political developments over the last century. Let us leave in suspension, then, for the moment, whether Marx's critical conception of political emancipation is adequate to its task.

The second question I raised concerned Marx's account of human liberation or emancipation. This is based directly, in his early work, on the theory of alienation and this must now be considered. For although Marx casts this theory in terms that only engage directly with the labour process and the wage relation, it is widely interpreted, and has become popularized, as a far more general theory. In particular, it is often argued that Marx's writings on alienation, and indeed the philosophical humanism and ethical emphasis in his early writings, constitute his major influence on feminism and other liberation movements.

II Oppression and Liberation

Marx's theory of alienation has proved one of the most popularly resonant of his works. Although there is a considerable gulf between the various colloquial uses of the word 'alienation' and the complex theory of self-objectification Marx himself elaborated under this heading, it remains the case that Marx here propounded a doctrine that goes straight to the heart of much radicalism. What finer and more elegant expression of injustice could take the place of Marx's words:

> Labour produces works of wonder for the rich, but nakedness for the worker. It produces palaces, but only hovels for the worker; it produces beauty, but cripples the worker; it replaces labour by machines but throws a part of the workers back to a barbaric labour and turns the other part into machines. It produces culture, but also imbecility, and cretinism for the worker.[14]

We can observe these processes today as Marx saw them in 1844. The significance of Marx's approach is that he identified the causal relationship between the enrichment of the product and the impoverishment of labour: he explained what might otherwise appear as coincidence, irony, tragedy. Marx's explanation is as simple as the basis of his hostility to religion: 'The more man puts into God, the less he retains in himself'. As he puts it: ' ... the more the worker externalizes himself in his work, the more powerful becomes the alien, objective world that he creates opposite himself, the poorer he becomes himself in his inner life and the less he can call his own.'[15]

Marx's theory of alienation is effective as a general theory of oppression and liberation for the reason that it has a strong *relational* character. It enables us to understand oppression not

                    Michèle Barrett

as an arbitrary imposition but as a process involving the oppressed. C.J. Arthur rightly notes that what distinguishes an alienating situation from one based on robbery and brute force is that ' ... the workers, in effect, continually *reproduce the conditions of their subservience*'.[16] It is this dimension of alienation theory that has made it so relevant to feminism, as indeed it has had its influence on work such as Fanon's on interior colonization. Feminist theory and practice has tended to emphasize the necessity of engaging with subjectivity and consciousness as well as with external structures and it has attempted analyses of how an oppressed group comes to live out the dynamics of oppression in forms of collusion. It is to these concerns that Marx's account of alienation speaks so eloquently. The engagement of feminism with psychoanalysis, even – through Simone de Beauvoir – with existentialist concerns of authenticity and good faith is widely recognised. But Marx's explorations of alienation, and his deployment of even such relatively crude concepts as 'false-consciousness' have made an indispensable early contribution to twentieth-century feminist thought.

It must be said, however, that this contribution has been extracted from the most general bearings of Marx's theory rather than from any explicit and detailed argument. Marx himself, unfortunately, poses the issue in such a way that a number of difficulties arise in *applying* the theory of alienation to the specific oppression of women. Consider the following passage:

> The alienation of man and in general of every relationship in which man stands to himself is first realized and expressed in the relationship with which man stands to other men. Thus in the situation of alienated labour each man measures his relationship to other men by the relationship in which he finds himself placed as a worker.[17]

To ask whether Marx intends 'man' to mean humanity or men is of more consequence than some 'tedious feminist pedantry'. If the generic meaning is intended Marx forgets that *precisely* the relationship in which a woman is placed *as a worker* differs from that in which a man is placed. (To what extent does the theory of alienation apply to a fulltime housewife? How do we analyse the dual role of many women, as wage-labourers but also as creators of use-values in the home?) Later Marx writes that 'The infinite degradation in which man exists for himself is expressed in his relationship to woman as prey and servant of communal lust ... '[18], recognizing that his use of 'man' is not the generic one. The more salient point, however, is the general significance of labour to Marx's definition of what it is to be human rather than animal. If, as we shall see later, Marx tends to construe the labourer as male, this will raise problems at some level in the applicability of the theory of alienation to questions of gender.

Ideology

A parallel example can be seen, although I wish to mention it only briefly here, in Marx's account of ideology. Nothing could be more opposite to the present hegemonic dominance of men in the media and in ideological and cultural processes than Marx's well-known remarks on 'ruling ideas':

> The ideas of the ruling class are in every epoch the ruling ideas, i.e. the class which is the ruling *material* force of society, is at the same time its ruling *intellectual* force. The class which has the means of material production at its disposal, has control at the same time over the means of mental production, so that thereby, generally speaking, the ideas of those who lack the means of mental production are subject to it.[19]

Certainly it is suggestive to consider the extent to which men could be said to control 'the means of mental production'. Virginia Woolf, for example, has constructed an argument along these lines in her well-known *A Room of One's Own*.[20] It would be another matter, however, to elaborate in respect of gender the arguments that Marx's outlines in theorizing the relationship of ideology to the mode of production. So we are left with an insight, a suggestive or illuminating metaphor, but scarcely a body of concepts or a theoretical account of gender ideology.

The theory of alienation, and Marx's early writings in general, have had a tremendous impact on political liberation movements outside the class struggle. These early works are held by many to represent the true revolutionary spirit of Marxism. It is easy to see how theories of 'human liberation' can be identified with a political stance such as feminism, and equally easy to see how the early Marx is read as just such a theory. Whether or not one subscribes to the view that Marx's mature works, including the detailed analysis of capitalism, constitutes a rejection of this youthful and idealistic humanism, it is necessary to consider the implication of Marx's later work for feminism. If, as I have suggested, the early work is difficult to apply to the question of gender, then we may be even less confident about the later works. In particular, I want to discuss the conception of the family employed by Marx in his analysis of wage labour under capitalism.

III The Family and Wage Labour

In theory, for Marx, both capital and labour are abstract categories and must be assumed to be sexless. In practice, however, although capital retains this conceptual purity, labour is historically constituted as the labour of concrete men and women.

There can be little doubt that Marx tended to assume a 'typical' wage-labourer who was male. This is because he tended to assume a rather naturalistic approach to the family without giving adequate consideration to this. It is perhaps not surprising that in Marx's early works, including those written with Engels, we find a naturalistic conception of sexual relations and the family. The *Economic and Philosophical Manuscripts* and *The German Ideology* tend to discuss phenomena such as 'the communal possession of women' exclusively from the point of view of the possessing men. Marx sees 'man's relationship to woman' as an index of the general level of culture – but the entire discussion is couched rather as if women were a barometer of the state of male civilization.[21] Certainly there are flashes of perceptiveness in these early works, just as there are in the iconoclastic discussion of the family in *The Communist Manifesto*, but it may reasonably be suspected that the best of these are indebted to the contribution of Engels.

Marx himself, in his later work, continues to use an analysis which casts female wage labour as intrinsically problematic. In *Capital*, for instance, he refers frequently to the labour of women and children as little other than a threat to the male worker. They are always invoked in terms of the moral degradation of women workers or in terms of the negative impact they have on male resistance. In a typical passage Marx writes, 'By the excessive addition of women and children to the ranks of the workers, machinery at last breaks down the resistance which the male operatives in the manufacturing period continued to oppose to the despotism of capital'.[22]

Marx's persistent assumption that the balance of forces in the labour-capital struggle was upset by women glutting the labour market was maintained over a curiously long period of time. *Capital* (Volume 1) was published in 1867 and yet seems surprisingly unaffected by some key passages in Engels's much earlier work *The Condition of the Working Class in England* (1844). The employment of women in large numbers was scarcely a new phenomenon, yet Marx describes it with an air of shock and surprise that is not strictly appropriate to the situation he is discussing. The tone of Marx's account suggests that the mass employment of women was an innovative strategy of capitalists in the mid-nineteenth century. Yet the data existed for Marx to see clearly that women had been wage-labourers from the earliest moments of wage labour. For one thing, it was known that they tended to earn less, so it must have been known that they earned something.[23]

Underlying Marx's 'common-sense' misapprehensions about female wage labour is his assumption that the norm from which to begin was the situation where a male worker's wage covered the reproduction of his family. Marx, as we see in the crucial passage where he puts forward the nub of his argument on the family and wage labour, assumes as a baseline that there is a (pre-given) housewife engaged in domestic labour in the home.

In so far as machinery dispenses with muscular power, it becomes
a means of employing labourers of slight muscular strength, and
those whose bodily development is incomplete, but whose limbs are
all the more subtle. The labour of women and children was,
therefore, the first thing sought for by capitalists who used
machinery. That mighty substitute for labour and labourers was
forthwith changed into a means for increasing the number of wage-
labourers by enrolling, under the direct sway of capital, every
member of the workman's family, without distinction of age or sex.
Compulsory work for the capitalist usurped the place, not only of
the children's play, but also of free labour at home within moderate
limits for the support of the family.[24]

At this point Marx explains in a footnote how, since women's
domestic work has to be replaced by buying ready-made things,
this situation raises the overall cost of keeping the family. The
simple implication of this leads to difficulties, however, since
domestic labour is not entirely replaceable with bought goods.
As is now abundantly clear to most women who work for wages
and work in the home, housework does not disappear as soon as
wage-labour begins. This point is glossed over by Marx (as
indeed it was by Engels) who goes on to make a more
substantial argument using this supposedly typical situation –
before the 'fall' of women into wage labour – of a male
breadwinner supporting his family on a single wage. A male
breadwinner *must* be assumed for Marx's argument to hold:

The value of labour-power was determined, not only by the labour-
time necessary to maintain the individual adult labourer, but also
by that necessary to maintain his family. Machinery, by throwing
every member of that family on to the labour-market, spreads the
value of the man's labour-power over his whole family. It thus
depreciates his labour-power. To purchase the labour-power of a
family of four workers may, perhaps, cost more than it formerly
did to purchase the labour-power of the head of the family, but, in
return, four days' labour takes the place of one, and their price falls
in proportion to the excess of the surplus-labour of four over the
surplus-labour of one. In order that the family may live, four people
must now, not only labour, but expend surplus-labour for the
capitalist. Thus we see, that machinery, while augmenting the
human material that forms the principal object of capital's

exploiting power, at the same time raises the degree of exploitation.[25]

What is not clear here is the implication of Marx having bound together his assumptions on women's domestic contribution to these broad generalizations on the value of labour-power. Eldred and Roth suggest, from an inspection of this and similar passages from *Capital*, that Marx by implication vitiates the category 'value of labour-power' in assuming that the women and children's labour-power 'have no value in themselves'.[26] Few Marxists would accept this suggestion, though it does indicate that disputes over the value of labour-power, the analysis of domestic labour and determination of female wages are of more than incidental significance. The 'domestic labour debate', however ensnared it may have become in irresolvable technicalities, was important for these reasons.[27]

The political implications of these debates are clearly of the utmost importance. Marx's view has naturally supported the argument that the standard of living of the working class is raised by a so-called 'family wage' system in which a male wage-labourer earns sufficient to reproduce his family without women or children being obliged to seek wage work. Critics of such a system – if 'system' it can be said to be when the history of wage-labour in Britain shows such a situation to be a rarity enjoyed only by a 'labour aristocracy' – can marshall various rather different arguments. In the first place Marx was in error in his assumption that women's employment 'cheapened' the value of labour-power since his comparison was with the fictitious situation of the woman as exclusively a housewife; in the second place he failed to see that the contribution made by domestic labour cannot be traded off against wage labour but exists where the housewife is also a wage-labourer; in the third place, such a strategy has tended merely to exacerbate the badly paid and marginal position of women workers thereby worsening rather than ameliorating the threat they objectively pose to male workers.[28] This last argument amounts to nothing less than the claim that Marx's unreflectively sexist presuppositions in regard to women, work and the family have contributed to one of the major divisions within the working class and the organized labour movement.

The difficulty in assessing these problems is that so much hangs on errors of omission. Marx persists, to the end of his life and in his posthumous writings,[29] in the assumption that the individual of whom he speaks is male and that occasionally cognizance will need to be taken of his wife and family. This is scarcely an unspeakable crime; on the other hand it is not what we might expect from a mind that did not rest at appearances, commonsense and an unreflective absorption of personal experience on any other matter. The problem has some light thrown on it by considering – some might think rather belatedly – the question of the relationship between Marx's work and that of Engels and the attitudes they both held on this issue.

IV Marx and Engels

Charles Wolfson has commented on a tendency for the 'errors' of Marxism to be laid at the door of Engels rather than at that of the 'great man' himself.[30] On the question of women, however, there is little danger of this occurring and indeed many feminists find the work of Engels by far the most useful of the texts of the Marx-Engels canon.

It is not necessary here to review the contribution made by Engels's much-debated account of *The Origin of the Family, Private Property and the State*. There exist several excellent discussions of this work from a contemporary feminist point of view[31] and perhaps the most striking aspect of the text is the purchase it still has on debate in this field. Scarcely a Marxist-feminist text is produced that does not refer somewhere to Engels's argument, and if one had to identify one major contribution to feminism from Marxism it would have to be this text, flawed and disputed as it is.

In general the writing of Engels often reads as more sympathetic to what we now identify as feminism than does the writing of Marx. Engels appears to be more modern in his touch on these questions and one has less sense of a Victorian patriarch worthily espousing doctrines that he believes correct rather than believes in. Random examples are somewhat unfair, and can be misleading, but they illustrate the point. Engels can deride Dühring's solemn comment on the demand for prostitution: '... *nothing of the kind is possible for the women*'. He simply remarks that 'I would not care, for anything in the world, to have the thanks which might accrue to Herr Dühring from the women for this compliment' and wonders how Dühring has managed to get by for so long without having heard of men living on the 'petticoat-pension'.[32] These sentiments would not disgrace a 'male Marxist' in 1983, let alone in 1878, and they are characteristic of Engels's empathy with women. Although no doubt a thorough search would reveal many sexist remarks in Engels's correspondence and private papers, one suspects that there would be little to match those 'howlers' that can be found in Marx.[33]

Nor is it irrelevant that it is Engels rather than Marx who has done most to settle fairly the question of the relationship between Marxist and utopian socialism. On the whole Marx sought to clarify the differences but Engels, although arguing that utopian socialism arose too early to rest on a proper analysis of industrial capitalism, is unstinting in his efforts to express solidarity with the earlier utopians against their critics. Owenite socialism, as Barbara Taylor has argued,[34] was in many ways more concerned with themes taken up in twentieth-century feminism than was Marxism, especially in its insistence on integrity and non-exploitativeness in personal relationships. Whatever differences arise between Owenism and Marxism, Engels was at least utterly open in his admiration, going so far as to say that 'Every social movement, every real advance in England on behalf of the workers links itself to the name of Robert Owen'.[35]

A comparison between Marx and Engels on 'the woman question' tends to favour the latter both in terms of personal and political attitudes and because of Engels's willingness to problematize the familial and sexual arrangements that Marx tended to take for granted. There is, of course, much controversy on whether the personal and family lives of Marx and Engels are relevant to an assessment of the value of their work for feminism. This is an issue on which, by and large, feminism's insistence that 'the personal is political' leads to different conclusions from those normally found among commentators. An acute instance arises over the paternity of Frederick Demuth – Engels on his deathbed having been reported as saying that Demuth was Marx's son rather than, as had been assumed privately, Engels's. A typical response to this is given by Terrell Carver who simply denies that the evidence exists to substantiate the claim. Carver's reference to the 'story' is prefaced by the following:

> Had Engels and Marx lived impeccably proletarian lives they would probably have had no time for their intellectual labours, and in any case subsequent critics might have attacked them for belieing their own middle-class origins and becoming phonies. The life-style of any radical critic of contemporary social arrangements is bound to look incongruous.[36]

In other words, personal conduct is completely irrelevant. Yvonne Kapp, in her discussion of the issue, maintains that Demuth *was* Marx's son but insists that ' ... Marx's importance to the history of mankind is not lessened by one jot because he fathered Frederick Demuth'.[37] In this Yvonne Kapp is right and Carver surely wrong – the issue is *relevant* although the outcome does not diminish Marx's *importance*. It does throw light, however, on Marx's unwillingness to challenge adequately the 'natural' family unit. Supposing that Kapp is right, the Demuth issue does identify the secrecy and hypocrisy that formed part of Marx family life.

The feminist critique of such hypocrisy is not the normal moralistic one: it simply demands that revolutionaries practise what they preach. These questions are relevant to an understanding of Marx because they help us to identify how and why his critique of the family is so flawed and contradictory. It could not be proved that his practice in this was the result of his theory, or vice-versa, but the relationship between them is worthy of note.

I say this not to score a point or to reiterate the painful fact that, as far as feminism is concerned, Marx's feet really are made of clay. To speak of 'Marxist-feminism' is not to invoke a systematic and integrated approach to the oppression of women in capitalism or in any other mode of production. The meaning that I would attach to it is that one's feminism exists alongside the recognition that Marxism provides an unrivalled explanation and analysis of the capitalist society in which we live. The task, if it be possible, of synthesizing Marxism and feminism was not attempted by Marx and to suggest that it was is to belittle feminism. We would do well, however, to heed Marx's views on comparable questions and refrain from taking too sanguine a view of this integrative project. Marx's discussion of the limitations of 'political emancipation' should alert us to the fundamental issue of what *kind* of feminism we are struggling for and in what context. Marx himself, as I argued earlier, poses this question in a way that is distinctly awkward for feminism in that it forces us to decide whether we seek a set of egalitarian demands or whether we can rise to the challenge of conceptualizing a truly revolutionary politics of gender. It is, of course, an ironic tribute to Marx's stature that his work raises the central feminist question – political emancipation or revolutionary liberation – in the course of discussing *not* the family or the position of women but in polemicizing on the Jewish question.

Notes

My thanks to Mary McIntosh and William Outhwaite for their helpful comments on this essay.
1. Marx and Engels, *The German Ideology*, London, Lawrence & Wishart, 1974, p. 65.
2. Engels, *Anti-Dühring*, Moscow, Progress, 1977, p. 347.
3. 'Marx and Equality', in *Issues in Marxist Philosophy*, Vol. 4 (Social and Political Philosophy), eds, John Mepham & David-Hillel Ruben, Brighton, Harvester, 1981, p. 196.
4. Yvonne Kapp, *Eleanor Marx*, Vol. 2 (*The Crowded Years*), London, Lawrence & Wishart, 1976; Virago, 1979, p. 85.
5. See the discussion of 'Women and Equality' by Juliet Mitchell in *The*

Rights and Wrongs of Women, eds, Juliet Mitchell & Ann Oakley, Harmondsworth, Penguin, 1976, pp. 379-399.

6.   Sebastiano Timpanaro, *On Materialism*, London, NLB, 1975.
7.   Raymond Williams, 'Problems of Materialism', *New Left Review*, No. 109, 1978, pp. 8-9.
8.   Karl Marx, 'Toward the Critique of Hegel's Philosophy of Right', in *Karl Marx and Frederick Engels: Basic Writings*, ed. L.S. Feuer, London, Fontana, 1969, p. 303.
9.   See Olive Banks, *Faces of Feminism*, Oxford, Martin Robertson, 1981.
10.   Marx & Engels, *The German Ideology*, London, Lawrence & Wishart, 1974.
11.   Marx, 'On the Jewish Question', in *Karl Marx: Early Texts*, ed. David McLellan, Oxford, Blackwell, 1979, p. 100.
12.   *Max Weber and Karl Marx*, edited by Tom Bottomore and William Outhwaite, London, Allen & Unwin, 1982, p. 78.
13.   'On the Jewish Question', p. 93.
14.   Marx, 'Economic and Philosophical Manuscripts', in *Karl Marx: Early Texts*, ed. McLellan, p. 136.
15.   'Economic and Philosophical Manuscripts', p. 135.
16.   *The German Ideology* (editor's introduction), p. 16.
17.   'Economic and Philosophical Manuscripts', p. 141.
18.   'Economic and Philosophical Manuscripts', p. 147. In the German Marx tends to use *Mensch* as the generic term and where, as here, a distinction betweem women and men is made or their relation noted he uses the specific, *Mann*.
19.   *The German Ideology*, p. 64.
20.   Penguin, Harmondsworth, 1972.
21.   'Economic and Philosophical Manuscripts', p. 147.
22.   *Capital, Vol. 1*, London, Lawrence & Wishart, 1970, p. 402.
23.   The kind of data I have in mind is that collected in, for example, Alice Clark, *The Working Life of Women in the Seventeenth Century*, London, Cass, 1977, and Ivy Pinchbeck, *Women Workers and the Industrial Revolution 1750-1850*, London, Cass, 1930.
24.   *Capital, Vol. 1*, p. 394-5.
25.   *ibid.*, p. 395.
26.   Michael Eldred and Mike Roth, *Guide to Marx's Capital*, London, CSE, 1978, p. 70.
27.   The following articles contain summaries as well as discussion of this debate: Sue Himmelweit and Simon Mohun, 'Domestic Labour and Capital', *Cambridge Journal of Economics*, Vol. 1, 1977; Maxine Molyneux, 'Beyond the Domestic Labour Debate', *New Left Review*, No. 116, 1979; Eva Kaluzynska, 'Wiping the Floor with Theory', *Feminist Review*, No. 6, 1980. On the question of the value of labour power and female wages the most salient text is Veronica Beechey's

'Some Notes on Female Wage Labour in the Capitalist Mode of Production', *Capital and Class*, No. 3, 1977.

28. These arguments are elaborated in more detail in 'The "Family Wage": Some Problems for Socialists and Feminists' by myself and Mary McIntosh, *Capital and Class*, No. 11, 1981.

29. See, for example, his discussion of private proprietors in *Grundrisse*, Penguin, Harmondsworth, 1973, pp. 474-476.

30. *The Labour Theory of Culture*, London, Routledge, 1982, p. 1.

31. For a general consideration see Rosalind Delmar, 'Looking Again at Engels' *Origin of the Family, Private Property and the State*', in *The Rights and Wrongs of Women*, edited by J. Mitchell and A. Oakley, Penguin, Harmondsworth, 1976.

32. Engels, *Anti-Dühring*, p. 393.

33. Some examples may be found in a collection that contains some items for good reason rarely anthologized, *The Essential Marx: The Non-Economic Writings*, edited by Saul Padover, New York, Mentor, 1978.

34. *Eve and the New Jerusalem*, London, Virago, 1982.

35. *Anti-Dühring*, p. 319. (Part of the extracts from Anti-Dühring reprinted as Engels's pamphlet, *Socialism: Utopian and Scientific*.)

36. *Engels*, Oxford UP, 1981, p. 72.

37. *Eleanor Marx*, Vol. 1. (*Family Life*), London, Lawrence & Wishart, 1972; Virago, 1979, pp. 289-297.

Ben Fine

Marx on Economic Relations under Socialism*

Introduction

To the extent that Marxists understand the workings of the capitalist economy, they owe an enormous debt to *Capital*. It has been the source of a mode of analysis as well as of fundamental theoretical propositions. Whilst the validity and interpretation of these may remain controversial, the central place occupied by *Capital* as the starting point for analysing capitalism, even one hundred years after Marx's death, is unquestionable. Yet no volume plays a similar role for the socialist economy.

It is worth asking why this should be so. Apart from the short-lived Commune in Paris of 1871, Marx himself had very little opportunity to examine the operation of socialism in practice.[1] The construction of ideal societies in advance of their materialisation often produced his most hostile criticism. Nevertheless, as we shall see, Marx had more to say about the nature of the socialist economy than is perhaps generally realised. Even so, apart from relying upon the genius of Marx, this still leaves unexplained the continuing absence of a volume called *The Economics of Socialism,* especially when we have available the experience of socialist societies from 1917 onwards. There are many well-worn explanations for this absence which are interrelated and do have validity. Socialism is a transitional society bridging the historical transformation from capitalism to communism. Socialist societies in practice have arisen in less developed countries and this has constrained and made divergent their economic forms of development. Finally, socialist revolutions have been made in different historical circumstances on different economic bases, and in the continuing presence of a hostile advanced capitalism. Consequently, there can be no uniform laws of development of socialism as for capitalism, even though bourgeois revolutions have similarly been made in different circumstances. Simply put, we have *Capital* because *capital* is the uniformly dominating aspect of bourgeois society. There is no corresponding category for socialism upon which the economic laws of socialism can be constructed.

Accordingly, the position adopted, and hopefully demonstrated, in this essay is that the search for the economic laws of socialism is as futile as the search for the Holy Grail. This has not prevented searches from taking place in either case, nor the belief that the treasure has indeed been discovered from time to time. In the case of the economic laws, the discoveries have usually been of two types. Either they have been pitched at such a level of generality as to defy both disagreement *and* applicability. Alternatively they have clearly reflected temporary expendiencies or political positions in which historically specific *policies* are paraded as general *laws*. Stalin, for example, in his *Economic Problems of Socialism in the USSR* neatly combined both of these types of law. He takes the most basic economic law of socialism to be the fulfillment of people's needs whilst simultaneously emphasising how socialism gives priority to heavy industry rather than to consumption. More generally, and this has been as true in China as it has in the Soviet Union and Eastern Europe, the economic 'laws' of socialism have tended to favour the market or not according to the extent to which the market is favoured by contemporary policy. In this there has been considerable fluctuation. For Russia, it is marked by the movement from War Communism to NEP, from NEP to collectivisation and the system of five year planning, and more recently by the tentative introduction of economic reform which makes greater concessions to market mechanisms.

To deny the existence of the economic laws of socialism is not to abandon analysis of the socialist economic formation at an abstract level altogether. To do so would be to adopt what might be termed for convenience the Eurocommunist position: that socialism involves freedom, democracy, workers' control, absence of exploitation, etc. but beyond this nothing much can be said without reference to a particular country at a particular time. But surely, Marxism informs us that the configuration of these highly desirable characteristics can only exist in forms which place definite limitations upon the nature of the structure and development of the society? To recognise this, it is not necessary to swing to the opposite extreme, for convenience termed Stalinist, in which it is presumed that socialism must take the form of a command economy in deference to which other economic and social relations must occupy a subordinate place.

The position adopted in this essay is to break with the (parodied) Eurocommunist and Stalinist positions rather than to seek a compromise between them. We begin in the first section by attempting to identify certain uniform characteristics of socialism. On this basis, the remainder of the essay will be concerned with the nature of the economic forms that arise in the socialist formation. In the second section, we shall be concerned with distributional relations and consumption. We shall find that undue prominence has traditionally been given to this aspect because of an understandable preoccupation with the *Critique of the Gotha Programme* in which Marx most systematically lays out his views on socialism and produces the dictum of distribution according to work. It is also suggested that this dictum has tended to be too narrowly or superficially interpreted. In the second section, the distribution of means of production will be considered followed in the third section by a discussion of the relationship between socialism and land. In each case, certain problems for the socialist economy can be identified and solutions can be seen in terms of furthering the development of the forces and relations of production. Such solutions, however, necessarily lie in the future and the means of accommodating these problems in the socialist economy are bound to be historically specific, and, consequently, non-analysable at an abstract level. To be specific with an example that combines the subject matter of both the second and third sections, it would be sheer idealism to propose a general solution to the problem of how to mechanise agriculture in the socialist economy.

The fourth and last substantive section focuses upon a subject which has more often been the starting point for an analysis of economic relations under socialism. It concerns the role of commodity production which has also been treated in terms of the role of the law of value. Here it will be argued that the very notions of commodity and value under socialism have to be considered very carefully. Indeed, they have to be specified historically in relationship to the socialist society under examination. In the absence of such an historically and empirically rooted analysis, the result is (and has been) to treat the socialist economy as if it were a capitalist commodity producing society. The positive or negative aspects of commodity production are then emphasised as the use of the market mechanism is or is not to be recommended.

Throughout the prime concern has been to distil Marx's views on economic relations under socialism. In doing so much of significance can be collected from *Capital.* As an expositional device, socialist economic relations are contrasted with those of capitalism. Finally, in order to bring down to earth what is necessarily an abstract discussion, reference is made to the experience of socialist countries, although these references cannot pretend to do more than to illustrate the arguments presented here rather than to shed a bright light on these experiences.

I *The Socialist Formation*

It is possible to propose certain uniform characteristics of socialism. As already observed in the introduction, it involves a transition between capitalism and 'a higher phase of communist society'[2] Marx is not silent on the nature of this higher phase. Considerable emphasis is placed upon the abolition of the division of labour in all of its forms, between town and country, men and women, head and hand. It is most eloquently proposed in *The German Ideology* (Marx and Engels (1976)) even if somewhat in the style of a country gentleman:

> For as soon as the distribution of labour comes into being, each man has a particular, exclusive sphere of activity, which is forced upon him and from which he cannot escape. He is a hunter, a fisherman, a shepherd, or a critical critic, and must remain so if he does not want to lose his means of livelihood; while in a communist society, where nobody has one exclusive sphere of activity but each can become accomplished in any branch he wishes, society regulates the general production and thus makes it possible for me to do one thing today and another tomorrow, to hunt in the morning, fish in the afternoon, rear cattle in the evening, criticise after dinner, just as I have a mind, without ever becoming hunter, fisherman, shepherd, or critic (p. 47).

Communism, as Engels argued (1968a), is also characterised by the withering away of the state. This is itself associated with the disappearance of social classes so that 'the government of persons is replaced by the administration of things, and by the conduct of processes of production'. p. 430, see also Lenin (1970). These two features of communism are deserving of emphasis since they represent a critique of bourgeois society in which individuals are confined within a division of labour and subject to class rule through state power. Equally, even of more importance, is the necessary implication that socialist society, that earlier phase of communist society, will continue to contain both a division of labour and a class state. For the latter is necessary to guarantee that the continuing administration of people as producers is not supportive of continuing or renewed exploitation:

> Between capitalist and communist society lies the period of the revolutionary transformation of one into the other. Corresponding to this is also a political transition period in which the state can be nothing but *the revolutionary dictatorship of the proletariat* (Marx (1968), p. 331).

At the economic level, the precondition for the abolition of exploitation is the social ownership of the means of production, and this is usually taken to mean state ownership or nationalisation of the means of production. This is the basis on which a planned economy can be constructed. In contrast to communism, the plan of the socialist economy continues to reflect the administration of producers even if, in contrast to capitalism, it is administration *for* the producers. The nature of this administration is difficult to specify at a general level, precisely because it is conditioned, or more exactly limited, by the degree of development of the productive forces which itself is reflected in the necessity of a continuing division of labour. Even more complicating, as experience of socialism in the twentieth century has demonstrated, is the continuing presence of private ownership of means of production, especially but not exclusively in agriculture, as in Poland for example.

Brus (1975) has discussed the problem of state ownership at some length, drawing the distinction between public ownership (which may be exercised on behalf of an exploiting class as for nationalisation within a capitalist economy) and socialised ownership in which effective possession resides in the hands of the working class. Even within socialist economies, it is possible to identify different forms of state ownership so that this most basic requirement of the socialist economy is far from unambiguous. By the same token, it renders notions of planning in terms of material balances highly technicist since the forms of state ownership may range from the ministerially regulated factory to the cooperatively run enterprise. The socialist economy can only be understood by reference to these diverse forms of ownership and there can be no presumption that one form of ownership is superior, or 'more socialist' than another. Indeed, the content of the ownership depends very much upon the overall economic and social relations in which the producing units are located. It is these alone that can be analysed at an abstract level. Otherwise we are forced to treat the Chinese Commune as equivalent to a Russian factory! By examining the economic forms that develop under socialism we intend to reveal the way in which different aspects of economic relations are connected together both structurally and in the process of change. We begin with distributional relations in so far as they affect consumption.

II *Distributional Relations and Consumption under Socialism*

Marx's discussion of distribution under socialism in the *Critique of the Gotha Programme* is well known but it has often been interpreted superficially as merely implying that distribution to individuals should be in proportion to labour contributed. This is certainly an implication, subject to certain reservations, but the analysis goes very much deeper. Marx is first, however, concerned to deflect the initial focus from distribution and to place it upon the relations and forces of *production*. Recall that it is distribution that has been brought to a place of prominence by the Gotha Programme itself, not by Marx.

> Quite apart from the analysis so far given, it was in general a mistake to make a fuss about so-called *distribution* and put the principal stress on it ... If the material conditions of production are the co-operative property of the workers themselves, then there likewise results a distribution of the means of consumption different from the present (capitalist) one. Vulgar socialism ... has taken over from the bourgeois economists the consideration and treatment of distribution as independent of the mode of production and hence the presentation of socialism as turning principally on distribution. p. 325.

Presently we shall examine how production relations under socialism lead to different distributional relations than under capitalism, quite apart from the difference in distribution and hence consumption itself. First, we observe that Marx was not apparently totally committed to this principle of distribution as has been commonly presumed. In *Capital* I, he argues as follows:

> Let us now picture to ourselves, by way of change, a community of free individuals, carrying on their work with the means of production in common ... The total product of our community is a social product. One portion serves as fresh means of production and remains social. But another portion is consumed by the members as means of subsistence. A distribution of this portion amongst them is consequently necessary. *The mode of this distribution will vary with the productive organisation of the*

*community, and the degree of historical development attained by
the producers. We will assume*, but merely for the sake of a parallel
with the production of commodities, *that the share of each
individual producer* in the means of subsistence is determined by
his labour-time (p. 82/3 [emphasis added]).

So, distribution according to labour-time is an *assumption*
contingent upon the level of development of the forces and
relations of production. It is in addition a bourgeois right of
equality, since it is within capitalism that workers alone tend to
be remunerated according to labour performed subject to
differences in skills, etc. Despite its being a *bourgeois principle*
of distribution, it is one that has never applied to the bourgeois
class. Under capitalism, distributional relations govern the
consumption not only of workers but also of capitalists and
other appropriators of surplus value. The principle only applies
within the proletariat, it does not apply to the population at
large, as for the socialist society, since exploiters consume but
do not work.

Paradoxically then the bourgeois principle of distribution
according to labour which is appropriate to socialism is
inapplicable to capitalism. This reflects deeper differences in the
relations of distribution which are in turn determined by
differences in the relations of production. Under capitalism,
distributional relations are based upon the monopoly ownership
of the means of production by the bourgeoisie and the
corresponding existence of labour-power as a commodity. The
value of labour-power is an *advance* of capital that is a
precondition of production. Surplus value is the *result* of
compulsion on the labourer to work over and beyond the
socially necessary labour-time required to produce the wage.
Such is the very basis of Marx's theory of capitalist exploitation.
It follows that the distribution between profits and wages is
interrupted and determined by the process of production (of
surplus value). The coercian to work harder, longer or more
skillfully is to the advantage of capital. Wages are the
precondition and profits the *result* of production whatever the
actual timing of the wage payment itself. Consequently,

capitalist distributional relations are not determined by a distribution of surplus product between the two classes in which wages gain at the expense of profits or vice versa.[3]

For socialism, the production and consequently the distributional *relations* are quite different. With the social ownership of the means of production, the surplus produced is not appropriated by one class at the expense of another, but is divided for consumption and other purposes according to a definite plan. It follows that labour power is not a commodity, as for the capitalist mode of production, even if it is remunerated in the form of wages.[4] Whatever the level of remuneration, it is the *result* of production and not its precondition. The clearest demonstration of this is the fact that capitalists will destroy a surplus product in the face of a glut, in the attempt to maintain profitability, a situation that is incompatible with socialism for which no purpose is served by the hoarding of products.

Such is the difference in distributional structure between the capitalist and socialist economies. In addition, there is the process of development of distributional relations to consider. In the *Critique of the Gotha Programme*, Marx is clear that *before* there is distribution for consumption, deductions must be made to replace and expand the use of means of production, to insure against calamities, etc., to provide for the cost of administration, to develop schools, health services, etc., and to provide funds for those unable to work. Here again, a contrast can be drawn with capitalism, for which the dictates of private accumulation alone are prior to the claims of 'social' expenses with the most notable exception being the costs of the military and law and order which form the absolute precondition for bourgeois society to be reproduced. Social expenses do increase under capitalism as is evidence by the rise of the welfare state but, as is sharply revealed in times of economic crisis and recession, these expenditures have a low, residual priority. They are always structurally constrained to conform to capitalism's needs for an exploitable workforce, this determining levels and types of education, for example, as well as, of course, unemployment benefit.

In contrast, under socialism in the light of the prior demands upon the product, it is possible to see how the bourgeois right of distribution according to work is *eroded* even as it is more fully *applied*. First, more and more goods are provided for collective consumption or at zero or subsidised prices and these can range from housing, health, transport and education through to the more immediate means of subsistence. It is here that socialist countries have exhibited a record of which they can be proud relative to the capitalist world. Consequently, the significance of differences in wages is reduced in proportion to the level of collective provision. Significantly, in all socialist countries, wage bonuses have taken the form of provision for collective consumption as for housing, for example. The closest substitute in capitalism is 'fringe benefits'. Secondly, however, the result of such collective provision under socialism will itself reduce the basis for wage differentials as a more equitable and rounded system of education is developed. In this context, Marx laid particular emphasis upon 'the germ of the education of the future, an education that will, in the case of every child over a given age, combine productive labour with instruction and gymnastics, not only as one of the methods of adding to the efficiency of production, but as the only method of producing fully developed human beings' (*Capital I* p. 454, see also pp. 438 and 460). The result will also be to allow progress to be made towards releasing individuals from the confinement to a particular role in the division of labour. This includes a breaking down of the sexual division of labour. Under capitalism, this has a number of separate but related components because of the subordination of women to men both within paid (wage) work and unpaid (domestic) work. Under socialism, the division between paid and unpaid work will persist with the survival of the principle of distribution according to work but it is a division that need no longer run along the lines of gender. To break down the sexual division of labour, it will be necessary to recognise work relations both for paid and unpaid labour and also for the connection between the two. As the women's movement has recognised within the confines of capitalism, this will require a reduction in the length of the (paid) working day, a conclusion that is also reached by Marx as necessary for the development of labour's potential in general (see *Capital III*, p. 819/20).

In these terms, the application of the principle of distribution according to work can under socialism be seen to contain the means of its own dissolution when it is connected to the development of the forces and relations of production. But it cannot be pretended that the application of the principle is itself unproblematical as has been recognised in the discussions over the priority of 'material' as opposed to 'moral' incentives. Greater work motivated by means of greater reward is a source of expanding the production possibilities open to the rest of society. It is also a potential source of differentiation and hierarchy. There is no solution to the conflict in the abstract except to recognise that it is extreme to rely exclusively on either material or moral incentives. Socialism is a stage of development precisely during which the worker labours for society *and* for self. This has to be recognised.

In this context, let us examine the role of piece-rates. The labour movement has a tradition of suspicion of and hostility to piece-rates, and with good reason. Marx's analysis of piece-rates under capitalism makes it quite clear why this should be so. For individuals, piece-rates lead to higher wages for faster, better quality work. The same is not true for the workers as a whole. The piece-rate can be adjusted and set at a level which leaves the average wage unchanged. The net result is to redistribute wages amongst the workers in accordance with work done at the same time as the average intensity and duration of work is increased. Recalling our earlier discussion, this can be seen to be a direct result of the capitalist relations of distribution. The wage is the precondition of production, profits are its result according to the amount of surplus labour that can be coerced. Wages in the form of piece-rates create the illusion, real in a narrow sense for an individual worker, that the level of wages is the result of production.

Under socialism, the different forms of distributional relations dictate that this need not be so. Wages can be increased in line with work and hence with output. Under capitalism, the piece-rate system has the function of coercing surplus labour on the basis of a given value of labour-power. For socialism, the system is motivated by the principle of distribution according to work both within and between factories. Marx appears to recognise that on this basis the piece-rate system is not obnoxious as for capitalism. First, at the level of management, even under capitalism, 'the cooperative factories of the labourers ... naturally reproduce, and must reproduce, everywhere in their actual organisation all the shortcomings of the prevailing system. But the antithesis between capital and labour is overcome *within them* ...' (*Capital* III, p. 440 [emphasis added]). Moreover, for capitalist management, 'that nothing is lost or wasted and the means of production are consumed only in the manner required by production itself, depends partly on the skill and intelligence of the labourers and partly on the disipline enforced by the capitalist for combined labour. This discipline will become superfluous under a social system in which the labourers work for their own account, as it has already become practically superfluous in piece-work' (*Capital* III, p. 83). Under capitalism piece-work is a surrogate for a discipline that is unnecessary under socialism. Accordingly, although Marx does not say this, piece-work can become the means of distribution according to work without acting as a disciplinary factor in the sense of coercing surplus labour at the expense of the labourer. Nevertheless, there is no guarantee in the abstract that surplus labour, induced by piece-rates or otherwise, benefits society as a whole. Quite clearly, the benefits could accrue within a hierarchy of management and, even if not, there are limits beyond which the labour of the worker should not be induced. Here a role for trade unions under socialism is defined which distinguishes it from capitalism. For the latter, there is a general principle of opposition to the coercion of surplus labour, whereas for socialism, trade unions have the role of guaranteeing that surplus labour is not only limited but also that it accrues to society rather than to individual managers, say, who supervise that labour. It is in this light, that the Stakhanovite movement must be seen. It is for the trade unions to place limits on surplus labour and upon the abuse of economic inducements as well as of political and ideological pressures.

To raise the question of management is to recognise another problem of applying the principle of distribution according to work since managers and many other workers contribute labour that is difficult to quantify by amount, intensity and quality. Clearly this problem is reduced to the extent that both production and consumption are collectivised: piece-rates apply over a body of workers rather than over individuals so that wage differentials cover a smaller proportion of total consumption. The same applies to the extent that the division of labour between mental and manual workers is broken down. These qualifications do not, however, solve the problem however much they may moderate it. In practice, the issue must be the subject of conflict, one in which the scarcity of skills involved has to be set against the principle of comparable pay for all classes of workers. In general, the skills involved are the product of society's contribution to their formation but they remain in the possession of the worker whilst distribution is according to labour. This is a source of privilege under socialism as indeed it is under capitalism.

There is nonetheless one major difference between the two. Distribution to labour under socialism is identical to consumption: 'because under the altered circumstances no one can give anything except his labour, and because, on the other hand, nothing can pass to the ownership of individuals except individual means of consumption' (Marx [1968], p. 323/4). By contrast, under capitalism, distribution involves the right to purchase means of production thereby combining or consolidating the work of management with the task of exploitation. By the same token, the skills of management or whatever tend to become the exclusive possession of those who are already economically privileged by more or less direct possession of the means of production. Accordingly, those who criticise the socialist countries for producing a class or an elite of managers can only do so on the basis of reproduced privilege in the hierarchy of management and differential access to education etc. This is certainly a *logical* possibility, and one that can yield simultaneously effective possession of the means of production. It is a *reality* that can only be guarded against by an independent trade union movement. Nevertheless, it is one that is limited both in possibility and in extent by the relations governing the distribution of the means of production themselves to which we now turn.

III *Distribution of Means of Production*

From the closing sentences of the previous section, it is apparent that distributional relations do not simply involve access to the means of consumption but also involve, indeed are based upon as Marx argued in Chapter LI of *Capital* III, distribution of means of production. Here, as for distribution for consumption, there are differences in the relations of allocation at the qualitative level as between the capitalist and socialist economies. For capitalism, the accumulation of capital is determined by the pursuit of profitability in which the production of relative surplus value leads to a rising organic composition of capital and a relative displacement of living labour from the production process by the substitution of machinery for living labour. Both within and between sectors of the economy these processes are coordinated by the anarchy of the market and the result is the generation of crises of overproduction from time to time.

For socialism, there is first a planned division between distribution for consumption and distribution for other purposes. The allocation of means of production can itself be broken down into various sectors. In this, most emphasis has usually been placed on the balance between material allocations to the various sectors. There is, however, the question of priority as between sectors and not only in terms of which sectors are to grow faster and/or be more advanced. Quite clearly such decisions also reflect and create other balances and imbalances, between town and country, etc. It is these considerations which tend to be absent in the process of capitalist accumulation, except in so far as the welfare state provides a retrospective corrective. Such are the consequences of capitalism's uneven development.

It is easier, however, to establish balance between sectors in theory than it is in practice. In Volume II of *Capital*, Marx examines the conditions for balance between sectors for simple reproduction and reveals the famous formula $C_{II} = V_I + S_I$. There is no guarantee that capitalism produces this balance through market related coordination of production at adequate levels of employment of labour and capital. Equally it must be recognised that planning under socialism does not guarantee a balance for simple (and extended reproduction) at the appropriate level. What it does do is to set targets for achievements which can be disaggregated further sector by sector and passed onto individual enterprises. But there is a considerable distance between the formulation of a plan and its implementation. Consequently, the formulation and guidance of a plan do distinguish socialism from capitalism, with the latter obtaining balance between sectors only through the anarchy of the market.

A more fundamental difference, however, and one that tends to be overlooked is how *imbalance* is dealt with as between the two economic systems. For capitalism, any imbalance has a tendency to be amplified through market repercussions as the effects say of overproduction in one sector are transmitted to other sectors with which it is related. In addition, the impact of imbalance tends to fall randomly across the economy and society through the market mechanism since it is simply the ability to pay which determines where shortages for example will or will not fall. For socialism there is the potential at least to deal with such imbalances at an appropriate level of central control and to give priority to particular sectors. What that appropriate level of control is does itself constitute a problem as is witnessed by the experience of socialist countries. Shortages, for example, can lead an enterprise to hoard the scarce materials in order to protect itself against plan underfulfillment thereby intensifying the shortage.

There is no economic solution to problems such as these although they have often been sought for this and other problems in the form of an appropriate incentive structure to enterprises. This can lead enterprises to seek easy targets so that the incentives become self-defeating. Rather the only guarantee or rather pressure against distortion due to imbalance is the appropriate *political* organisation of relations within and between enterprises. To the extent that workers and other interested parties are and can be involved in both plan formulation and implementation, the recognition and response to imbalance can be improved and distortions limited. These general remarks do not solve or eliminate the problem but only show how it is to be accommodated precisely because workers and others (such as consumers) are interested parties. Under socialism, however, it is the political representation of these parties which distinguishes it from capitalism for which the only represented parties in case of imbalance are those with the money to pay.

The question of balance between sectors is worth pursuing in the context of the division of labour because of the central place that this occupies in Marx's discussion of the transition from socialism to communism. The relationship between the two has often been neglected. For capitalism, Marx identifies two tendencies in the development of the division of labour in conformity to the two forms of the division of labour within society. The social division of labour is synonymous with the boundaries of exchange relations, the frontiers across which products move as commodities. On the other hand, within the factory there is a developed division of labour along the production process, as in assembly work for example. As capitalism develops, what were formerly parts of a production process may be divided up into separate trades and become part of the social division of labour. Equally, what were formerly separate trades may be combined into a single production process by excluding the direct intervention of market relations. Here we have what is termed vertical disintegration and integration, respectively. Marx identified both as systematic results of capitalist development but considered that the two tendencies interacted anarchically to produce a division of labour in society as a whole that was subject to the vagaries of competition. Whichever tendency, if any, dominates, the result is nevertheless to confine individual workers to particular tasks.[5]

For socialism, there is no such necessity for specialisation to develop in this way. The issue of what constitutes a sector has itself to be determined before an allocation can be made by a plan between sectors. Moreover, for socialism the planning of material balances is itself to be identified with the planned but indirect allocation of labour. The labourer under socialism does not give work freely and cannot do so until the productive forces have developed to the level where planning merely involves providing a division of labour in which the worker can make a choice to be a shepherd or whatever. Planning material allocations before this full phase of communism is the determination of what jobs are available to be done by individuals. The more collectively these jobs can be done the greater is the scope for breaking down confinement within a division of labour, although this is mediated by the continuing distribution of consumption according to work. Because labour-power remains in the possession of the individual under socialism, confinement to a division of labour persists in conformity with the principle of distribution according to labour. It is a reflection of the level of development of the forces and relations of production. In the full phase of communism, the worker is freed, paradoxically, from the confinement to a division of labour by the same process that places that individual labour completely in the possession of society as a whole and distributes consumption according to need: 'only then can the narrow horizon of bourgeois right be crossed in its entirety and society inscribe on its banners: From each according to his ability, to each according to his need' (Marx [1968], p. 325).

The allocation of labour through the allocation of means of production is entirely different under capitalism, most clearly because there is no commitment nor possibility of full employment, whatever the claims of a now discredited Keynesian ideology. For Marx, capital accumulation produces a law of population unique to this mode of production, the systematic creation of a surplus population in the form of a reserve army of labour. Nevertheless, within the factory itself, where exchange relations do not intervene directly, there is the most careful organisation of production:

The same bourgeois consciousness which celebrates the division of labour in the workshop ... as an organisation of labour that increases its productive power, denounces with equal vigour every conscious attempt to control and regulate the process of production socially, as an inroad upon such sacred things as the rights of property, freedom and the self-determining 'genius' of the individual capitalist. It is very characteristic that the enthusiastic apologists of the factory system have nothing more damning to urge against a general organization of labour in society than that it would turn the whole of society into a factory (*Capital* I, p. 477).

More generally, Marx frequently employed the 'model' of the capitalist factory as the model for planning in a socialist society and indeed he saw it ultimately as the material basis of socialism, particularly in the context of large-scale joint stock companies where control is divorced from ownership and profitability is reduced to the rate of interest:

This result of the ultimate development of capitalist production is a necessary transitional phase towards the reconversion of capital into the property of producers, although no longer as the private property of the individual producers, but rather as the property of associated producers, as outright social property ... This is the abolition of the capitalist mode of production within the capitalist mode of production itself, and hence a self-dissolving contradiction, which *prima facie* represents a mere phase of transition to a new form of production (*Capital* III, p. 437-8).

The factory system is based upon the use of machinery or fixed capital. This is subject to renewal over periods much longer than the production period itself. Consequently, under capitalism the various turnover times and replacements of the fixed capitals in relationship to the sectors that produce their machinery must be coordinated through the market mechanism. Capitalists have to hold reserves in order to allow for the renewal of their fixed capital, and the operations of the machinery producing sectors are highly contingent upon the time profile of renewal. Indeed, there tends to be cyclical movements in the economy in line with the renewal of fixed capital which in turn tends to be synchronised across capital as a whole. For the socialist economy, Marx argues that there is a continued need for a reserve precisely because the different portions of fixed capital depreciate at different rates and need to be replaced at different times. Whilst this function is undertaken through the market for capitalism, it is open to conscious planned coordination under socialism (see *Capital* II, p. 473).

Marx argues that overproduction does indeed occur under socialism but that it has the function of providing for the smooth periodic renewal and replacement of fixed capital. In contrast, for capitalism, the same process of renewal tends to lead to and to be associated with overproduction of crisis proportions. This role of overproduction under socialism can be related to the earlier discussion of the problem of imbalance since it is a special case of the problem, viz with respect to fixed capital. More generally, the case can be made for overproduction in the socialist economy as a whole to mitigate divergencies between plans and their outcomes. This runs against the experience of the socialist economies where high priority has been given to what has been termed taut planning and limited measures are taken to guard against contingencies. The result has often been that taut planning is associated with slack implementation with shortages arising and the effects of this are transmitted through the economy. This has been particularly true of large scale capital investment which tends to be pushed beyond its possible limit. In Poland (and in China) in the 1970s, this has often led to foreign exchange problems, because the investment is associated with foreign technology.

Marx also argues that machinery will be used more extensively under socialism than under capitalism (see *Capital* I, p. 370/1 and *Capital* III, p. 261/2).[6] In addition, for capitalism the organisation of finance for investment is based on the speculative determination of the rate of interest which itself reflects the conflict between the fractions of industrial and banking capital. These considerations have led some to deny absolutely the role of a rate of interest in a socialist society since investment should be materially allocated and the vagaries of market allocation be eliminated. This is a view that is as single-minded as the opposite extreme, the one associated with the theory of market socialism, that sees socialism as providing the conditions under which the bourgeois fiction of a perfectly working market for finance (and all goods) can be realised. In contrast, we emphasise that it is not a question of *whether* the rate of interest should be a mechanism of planning in a socialist economy or not but at what level it should operate and in what circumstances. Certainly, the rate of interest need no longer reflect the antagonism between industry and finance and thereby be an irrational basis on which to allocate investment. As such, the rate of interest can reflect a single factor alone, the scarcity of resources available for accumulation. To accommodate the many objectives of socialist planning the rate of interest can only play the single and subordinate role of reflecting this. For major commitments, it can play no role at all since these will be determined independently of financial flows, although it can be used for accounting purposes to measure the time profile of surplus generated. But it cannot be presumed that a Central Planning Board can mobilise and allocate scarce (financial) resources at all levels of the economy and in all circumstances. Accordingly, there is a place for the use of the rate of interest under socialism but it is one which is limited and contingent upon economic *and* political circumstances (since interest is a mechanism of consolidating and encouraging class differentiation).

These remarks are of relevance to the experience of the socialist countries as they face the transition from what has been termed 'extensive' to 'intensive' economic expansion.[8] Historically, it would appear that initially the problems of organising a planned economy dictate that there be extensive coordination through material planning and little scope for decentralised initiative within the plan and consequently a minimal role for credit and interest payments. More recently, particularly in Hungary, economic reforms have recognised the role that can be played in decentralising investment decisions by the introduction of a market for capital (i.e. investment finance).[9] Much discussion of these reforms has emphasised their significance in principle but their limited application in practice.[10] This is thought to be due to a heritage of over-centralisation[11] and bureaucratisation[12] that structurally preempts and retrenches upon moves to decentralise and liberalise the economy. As such, the experience of opposition to economic reform is often seen as a defence of incumbent political interests against the pressing needs of economic development (which itself may be associated with the political interests of a managerial strata whose own position is enhanced by such reforms). These arguments concerning such political factors cannot be discounted but our analysis has suggested that the phenomena of centralisation/decentralisation and reform/planning are complex at the economic level alone in so far as socialist development promotes each couplet together. Put another way, the process of economic decentralisation has the potential to improve central coordination just as economic reform need not be at the expense of the planning mechanism. In a later section, we will take up these issues again in the more general context of commodity production under socialism where the discussion will not be restricted simply to the capital market.

IV *Socialism and Land*

No discussion of the distribution of the means of production is satisfactory if it excludes consideration of land. It is a source of both the most immediate means of consumption as well as of raw materials for industry. The socialist countries have experienced considerable economic and political difficulties with agriculture, problems that could hardly have been anticipated by texts such as the *Critique of the Gotha Programme*. This is not the place to rehearse an analysis of Marx's theory of (agricultural and mining) rent.[13] His main conclusion is that under capitalism rent is an economic form in which surplus value is appropriated by landlords. There are two types of rent, differential and absolute. Differential rent reflects differences in fertility and location and in the uneven distribution of intensive cultivation across the land. Absolute rent represents the price paid for the movement of capital onto new land. But rent is not simply nor predominantly a distributional category. Since it reflects the conditions of access of capital to the land it influences the accumulation of capital on the land and potentially impedes the development of intensive methods of production. As an attack on private property[14] there is a marked:

> reluctance by capitalists to regulate raw material production ... The moral of history, also to be deduced from other observations concerning agriculture, is that the capitalist system works against a rational agriculture, or that a rational agriculture is incompatible with the capitalist system (although the latter promotes technical improvements in agriculture), and needs either the land of the small farmer living by his own labour or the control of associated producers (*Capital* III, p. 120).

Despite admitting that the small farmer may be the basis for a 'rational' agriculture, Marx is clear elsewhere that this is incompatible with socialism in so far as the farmer enjoys private property in the land:

> From the standpoint of a higher economic form of society, private ownership of the globe by single individuals will appear quite as absurd as private ownership of one man by another. Even a whole society, a nation, or even all simultaneously existing societies taken together, are not the owners of the globe. They are only its possessors; its usufructuaries, and like *boni patres familias*, they must hand it down to succeeding generations in an improved condition (*Capital* III, p. 776).

State ownership of land is compatible with capitalism but land cannot become *common* property since capital must exclude labour from independent access to the means of production and hence consumption (*Theories of Surplus Value* II, p. 44). State ownership of land is a means by which the state can in part appropriate rents and thereby reduce taxes on the capitalists as a whole (*Theories of Surplus Value* III, p. 472). This is the means by which absolute rent can be abolished within capitalism (ibid., II, p. 103/4). But differential rent remains as long as there is a market price as a result of capitalist production. Under socialism, however, these differentials can be used collectively to iron themselves out by more intensive cultivation of the worse lands (ibid., p. 105/6). Nevertheless, we can observe that even with state-ownership of land and associated taxation policy of better lands, there are limitations on the rational development of agriculture in so far as there is any persistence of private *possession* of land. If farmers have only a life-time or more limited right of cultivation of the land, then they will not act fully as 'godparents' to succeeding generations. Moreover, taxation of differential output will further serve to limit improvement in more immediate conditions of productivity. For landed property, the ultimate goal of communism requires social ownership and possession of the land, but the path of transition on the basis of distribution according to work is further complicated by the existence and generation of fertility differences. It is only with social possession of the land in which the farm becomes a factory in parallel with those of the city that the division between town and country can be broken down.[15]

It is precisely the absence of such conditions in existing socialist countries and the problems of creating these conditions that helps to explain both the problems of agriculture and the diverse forms in which it has been organised from the collectivisation in Russia from the late 1920s to the communes of China and yet again private agriculture in Poland. In each case the problem exists of distributing according to work *within* agriculture and by equity with industry even as there remains systematic differences in the conditions of production governed by the fertility and location of land. The means of ironing out and reducing the significance of these differences is by intensive cultivation through mechanisation of farming. But to the extent that land remains in private possession this leads either to difficulties in gaining control of surplus for social consumption or investment through the state or to difficulties in inducing farmers to introduce mechanisation unless they receive the major part of the surplus generated by it.[16] On the other hand, effective collective possession of the land requires that intensive cultivation be already well-developed since, otherwise, the production process does depend significantly upon the effort and hence rewards of the individual unit of production.

V *Commodity Production Under Socialism*

Much of the previous sections are concerned, although this has not yet been made explicit, with particular instances of a more general problem: the role of commodity production under socialism. Whether in the context of distribution for consumption, distribution of means of production, economic relations on the land, or more generally, the nature and significance of commodity relations under socialism has been an important theoretical and practical issue. It is, for example, intimately related to the problems of economic reform in the socialist countries.[17] In our view, much of the debate over commodity production under socialism has been misguided. It has often been concerned with the question of whether commodity production does or does not exist under socialism or whether it should or should not exist. This approach tends to avoid the question of the differing nature of commodity production itself under different forms of economic and social organisation. As it were, it tends to assume that commodity production and commodities are the same irrespective of the conditions under which they occur be it feudalism, capitalism or even socialism. As the view adopted here is quite different, it is worth digressing initially to consider the nature of commodities and their production.

Marx began *Capital* with an analysis of commodity production in general. A commodity seems simple enough in so far as it is characterised as a use value and as an exchange value. Matters are, however, much more complicated. Whilst use value and exchange value are properties of a commodity they neither define the commodity nor its nature. Marx gives at least two examples of objects which have both use value and exchange value without being commodities. One is bribery which has both a definite use and a negotiable price.[18] The other is land for which the price merely represents the discounted value of surplus value appropriated in the form of rent and whose use is related to its properties of fertility etc.[19] Neither bribery nor land constitutes a commodity and this follows from the fact that neither is the product of labour.[20] In addition, interest bearing capital, or finance provided to capitalists by banks for the purposes of accumulation, is a very special commodity. Its use value is that it enables industrialists to employ labour to produce surplus value. Its exchange value is the rate of interest which has no direct relationship to the labour time required to produce the 'commodity' concerned, that is money to be used as capital whether it be in a paper or commodity (gold) form.[21]

The examples above suffice to demonstrate that an understanding of the commodity based on its properties of use value and exchange value is inadequate. Land and bribery have both without being commodities. Interest bearing capital is a commodity which is only comprehensible in terms of its relationship to industrial capital. Leaving aside these exceptions, commodity production in general must be analysed as *value* production. This is not simply a quantitative relationship involving socially necessary labour time, it is a social relationship in which different types of labour are brought into equivalence with each other through the market mechanism. Such is the weight of Marx's analysis in the opening chapter of *Capital*.[22]

This can and must be taken further. In so far as commodity production is not simply use value and exchange value production but production based on definite social relations between producers, so commodity production itself differs according to those production relations under which it is organised. For the capitalist mode of production CMP, commodities are produced in the context of capitalist relations of exploitation which involve the creation of both value and surplus value. Commodity production under the CMP can only be understood adequately on this basis. By the same token, commodity production under other modes of production such as feudalism, for example, must be understood differently. Because feudal differs from capitalist production,[23] it follows that commodities are different under feudalism than under capitalism even if both share the use value and exchange value characteristics.

This does not render the discussion of commodity production

in general a fruitless one,[24] but it does impose limitations upon it. The point being made here may be clarified by appeal to an analogy. Marxism has long recognised that there are general characteristics of the state, the means of exercising ruling class power or the monopoly of violence, for example. Yet few would identify the state associated with one mode of production with that associated with another. Unfortunately, this is precisely the confusion which surrounds much analysis of commodity production. In addition, there is a tendency within Marxism to identify commodity production with capitalist production. This is hardly surprising since it is under the CMP that commodity production is both most generalised and most developed. Here there is a contrast with the state, for example, for which overt oppression may be less pervasive for capitalism than for pre-capitalist societies. We do not for this reason model views of non-capitalist state power upon the capitalist state and by analogy we should not base our understanding of commodity production in general upon capitalist commodity production in particular.

An immediate corollary of this discussion is that it is not only commodity production that has to be understood in the context of the specific social relations in which it occurs. For Marx, whilst use value and exchange value are the most obvious properties enjoyed by a commodity, they are so only because the commodity also has the property of being a value. It follows that value production differs according to the mode of production under which it is organised, again because the nature of the production *and* of the value is different. Even within the CMP, value must be understood differently depending upon the stage of development attained by the mode of production. Under laissez-faire capitalism, Marx argues that commodities tend to exchange at their values and that these are definite limitations upon the formation of socially necessary labour time because of the restrictions in the mobility of capital, labour and commodities. For monopoly capital, a developed credit system and mobility of labour tend to guarantee the reduction of individual labour times of production to a common standard.[25] The nature of the value produced in these two cases is different since the relations and forces of production are different even though both involve capitalist production.[26]

The implication of the varying nature of value according to the relations under which it is produced is that the law of value must either be conceived at a very general level or be analysed on the basis of specific forces and relations of production. At the general level, the law of value can be seen in terms of the allocation of labour to different sectors of the economy. At a more specific level, the danger must be avoided of presuming that the law of value in its most developed form necessarily operates as if the law were identically applicable say to feudalism, or to monopoly capitalism. *Capital* is predominantly concerned with how the law of value operates under various stages of development of capitalism. Consequently, the results of this analysis cannot be imposed to represent the workings of the law in other forms of organisation of society.

Let us now turn directly to the issue of commodity production under socialism. The preceding lengthy digression gives rise to a few elementary propositions, if little else. Experience teaches us that commodity production does persist in the socialist economy. There are no ready-made or general laws with which to understand this commodity production since the forces and relations of production involved will exhibit great variety and these are the basis on which the nature of that commodity production is to be understood. What must be avoided is the substitution for this understanding of an analysis appropriated from the examination of other modes of production, the most likely being the CMP.[27] This is best illustrated by reference to two polar extremes which have recurred in the debates over commodity production under socialism, specifically in the discussion of economic reforms in the Soviet Union in the 1960s and subsequently in Eastern Europe and more recently in China.[28] The first position emphasises that commodity relations belong to the CMP and that this suggests a policy of eliminating commodity production in order to eliminate continuing capitalist influences. The strategy implied is one of gradual or even violent attacks on commodity relations. No doubt this strategy would involve political considerations, but theoretically it is based upon the erroneous notion that all commodity production is capitalist. It is a strategy that is particularly disadvantageous for a socialism based upon an underdeveloped level of productive forces. Here, particularly in agriculture, for example, commodity relations whether capitalist or otherwise, are liable to be extremely underdeveloped. The implication of discouraging commodity relations is liable to be the isolation of the producers concerned under the name of attacking capitalism. This is the consequence of imposing the analysis of *Capital* upon the socialist economy, with particular emphasis being placed upon the deficiencies of capitalist commodity production, as for the anarchy of the market, for example.

The other extreme position is to argue that commodity production under socialism is not capitalist because of the underlying socialist relations of production, particularly as reflected in the state ownership of means of production, and because of the absence of exploitation. This is essentially correct, although there is nothing in state ownership as such which guarantees either an absence of capital or of exploitation, as can be seen from the experience of nationalised industries in capitalist economies. However, this starting point of the distinction between socialist and capitalist commodity production is often taken to imply that the deficiencies of capitalist commodity production can be throw-away whilst the benefits can be retained. These include the automatic, and supposedly efficient, allocation of resources between sectors by the market mechanism with the associated stimulus to socialist competition and incentive. The socialist economy is seen as identical to the capitalist economy except that the latter has been stripped of exploitation and crises.

The differences between these two schools of thought are irreconcilable at the theoretical level. The first emphasises the significance of class relations within the socialist economy and identifies these with commodity production. The second emphasises the development of productive forces through commodity production. The understanding of the relations and forces of production are respectively drawn from the CMP. Consequently, the debate can proceed without reference to the specific nature of the forces and relations of production of the socialist society under consideration.

Marx is not silent on this dispute. The second position is vehemently and frequently criticised by him.[29] It is a utopian socialism that seeks to retain the commodity form of production whilst abolishing its capitalistic basis by making credit free or by more evenly distributing means of production. But Marx does not explicitly deny the existence of commodity relations nor their development under socialism, although for a fully-fledged communism they will have been abolished. Interestingly, Marx rejects the idea that commodities can be distributed through the use of a money, or labour chits, which *directly* represents the labour embodied in their production. This follows from the impossibility of guaranteeing that commodities are produced in the proportions in which they are demanded, so a labour chit would simply become a paper money like any other except in so far as it had a peculiar name. Consequently, it must be recognised that commodity relations under socialism require money and remain fetishized.[30] The relationship between producers is not direct but continues to be mediated by the exchange of things. Further, the persistence of commodity production is the persistence of labour power in the commodity form. Even so, as has been revealed earlier, the nature of labour under socialism is entirely different because of the absence of relations of exploitation.

VI *Conclusion*

It is possible to anticipate two different and extreme reactions to this paper. One will be to consider it an apology for 'actually existing socialism'.[31] Here we have attempted to demonstrate the necessity of the existence of economic forms under socialism which have their counterpart under capitalism. Let us remind ourselves that socialism is considered to continue to be characterised by the bourgeois right of distribution (according to work even to the extent of piece-work), labour power in the form of a commodity, an interest rate as a means of allocating investment between sectors, private possession of land, etc. The society seems barely distinguishable from capitalism. Yet, it has been so distinguished precisely because these economic forms under socialism are found to correspond to definite directions of change: the collectivisation of consumption, the breaking down of the division of labour between head and hand, man and woman, town and country, and so on. This is the source of a second reaction to this paper which, in contrast to the first, sees it as hostile to the socialist countries since it sets a standard against which they are to be judged: in providing an adequate reserve for the renewal of fixed capital, in abolishing private possession of land, in planning the division between consumption and investment and allocation of resources across sectors, etc.

Both of these positions misunderstand the object of this paper (and believe socialism can be understood independently of its concrete existence). It is to provide an analysis of the economic forms that develop under socialism in general as the basis on which to understand specifically developed relations and forces of production. Without the latter, unique to each socialist formation, there cannot be a satisfactory assessment of the developments concerned. As Engels (1968b) remarked in the context of distributional relations:

> There has also been a discussion ... about the distribution of products in future society, whether this will take place according to the amount of work done or otherwise. The question has been approached very 'materialistically' in opposition to certain idealistic phraseology about justice. But strangely enough it has not struck anyone that, after all, the method of distribution essentially depends on *how much* there is to distribute, and that this must surely change with the progress of production and social organisation, so that the method of distribution may also change. But to everyone who took part in the discussion 'socialist society' appeared not as something undergoing continuous change and progress but as a stable affair fixed once for all, which must, therefore, have a method of distribution fixed once for all. All one can reasonably do, however, is (1) to try and discover the method of distribution to be used *at the beginning*, and (2) to try and *find the general tendency* of the further development. But about this I do not find a single word in the whole debate.

The same applies to economic forms including the comment that continues:

> In general, the word 'materialistic' serves many of the younger writers in Germany as a mere phrase with which anything and everything is labelled without further study, that is, they stick on this label and then consider the question disposed of. But our conception of history is above all a guide to study, not a lever for construction after the manner of the Hegelian. All history must be studied afresh, the conditions of existence of the different formations of society must be examined individually before the attempt is made to deduce from them the political, civil-law, aesthetic, philosophic, religious, etc., views corresponding to them (p. 689).

In the spirit of this last quotation we hope to have shown that socialism can only be understood on the basis of a careful empirical analysis. The alternatives of projecting the laws of motion of capitalism onto socialist societies or of projecting a vision of a future utopian society onto them, whilst remaining blind to aspects which do not scan, must be rejected.

Notes

* This is a modified and expanded version of a lecture delivered in Jinan on 10 September 1981. The lecture was given upon the invitation of the Shandong Academy of Social Science whilst the author was on an academic exchange organised under the auspices of the Chinese Academy of Social Sciences, the British Academy and the Social Science Research Council. The essay has benefited considerably from comments by Betty Matthews, Kathy O'Donnell and Jeff Skelley on an earlier draft.

1. See Marx (1971b).
2. See Marx (1968) p. 324 and Lenin (1970).
3. This is an element of bourgeois ideology, the notion of the division of a fixed 'cake' between the two classes, and it is used as an argument to hold down wages. This view is also reflected in the neo-Ricardian school of Marxism which focuses upon distributional struggle between capital and labour as the determinant of the rate of profit. Note that the argument here is not that increases in wages have no effect upon profitability only that the effect is indirect and not exclusively nor

necessarily predominantly distributional.

4. We discuss below the nature of commodities in general under socialism.
5. For a discussion of the place of the division of labour in Marx's analysis (and for a contrast with Adam Smith), see Fine (1982) Chapter 2.
6. The arguments of this paragraph have been condensed from an earlier version which is available from the author on request.
7. This is a heroic one sentence summary of *Capital III* Part V.
8. The need for the transition arises as soon as surplus labour available for industrial expansion is exhausted.
9. Similar but less extensive developments towards a more active banking sector in China are also to be found in the economic reforms following the Cultural Revolution. For a discussion of the Hungarian experience, see Hare (1977).
10. See Hare (1977).
11. See Dobb (1970).
12. See Mohun (1980).
13. See Fine (1979), Ball (1980) and Fine (1980a).
14. See also *Theories of Surplus Value* II p. 42-3.
15. For a further discussion of Marx's views on state ownership of land, see Fine (1982a), Chapter 4.
16. This is well demonstrated by the problems leading up to and following collectivization in the USSR. See Ellman (1975) for example.
17. For a history of the debate over economic reform in Eastern Europe, see Brus (1972), for China see Lin (1981), and for contributions in China recently, see the newly restored *Social Sciences in China*.
18. Marx makes this observation in the *Grundrisse* but I am unable to find the exact reference.
19. See *Capital* III, Chapter XXXVII.
20. See *Capital* I, Chapter I.
21. See Capital III, Chapter XXI in which interest bearing capital is characterised as a commodity 'sui generis' for which the rate of interest is an 'irrational' price.
22. The relative emphasis and content given to this qualitative aspect of value theory goes to the heart of controversies over the subject and consequently over Marxist economics in general. See Fine and Harris (1979) Chapter 3, Elson (1979) and Steedman *et al.* (1981).
23. It is widely but not universally recognised, even within Marxism. The school of underdevelopment associated with Andre Gundar Frank associates all commodity production with capitalist commodity production. For a critique see Brenner (1977).
24. For example, even at this general level, Marx can produce important propositions concerning the nature of money and of commodity fetishism.

25. For the implicit recognition of these stages of capitalist development in Marx's economic analysis, see Fine and Harris (1979), Chapter 7. The question of value at different stages of development of (capitalist) commodity production has usually been discussed in terms of the relationship between value and price under the name of the historical transformation problem. As suggested in the text, this neglects the nature of value itself at different stages of development, thereby presuming that it is undifferentiated. For a treatment of the historical transformation from the point of view of value rather than price see Fine (1979), Appendix IV and the debate between Catephores (1980) and Fine (1980b).

26. That these are different levels of development of the forces and relations of production is recognised by Marx by his distinguishing them as the formal and real subsumption of labour to capital, respectively. See Marx (1976), Appendix: Results of the Immediate Process of Production.

27. As Mohun (1980) has suggested: 'the aridity and emptiness of analysis which superimposes categories of the capitalist mode of production upon a particular society'.

28. The positions described here necessarily have their counterparts in the west. The first, for example, is characteristic of Bettelheim (1976). The second is to be found in the schools of market socialism. Within bourgeois economics, this is reduced to formal models of decentralised planning through central price fixing. Interestingly, here the bourgeois economist imposes an understanding of socialism drawn from capitalism. But capitalism is itself understood as a system of simple commodity production. It is simply a question of coordinating the markets for the commodities (including labour) that individuals bring to exchange. The notion of socialism as a decentralised market economy in which a central planning board sets prices has its origins in the debate between von Mises and Lange and Taylor. See Lange and Taylor (1938).

29. See *Capital, The Communist Manifesto, the Poverty of Philosophy, Grundrisse, Contribution to a Critique of Political Economy*, etc.

30. Here, it is very important to understand commodity fetishism properly, that relations between producers are and are expressed as relations between things. This does not render these relations necessarily exploitative. Only when abundance eliminates the need for relations between producers to be mediated by a market will commodity fetishism be abolished. For an analysis of commodity fetishism, see Geras (1972), Fine (1980c) Chapter I and Mohun (1979).

31. The term is Bahro's (1978).

References

Bahro, R. (1978), *The Alternative in Eastern Europe*, London, New Left Books.

Ball, M. (1980), 'On Marx's Theory of Agricultural Rent: A Reply to Ben Fine', *Economy and Society*, Vol. 9, No. 3.

Bettelheim, C. (1976), *Economic Calculation and Forms of Property*. London, Routledge and Kegan Paul.

Brenner, R. (1977), 'The Origins of Capitalist Development: A Critique of Neo-Smithian Marxism', *New Left Review*, 104.

Brus, W. (1972), *The Market in a Socialist Economy*, London, Routledge and Kegan Paul.

Brus, W. (1975), *Socialist Ownership and Political Systems*, London, Routledge and Kegan Paul.

Catephores, G. (1980), 'The Historical Transformation Problem – a Reply', *Economy and Society*, Vo. 9, No. 3.

Dobb, M. (1970), *Socialist Planning: Some Problems*, London, Lawrence and Wishart.

Ellman, M. (1975), 'Did the Agricultural Surplus Provide the Resources for the Increase in Investment in the USSR During the First Five Year Plan?', *Economic Journal*.

Elson, D. (ed.) (1979), *Value: The Representation of Labour in Capitalism*, London, CSE Books.

Engels, F. (1968a) in Marx and Engels, *Selected Works,* London, Lawrence and Wishart.

Engels, F. (1968b), 'Engels to C. Schmidt in Berlin', in Marx and Engels, *Selected Works*, Moscow, Progress Publishers.

Fine, B. (1979), 'On Marx's Theory of Agricultural Rent', *Economy and Society*, Vol. 8, No. 3.

Fine, B. (1980a), 'On Marx's Theory of Agricultural Rent: A Rejoinder', *Economy and Society*, Vo. 9, No. 3.

Fine, B. (1980b), 'On the Historical Transformation Problem', *Economy and Society*, Vo. 9, No. 3.

Fine, B. (1980c), *Economic Theory and Ideology*, London, Edward Arnold.

Fine, B. (1982), *Theories of the Capitalist Economy*, London, Edward Arnold.

Fine, B. and Harris, L. (1979), *Rereading 'Capital'*, London, Macmillan.

Geras, N. (1972), 'Essence and Appearance: Aspects of Fetishism in Marx's *Capital*' in R. Blackburn (ed.), *Ideology in Social Science*, London, Fontana.

Hare, P. (1977), 'Economic Reform in Hungary: Problems and Prospects', *Cambridge Journal of Economics*.

Lange, O. and Taylor, F. (1938), *On the Economic Theory of Socialism*, Minneapolis.

Lenin, V. (1970), 'State and Revolution', *Selected Works* in three volumes, London, Lawrence and Wishart.

Lin, C. (1981), 'The Reinstatement of Economics in China Today', *China Quarterly*.

Marx, K. (1980), *Capital, Volume I*, London, Lawrence and Wishart.

Marx, K. (1968), 'Critique of the Gotha Programme', in Marx and Engels, *Selected Works*, London, Lawrence and Wishart.

Marx, K. (1969), *Theories of Surplus Value*, Part II, London, Lawrence and Wishart.

Marx, K. (1971a), *Capital*, Volume III, London, Lawrence and Wishart.

Marx, K. (1971b), *Writings on the Paris Commune*, H. Draper, ed., New York, Monthly Review Press.

Marx, K. (1973), *Grundrisse*, Harmondsworth, Penguin.

Marx and Engels *Collected Works*, Vol. 5, Lawrence and Wishart.

Mohun, S. (1979), 'Ideology, Knowledge and Neoclassical Economics', in F. Green and P. Nore, *Issues in Political Economy*, London: Macmillan.

Mohun, S. (1980), 'The Problem of the Soviet Union', in P. Zarembka (ed.), *Research in Political Economy*, Vol. III, JAI Press Inc.

Steedman, I. et al. (1981), *The Value Controversy*: London, Verso-NLB.

Peter de Francia

Marxist Criticism and Painting

The controversies of the late fifties and early sixties concerning the nature of realism and the necessity of developing a visual language suited to the ideological content of Marxism now tend to be forgotten, or at best, are referred to as an example of sterile wrangling associated with the − then − Cold War. It is unfortunate that these conflicts and debates are so neglected at the moment. It is equally unfortunate that owing to this neglect there is little opportunity to evaluate the achievements of art in the period, as well as its failures. An example of the type of difficulty to be encountered in any attempt to make a critical evaluation of the work that was produced is illustrated by a suggestion made some six years ago in Hungary that the National Museum in Budapest should organize a major retrospective of Socialist Realist painting and sculpture. Conceived as an international exhibition, the project was turned down, as it was thought that this art would be equated with 'Stalinism'.

The essential issues raised in the debates at that time remain largely unanswered. What, for instance, constitutes a viable visual language capable of encompassing a political or social content without making use of a petrified, or at best outmoded syntax? Do the political imperatives of a work allow an active dialectic to form an essential element of the language employed? Or does this dialectic, within the context of bourgeois societies, simply result in a process, constantly repeated, of reification and fragmentation? The latter problem remains central to the issues raised, for instance, by Cubism. Can 'revolutionary' modes of conveying ideological issues exist outside revolutionary

societies? Or do these modes simply result in stylistic
manipulation of visual language, relegating art to an area that
has been aptly described as that of the feudal limits of the
bourgeoisie?

Part of the problem at this time, in Britain and elsewhere,
certainly lay in the type of models proposed for the arts based
on socialist ideology, and for the different media in which they
were supposed to operate. These models in fact were first
formulated in the early thirties. They nevertheless tended to be
central to the discussions some thirty years later. All were based
on the concept of a mass public, a factor which in itself was
hedged with difficulties, and was frequently construed in idealized
terms. Literature was seen as being best embodied in the vehicle
of the long novel; the epic poem was seen as possessing the
qualities most suited to historical or political events. The cinema
was envisaged as being essentially narrative in form (despite the
innovations of early Soviet film), the theatre as realistic in terms
of production and acting techniques. The symphony was seen as
an ideal means of musical creation. Painting and sculpture were
invested with an essentially civic role; for this reason stress was
laid on the mural function of painting.

Initially these models possessed considerable viability. Except
for the cinema they were rooted in nineteenth century traditions
which, as in the case of literature, were closely associated with
the Soviet Union, but were equally applicable in all countries
with a sustained literary history. Authors whose work was
rooted in the nineteenth century were able to develop and
expand the novel for political ends and did so with considerable
success. In the late twenties and early thirties it was possible to
adapt the type of autobiographical trilogy developed by Maxim
Gorki with compelling and authentic results. The Danish writer
Martin-Anderson Nexö provides a valid example of this. This
tradition also formed the basis of what is perhaps the greatest
Marxis work of fiction written in Britain in the thirties – Lewis
Grassic Gibbon's unique and ofted neglected trilogy, *A Scots
Quair*. Louis Aragon's multi-volume novel, *Les Communistes*,
which appeared in the immediate aftermath of the Second World
War, the roots of which can be traced to both Balzac and Zola,

provides a compelling example of the vitality of the political novel.

The complex manner in which changes have modified these original models, the shifts of emphasis and the manipulation of techniques, is best seen in the development of the political cinema. Basically almost every country with a cinema industry has at various periods developed a highly politicized school of directors. Because of its precise historical origins, its international ramifications in terms of production and viewing public, the cinema provides the richest material for political and historical analysis.

However, over a long period of time, and paradoxically because of the class structure of its audiences, it is probably through the medium of the theatre that Marxism has had the most sustained influence and – especially in the case of Bertolt Brecht – has been the catalyst influencing other art forms. In Western Europe as a whole this remains true today. The theatre has been able to fuse innovatory production methods with ideological content from its origins in pre-Hitler Germany to the present, and in widely varying circumstances it has maintained much of its original impetus. One of the reasons for its vitality is certainly to be found in the wide-ranging opportunities offered by the reinterpretation of plays from the historical repertoire. This partially accounts for the fact that in a large number of Western countries there exists, to a degree not found in the other arts, a *political* theatre.

Although the initial models outlined above were never methodically formulated they contained a feature common to most cultural ideas – then aimed at the future: that of inbuilt geological faults. One of these concerned the contexts in which it was postulated that Marxist art could develop. The other that of the developments of bourgeois culture in Western Europe and the United States.

In the case of the former it was evident that the specific social structure of the majority of Western European countries, and notably of Britain, precluded entire categories of literary and visual revolutionary art, notably in terms of the treatment of epic themes. The magnificent achievements of a poet like Pablo

Neruda for example, are not easily adaptable outside the context of Latin America. This is also true of the Mexican muralists of the thirties, the quality of whose work remains unique, but which are all too frequently cited as examples for Western painters today, though they represented a valid and legitimate example to American artists working under Roosevelt's New Deal programme (W.P.A.) in the thirties.

It is correct to make use of an inheritance which permits a reactivation for both the present and the future of the revolutionary impetus embedded in traditions of the past. But such an impetus cannot be transmitted directly or in a simplistic manner without the mediation of the enormous historical changes of the past half century.

The cultural problems stemming from developments within capitalist societies, and ones which have a direct bearing on virtually all attempts to formulate a basis for both a socialist art and the criticism essentially needed for such an art, are of great complexity. They particularly affect the visual arts, and notably painting.

The ideology of bourgeois capitalism is that of expropriation, veiled in cultural phraseology by a constant reference to 'principles' derived 'from history' or 'values' totally unconnected with need. The immense accumulation of historical documentation on the visual arts, and especially of the art of the first two decades of the twentieth century, has offered the most fertile source of this expropriation. The greater part of art historical teaching, with some notable exceptions, has been either based on pure historicism or on a kind of technocratic handling of the subject, and has been able to present virtually every development in twentieth century art in terms of innovatory or revolutionary intentions, inseparable from the concept of avant-gardism. The ever-increasing fragmentation of British bourgeois philosophy, e.g. logical positivism, has been reflected in the methods and terminology of most art criticism.

Paradoxically it has been through a parody of political concepts that the basis of avant-gardism has, until the last few years, been maintained. 'Revolutionary art', it was argued, was under constant attack by the cultural establishment, who viewed it as both subversive and potentially threatening. A form of jousting was thus evolved in which the assumed subversion, more often than not confined to a permutation of types of formal visual language, was quietly and efficiently expropriated and absorbed.

Marxism, when intelligently used, offers an immense range of creative energy to artists and critics. In retrospect it is evident that in Britain its potential has been neglected and, especially in the field of criticism, has frequently been used in such a way as to alienate rather than constructively encourage those – more numerous than is often assumed – whose sympathies and interests are potentially oriented to socialism.

Part of this failure must be ascribed to the use of repeated formulae and an epistemology that is frequently presented as scientific whilst lacking the clarity and discipline necessary to scientific investigation. It has tended to stress the conditions under which a socialist art could come into being whilst at the same time neglecting an analysis of the possible formal languages that would form the syntax of such an art. It has, more unfortunately, all too often neglected an analysis of practice. More important – and this is perhaps central to the problem – it has neglected what *has been available*, i.e. the work of those few major artists whose contribution to Marxist parties in Western Europe was continuous and sustained.

The work of both Pablo Picasso and Fernand Léger is of particular relevance in this connection. The case of Picasso presents a particular example of lost opportunities, and is perhaps best illustrated by the fact that his *War and Peace* murals at Vallauris, political in content and based on a specific political event – the Korean War – are the works by Picasso least discussed by those claiming to be Marxist critics. The fact that they are virtually ignored in bourgeois publications should provide an added incentive for Marxist criticism and evaluation.

Marxism is not a dogmatic cult and is thus not in need of repeated litanies and repetition. Powerful and valid arguments exist which can be directed against formalism in the visual arts. But it can be demonstrated that the repeated use of the term 'figuration' or 'figurative art' was, in the long run, a singularly ineffective polemical weapon, and is all the more inappropriate at the moment when purely abstract, or informal, art is so visibly declining. But orthodox Marxist criticism was so heavily dependent on the term that it was unable to cope with the advent of bourgeois modes like that of photo-realism, an art whose counterpart is to be found in the writings of authors like Alain Robbe-Grillet, based on the fetishism of objects. Extreme objectivization in art is far more abstract – especially when associated with the term 'realism' – than a great amount of non-figurative painting.

Initial discussions of the role of Marxism in the visual arts some thirty years ago were frequently linked with premises based on Soviet painting and sculpture. This tends to be less true at present. It is not the purpose of this article to add to the chorus of attacks against the art produced in the Soviet Union except to suggest that, in the words of Brecht 'because things are as they are they will not remain as they are'. The reported favourable response to the Soviet exhibition at the 1982 Venice Biennale should however be treated with a degree of care. Very powerful gallery and art market interests are currently engaged in promoting 'a return to realism' which may account for these reactions. It is an operation to be treated with extreme caution and one based on most questionable premises.

It is more than probable that the painting and sculpture produced in the coming decade will contain an increasing amount of political content. The current work of the French sculptor Ipoustéguy provides a most important example of such an orientation. The principal characteristics of such work will consist of the brusque and often unexpected intrusions of political truths, often ill-defined ones. It will be the task of Marxist critics to detect, evaluate and encourage these intrusions. This does not mean, as is frequently implied, that a dyke should be breached and every manifestation of art produced in bourgeois countries should be passively accepted, as suggested some years ago in Roger Garaudy's *Un realisme sans rivages*. Garaudy's boundless horizons were in fact an abdication of criticism and it was not by accident that his book was renamed 'The Flood' by Italian critics. What is implied however is that Marxist artists and critics should cease huddling behind stockades and become far more aware of the still untapped potential of creative energy waiting to be used.

The bunker mentality was in fact far less prevalent amongst some of the major artists in the decade following the second world war than is often assumed, and the 1981 *Paris-Paris* exhibition at the Baubourg centre in Paris clearly demonstrated the fact. A number of important painters working in the late forties were fully committed to the necessity of evolving a visual language which could be used to promote political issues. In Italy Renato Guttuso's numerous paintings on the theme of the occupation of the land in Sicily and Calabria by unemployed agricultural labourers and dispossessed peasants remain a major landmark in the history of twentieth-century art in Western Europe. In the early fifties Fernand Leger planned a huge picture based on the defence of Stalingrad, and the numerous surviving drawings for this uncompleted work give some idea of the potency of the tradition of historical painting. Artists in, and from, Latin America have frequently been in the forefront of attempts to create a modern pictorial political language. The work of Roberto Matta, whilst frequently tinged with an apparently surreal anarchism, is clearly and often directly political in both theme and content. The task of analysing such works is to perceive in what manner pictorial language − like any other − mediates between a concept of history and the essence of reality.

One of the most difficult problems facing any artist wishing to base a work on a contemporary political event is that of making the choice between a thematic interpretation of such an event or of producing what is essentially a 'work of circumstance', a document which can serve an immediate and urgent purpose based on factual imperatives. Such works are, in essence, documentary ones through the manner in which ideas or information are presented. But documents only offer a possibility of verification. They are concerned with offering proof of something. Used in a simplistic manner they do not offer any information and, on a deeper level, are unmemorable since they rarely achieve an associative link with concepts underlying the subject matter, political or otherwise.

In addition, works of circumstance of this type can only be effective if linked with mass revolutionary movements. The Agitprop art developed in the USSR, entirely valid in the early twenties, relied very heavily on typification of imagery. A work of circumstance is essentially expendable. It is the visual equivalent of a manifesto. It is interesting to note in this connection how uninventive and repetitious this type of 'mass' art has become within the last twenty years when used in countries in which innovatory developments might well have been expected, especially those with a strong tradition of popular folk imagery.

Paintings and sculpture that have sought to transcend the limitations of a work of circumstance, but for which the catalyst was a specific historical event or series of events, are exceedingly rare in the twentieth century. Those that have been created, with a few exceptions, are inseparably bound to the work of Picasso.

It has become fashionable within the last twenty years to denigrate the achievements of this extraordinary man whose death, in Neruda's works, was like that 'of the disappearance of a whole continent'. Criticisms have ranged from puritanical disapproval of his life-style to accusations of fickleness in his attitude to politics.

Picasso's political commitment was in fact sustained, and his contribution to the cultural life of the French Communist Party, notwithstanding systematic attacks against much that he produced, is well-demonstrated by his continuous production of posters and illustrations, and works on political and social themes. Writers and critics who have a vested interest in denying the validity of any political commitment held by artists and intellectuals resort to the simple expedient of completely ignoring his political works.

The two historical events which evoked the strongest political response in Picasso occurred in 1936 and 1950. They were the Spanish Civil War and the Korean War.

His most profound and sustained emotional links, together with a very substantial part of his pictorial language were with Spain. Picasso's *Guernica* and the numerous paintings, drawings

The 12th century deconsecrated chapel at Valauris, known as the *Temple de la Paix*, with Picasso's murals mounted on the barrel vaulted interior. © Editions Cercle d'Art

War by Picasso

Peace by Picasso

and etchings linked to this epic work have been extensively commented on, analysed and interpreted. His paintings and drawings stemming from the Korean War, notably his 1950 picture *Massacre in Korea*, have received less attention and, as has already been noted, the *War* and *Peace* murals in the Temple of Peace at Vallauris in the South of France, begun in the summer of 1952, remain the least discussed and least reproduced of any of his works. Yet they are certainly amongst the greatest that he ever produced.

Picasso had come to Vallauris in the late forties and had worked intensively in its ceramic workshops. On his seventieth birthday he agreed to decorate the walls of a low twelfth-century barrel-vaulted deconsecrated chapel in the town, formerly used to house an olive press.

In the summer of 1952 he began work on two huge paintings in a large temporary studio whilst an armature, designed to insulate the panels from the damp of the stone walls, was being erected in the chapel. The *War* and *Peace* panels measured 15′ 5″ x 33′ 6″ each and were designed to cover either side of the low vault from floor to ceiling. They were painted in oil on Isorel (a type of synthetic board). Completed in the same year, they were exhibited in Milan and Rome before being definitely installed in the chapel in the autumn of 1953. Picasso was to say of them that 'none of my paintings had been painted with such speed, considering its size'.

Both panels represent in very different ways a summation of Picasso's attitude to mankind. Both are entirely thematic works. The *Peace* mural is stylistically far more formalized and perhaps for this reason seemingly more generalized and less compelling than that of *War*. But this is due to the fact that it is far more difficult in this century to depict images of plenitude than of violence and tragedy. The colours used in both paintings are relatively sombre.

The *War* mural depicts an extraordinary funereal procession moving from right to left across almost the entire length of the wall. Against a background of massed greyish greens, a black hearse-like cart advances like some archaic war chariot, its centrally-pivoted wheels derived from the chassis of small ancient agricultural handcarts. Two of the three lurching horses dragging the cart are partially decked in the white head-coverings which were part of the processional trappings of horses formerly used in Mediterranean funerals, and which featured frequently in imagery used in Italian neo-realist films of the fifties. The procession lurches forward, the horses hooves trampling over already burning books. Near to and below the guide reins, and about to be crushed by the forward wheels of the cart, a solitary pair of hands emerge from darkness, their expressiveness bearing comparison, though in a reversed position, to those in the sculptures of the tympanium of Autun Cathedral. Behind the horses, depicted as shadows thrown from figures engaged in some barbarous ritualistic war-dance, a group of warriors brandishing archaic weapons charge forward in a kind of hysteria. They are painted in flat black as is the smoke-laden cloud descending on the scene from the right. The overall colour of the mural conforms well to an old dictum of Spanish painters: 'If you want more colour, use black!'

Confronting this triumph of death, on the extreme left of the picture, stands the figure of a young man who, guardian-like, carries the scales of justice in his right hand. He is protected by a shield on which is inscribed the dove of Peace.

But it is the grimacing demon-like figure standing on the cart which, brandishing a blooded blade and carrying a great load of skulls strung in a net on its back, is an image of such arresting intensity. For this figure, with a wide sweeping gesture of the left hand usually associated with that of a sower, is scattering, as though in some ritual, a mass of hairy insect like shapes. This is a direct reference to the American General Ridgway and the repeated claims of the use of germ warfare by the Americans in Korea.

The *Peace* mural naturally reflects a completely different attitude to the human condition. It has been criticized for being 'profoundly humanistic', for its avoidance of any references to the twentieth century, and for being 'legendary' and even 'proverbial' and thus idealistic in content, since it depicts what is essentially a kind of Arcadian innocence. This in fact was intentional and is reflected in every aspect of the imagery used.

On the extreme right of the mural the naked figures of two men and a woman are depicted beneath a fruit-laden tree. One man tends a fire on which a cooking-pot is placed, another writes, and the woman – lying on her side and reading – suckles a child.

Towards the centre of the painting the giant image of Pegasus, tamed by a small boy, draws a plough. On the extreme left a seated figure plays on pipes, and two dancing women in the foreground respond to their rhythm, providing what is almost the only source of movement in the calm context of the work. Above the women the diminutive figure of an acrobat balances a long pole on his head. At one end hangs a birdcage containing fish; at the other is balanced a bowl full of fluttering birds. The colour of each of these images is reversed. The fish swim in yellow evoking the sky, the birds, above, in blue water. On the acrobat's head is perched the Owl of Minerva. Dominating the entire scene and containing the strongest colours to be found in the mural, a gigantic sun is given an iconic significance. The duality of its configuration is both that of a sun and a gigantic eye, the lashes of which are depicted as ears of sprouting wheat.

Both murals raise a number of problems that are directly relevant to the use of imagery in the context of works of political significance. They are essentially allegorical works. In addition they make direct reference to renovated myths of antiquity. They also make use of – and this is especially true of the *War* mural – a considerable degree of visual rhetoric. Both these factors probably account for the criticisms and reservations directed against them.

However it seems increasingly probable that allegory could present an indispensable way of using narrative in our time and notably in connection with ideological works. Its use carries the ever-present danger of sentimentality or that of obscurity in the selection of sources used. Its virtue lies in the fact that ideological content must be presented in such a way as to stimulate the imagination. It can be used in a way which avoids idealization.

Rhetoric presents other problems, notably in its associative links with theatricality. But this may be necessary in the projection of epic themes carried not on a very large scale.

Both factors — allegory and rhetoric — are of critical significance in the creation of ideological works. We are all the poorer, and the weaker, in ignoring or dismissing them.

Yvonne Kapp

Karl Marx's Children: Family Life 1844-1855

Note: *The translation of direct quotations from letters is, because of their subject, slightly freer than would be permissible for sacred texts. While the feeling of loving parents for their children has not vastly changed in the last 150 years, its expression has. Rather than expose the Marx family, and in particular the mother, to a charge of false sentimentality or heightened melodrama, the language, here and there, has been triflingly modified to accord more nearly with modern diction.*

I

It has frequently been said, for reasons which escape me, that Eleanor was Karl Marx's favourite child. The truth is that Marx was devoted to all his children, without distinction; though in later life he cherished above all, it may be, his first-born, Jenny. But in the early years of parenthood the one he most loved was undoubtedly the third child, Edgar, whose death at the age of eight he never ceased to mourn.

The circumstances of Edgar's brief life have been fairly well documented, though I have not – and nor has anybody else – discovered the exact date of his birth in December 1846 or January 1847 at 42 rue d'Orléans in Brussels, where the family had resided since the previous October.

Marx had arrived in Brussels early in February 1845 following his expulsion from Paris by Guizot[1] on orders from the Prussian government. He was shortly rejoined by his wife and their nine-months-old daughter, Mrs Marx having used the few days' grace allowed her by the police to sell the contents of their dwelling at 28 rue Vanneau in the faubourg St Germain in order to pay for her journey and not go penniless to Brussels. Before this, on 7 February, Marx had petitioned King Leopold I[2] for domiciliary rights. These were granted on 22 March on condition that he signed an undertaking to publish nothing on current political affairs while in Belgium. With this he complied; though even then his friend, Frederick Engels, foresaw that he would nevertheless be harried by the Belgian authorities and that, in the end, his only recourse would be emigration to England.

In the meantime, the first work on which Marx and Engels had collaborated during the autumn of 1844 in Paris, *The Holy Family*, was published in Frankfurt towards the end of February, at which point Mrs Marx reached Brussels to put up at the *pension* Bois sauvage, 19 Plaine Ste Gudule, and thereafter, for the next few weeks, at various addresses. However, in April, her mother, the Baroness von Westphalen, dispatched from her household to help the young family a much-prized servant, Helene Demuth, then aged 25, who was to remain with the Marxes for the rest of their lives and to become 'the axis around which everything in the house revolved'. So, early in May, they took a small house outside the Porte de Louvain at 5 rue de l'Alliance.

That spring Marx wrote his *Theses on Feuerbach* and in the summer, from 12 July until 24 August, he made his first visit to England, under Engels' guidance, staying in London and Manchester, meeting such leading Chartists as Ernest Jones and Julian Harney and being introduced to the social, economic and industrial constitution of this 'workshop of the world'.[3] During Marx's absence his wife set out at the beginning of August with her little daughter Jenny, then aged 16 months, to stay for six weeks with her mother in Trier.

II

This was not the first time Mrs Marx had returned to her girlhood home since her marriage on 19 June 1843. Almost exactly a year later, when her first baby was six weeks old, she had been there on a three months' visit. In two of the letters that have come down to us which she wrote to her husband during that time she expressed not only her deep and, as it proved, undying love for Marx but also her intense joy in motherhood. She observed in minute detail and recorded every sign of her infant's development. The mixture of adoration, pride, gentle amusement, tenderness, solicitude and delight here manifested was characteristic of her attitude towards her children all her life.

She travelled from Paris by mail coach. The baby, already overfed, was completely upset by the journey so that, immediately upon arrival at her grandmother's house, the family physician, Dr Robert Schleicher, a figure of some prominence in the town, was called in and decreed that she should have a wet-nurse. This move was successful – Mrs Marx did not believe the child would have pulled through otherwise – and the healthy young woman, called Gretchen, who was engaged from Barbeln, a suburb of Trier, turned out to have been as a child the recipient of the Westphalens' charity in their better days, which *quid pro quo* enchanted Mrs Marx. Presumably Gretchen's own baby had died, or been fostered, for there is no mention of it at all; and she, who had been in service for three years in Metz and therefore spoke French, agreed with enthusiasm to accompany Mrs Marx back to Paris at the end of her stay.

While the baby was being nourished back to health Mrs Marx was fêted by the small gentry of Trier who had known her as a girl and whose kind hearts were naturally wrung by the thought of this beautiful woman's unprofitable marriage.

Although my whole manner and being express contentment and *plenitude* [she wrote], everyone still hopes you will decide to take a permanent post ... the asses ... All Trier gapes, goggles, admires and pays court, but my heart and soul are turned towards you ... They all talk too much about a *steady* income. To this my only answer lies in my rosy cheeks, my healthy body, my velvet cloak, feather hat and stylish *coiffure*. That makes the best and the deepest impression ...

A few days after her arrival – on the anniversary of her

wedding-day – she went with trepidation to pay a call on Marx's widowed mother whose relations with her son had been far from happy and who shared, if she had not inspired, the prevalent opinion that he should be regularly employed in some highly-paid profession rather than frittering away his time upon useless pursuits. However, Mrs Marx's visit, despite her fears, went well. She was affectionately greeted by her sister-in-law, Henriette, known as Jettchen, then 24, who led her into the room where Mrs Marx senior and her daughter Sophie received her with unexpected warmth. Sophie, Marx's elder sister, was evidently there on a visit, for she had married in 1842 a Netherlands lawyer, Wilhelm Schmalhausen, and lived in Maastricht. According to Mrs Marx she looked ravaged by illness and as if she were unlikely to recover.[4]

> But Jettchen [she added] looks far worse. Only your mother is flourishing and well and gaiety itself, almost frolicsome and skittish. This skittishness is positively eerie.[5]

A third sister – the youngest, Caroline, then 21, who was to die, unmarried, of consumption three years later – was also there and all these ladies paid gracious calls on the Westphalen house to inspect the baby. Mrs Marx was much surprised, but well pleased.

> Can you imagine such a change? [she wrote] Why, all of a sudden? What a difference success makes, or rather, in our case, the *appearance* of success which I know how to maintain by the subtlest tactics …

Her own mother, who lavished loving attentions upon her and the little Jenny, was plagued by worries caused for the most part by her son Edgar, then studying to qualify as a (non-practising) County Court lawyer.

> He makes use of all the significant signs of the times, all the ills of society, only to cover up and gloss over his own worthlessness. Now the vacation will be starting again and nothing will come of

the examinations. Mother has to deny herself everything while he goes merrily to all the operas in Cologne, as he himself writes. He speaks with the utmost tenderness of his little sister ... but I find it impossible to feel tender towards the scapegrace ...

While much of this letter, written on 21 June, eight days after leaving Paris, dwelt upon the baby's beauty, charm and constipation, the extreme youth of their subject renders these passages of but moderate historical interest. Seven or eight weeks later, however, in a further letter written when, at three months, Jenny's gifts were unmistakable, the mother's observations provide an engaging glimpse of them both.

... when she cries [wrote Mrs Marx], we immediately draw her attention to the little flowers in the wallpaper; then she becomes as quiet as a mouse and stares so fixedly that tears come to her eyes. We must not talk to her quite so much any more because it over-taxes her. She tries to imitate and respond to every sound, but the swelling and flushing of her forehead are surely signs of too great exertion. For the rest, she is happiness personified. She chuckles at the sight of every face ... As soon as she hears a voice she turns that way and goes on gazing until something else distracts her attention. You have no idea of the child's liveliness. For whole nights she does not shut her eyes and if you peep at her she laughs aloud ... Karl, my love, how long will this poppet play a solo part? I fear, I fear, that when papa and mama are together again, living in joint ownership, a duet will soon be produced ... I can scarcely go on writing; the child constantly distracts me with her adorable gurglings and attempts to talk ...

Jenny's strong resemblance to her father which, with her dark eyes and black hair, increased as she grew, was also noted at this early age with extreme pleasure.

In this letter Mrs Marx reverted to the poor sick girl, her sister-in-law Jettchen, the elaborate preparations for whose marriage to an architect, Theodor Simons, were now in full swing, so that the members of that household were too busy to visit her and she too tactful to call on them.

... The wedding is on 28 August, [she wrote]. ... Despite all the splendour Jettchen's health deteriorates daily; her cough and hoarseness grow worse. She can hardly walk. She goes about like a ghost, but married she must be. It is generally looked upon as horrible and infamous ... I cannot imagine how your family can feel pleased and joyful about it ... I do not understand your mother, she baffles me. She told us herself that she believes Jettchen has consumption, and yet she lets her marry ... I wonder what will happen ...

What happened was that in less than six months, on 3 January 1845, Jettchen died.

At about the same time Mrs Marx's fears under another head were also realised: when she went back to Trier in August 1845, this time from Brussels, she was seven months pregnant and returned to the rue de l'Alliance only a fortnight before the birth of a second daughter on 29 September who was named Jenny Laura.

It may be said that all Marx's daughters were given the name Jenny, after their mother, though only the eldest – Jenny Caroline – ever used it.

III

In the winter of 1845-6, during which Marx worked with Engels on *The German Ideology*, Mrs Marx's brother, the unsatisfactory Edgar, came to stay with the family in Brussels. Though she had disclaimed tender feelings for him, and disapproved of this inveterate sponger of no settled occupation at the age of 26, she was genuinely fond of him and glad that he now sought and found employment in a newspaper office. There he was joined in the spring by one of Marx's closest friends and a fellow revolutionary, Wilhelm Wolff, known as Lupus, to whom Marx was to dedicate the first volume of *Das Kapital*.

At the start of the year 1846 Marx and Engels set up the Brussels Communist Corresponding Committee with the aim of providing information and an exchange of ideas between German, French and English socialists. It was not a political party but a loose organisation whose main adherents were in

Paris to which, in August, Engels was sent as a delegate from the Brussels Committee, living from October that year until the following March at 23 rue de Lille.

Meanwhile that spring, Mrs Marx, this time alone, visited her mother who was ill and thought to be dying. She was in fact to live for another ten years and, once her recovery was assured, Mrs Marx returned to Brussels where, for reasons of financial stringency, the family gave up the house in the rue de l'Alliance and in May – Jenny now just two and Laura eight months – went back to live in the little Bois sauvage *pension* until 23 October when they moved to 42 rue d'Orléans in the faubourg d'Ixelles.

Here the boy Edgar, named after the uncle who stood as titular godfather, was born. Though he was given the name Edgar, and only Edgar, his mother later confided to a friend that, should her mother-in-law, improbably, ever loosen the purse-strings again, the 'Edgar' might, for the occasion, be suppressed and the name Henry (Heinrich) – that of his father and paternal grandfather – be assumed. This did not happen and Edgar he remained, though generally known as Musch, or Mouche.

It was at this period that the League of the Just – originally founded in the mid-30s in Paris by German workers and spreading to England, Germany, Switzerland and Sweden – was reorganised and changed its name to the Communist League, having persuaded Marx in Brussels and Engels in Paris to join its ranks, they in their turn having persuaded the League to adopt their principles of socialism. That was in February 1847 and, under its new title, the League held its first congress from 2 to 9 June – to which Engels and Wilhelm Wolff went – in London where the executive committee established itself in November 1846 following ceaseless persecution by the Paris police. A second congress was held in the same year, from 29 November until 8 December, attended by both Marx and Engels who played a leading part in the proceedings and were assigned the task of writing a manifesto.

During this first year of Edgar's life, when his father was writing *The Poverty of Philosophy* – published simultaneously in

Brussels and Paris in July 1847 – he thrived, though he was not, it appears, of those who have only to be seen to be admired. His mother, indeed, took an exceedingly poor view of his looks. Her girls were lovely, she wrote to Mrs Herwegh, the wife of the poet, but 'the boy, the boy', she moaned, 'is a little monster'; while she told Lina Schoeler, the long-term fiancée though never the bride of Edgar von Westphalen, that he was assuredly no Adonis. She was thankful, she said, that, at a year, he had lost some of his earlier frightfulness (she used the word *Schrecklichkeit*), but she did wish this whey-faced infant would not always wear such a bellicose expression.

That was in January 1848, at the onset of the year of revolutions, 'the Springtime of the Nations', as it has been called, one of whose early side-effects was Engels's expulsion from France on the 29th. He was back in Brussels two days later, by which time the central authority of the League had been pressing for the manifesto, going so far as to say that if Marx did not deliver it by 1 February, he should return all the documents entrusted to him. It must have arrived by that date, for *The Manifesto of the Communist Party* was published in London on or about 24 February, in German, with the imprint *Gedruckt in der Office der Bildungsgesellschaft für Arbeiter* (printed in the office of the Workers' Educational Society).[6]

Though conceived by both Marx and Engels, to some extent derived from ideas already expressed in their joint work *The German Ideology*, and largely based upon Engels' two documents – the so-called *Credo* (or *Draft of a Communist Confession of Faith*) and the *Principles of Communism* – the *Manifesto* was in fact written by Marx alone, Engels having gone back to Paris. The manuscript, save for one page in a notebook dated Brussels, December 1847, has vanished.

Events now moved swiftly: the French government collapsed, the King[7] abdicated, fleeing to England, and on 26 February the French (Second) Republic was proclaimed. It did not take long for the Belgian authorities to pounce. On 2 March King Leopold issued a decree expelling Marx forthwith. Two days later, after nightfall, as he was preparing to leave, the police burst into his house and arrested him. As they took him away to the Amigo prison his wife rushed out in a vain attempt to follow, then frantically sought help, hurrying in the dark from one friend's house to another until she, too, was seized by the police and unceremoniously flung into a lock-up with vagrants and prostitutes. From its window the next morning she saw her husband being marched off under military guard. Later that day she was lengthily interrogated and only in the evening allowed to go home to her children. Meanwhile Marx reached Paris where he put up on the boulevard Beaumarchais in Ménilmontant.

It could be said that they got off lightly: Wilhelm Wolff was taken into custody on 27 February, before the formal order for his arrest and expulsion, and was so brutally maltreated that, being punched and kicked in the face, he almost lost the sight of one eye.

With the new situation in France, the family could now have settled there; but events in Germany, where insurrections broke out in mid-March, determined Marx to go back to his native country. Early in April both he and Engels went to Mainz and, on the 11th, Marx reached Cologne where he intended to stay.

Mrs Marx, having abandoned or pawned her belongings in Brussels, briefly to rejoin her husband in Paris, now went to Trier again where she was able to introduce Laura and Edgar to their grandmother. She did not go to Cologne until Marx had permission to reside there. Then, on 1 June, the first number of the *Neue Rheinische Zeitung* appeared under the editorship of Marx and Engels. The editorial staff included Wilhelm Wolff, their old companion, a teacher by profession; Ferdinand Wolff, a journalist, known as Red Wolf; Ernst Dronke, a writer; George Weerth, a poet and the features editor of the paper; and Ferdinand Freiligrath, also a poet. All were members of the Communist League and all of them at some stage emigrated to England.

By mid-August the paper had reached a daily circulation of 5,000 copies; but by then the financial backers had lost their nerve and withdrawn their support. Marx travelled to Berlin and Vienna to try to raise funds. However, on 26 September Cologne was declared in a state of siege, an order was out for Engels' arrest and the paper was suspended for a week. This further undermined its precarious finances which Marx then personally shouldered, using up the remains of the inheritance from his father who had died ten years earlier.

Before the year was out counter-revolution was gaining ground throughout Europe: a state of siege was declared in Berlin on 12 November while, in France, Louis Bonaparte – according to Marx's 'a crafty old roué' who bore the name simply because French law forbade enquiries into paternity – was elected president of the Republic a month later and, following an investigation by the Cologne Public Prosecutor, both Marx and Engels were formally charged in early February 1849 with 'insulting the authorities'. A separate case was brought against Marx for 'incitement to revolt', though at the end of the two court proceedings they were acquitted. On 10 May martial law was imposed throughout Prussia. Nine days later, availing themselves of the fact that in December 1845 Marx had renounced his Prussian citizenship, the authorities declared him a foreigner who had 'disgracefully abused' the benefits of hospitality which were therefore revoked and he was expelled at 24 hours' notice, together with his colleagues Dronke and Weerth – also not Prussian citizens – while Freiligrath and Wilhelm Wolff – who were – faced legal action. On that date, 19 May 1849, the last number of the *Neue Rheinische Zeitung* came out, printed in red.

For the rest of the month Marx and Engels travelled about southern and western Germany, then in a state of insurrection, visiting Frankfurt, Baden, the Palatinate and, finally, Marx went to Bingen where he met his wife with Helene Demuth and the children on their way to Trier. Mrs Marx now made a detour to Frankfurt to pawn yet again the silver she had just redeemed from Brussels, in which transaction she was helped by Joseph Weydemeyer – at that time the leader of the Frankfurt circle of the League of Communists – who, with his wife Luise, gave the little travelling party hospitality. She then went on her way to remain with her mother until July.

In the first days of July, after Engels had joined the Baden-Palatinate insurgent army, fighting in a number of engagements until it was forced into retreat at Ratstatt, Marx reached Paris, using the name of Ramboz for his correspondence. He was not allowed to remain in peace for long. On 19 July, less than a fortnight after the family had been re-united and when they had just found what Mrs Marx described as 'pretty, convenient lodgings in a healthy neighbourhood' (at 45 rue de Lille, the same street in the faubourg St. Germain where Engels had lived in 1846) where, although it was rather expensive, they planned to stay for a while, the Minister of the Interior, Dufaure, banished Marx from Paris to what he, Marx, believed to be the particularly unhealthy department of Morbihan. (A contemporary atlas speaks of its climate as '*doux et uniforme*'.) He strongly objected and appealed against this order but a month later he was informed that it must be obeyed, without delay.

That was on 16 August 1849. Thereupon he realised, as Engels had predicted four years earlier, that England was the only place left for him. Eight days later he embarked with Ferdinand Wolff from Boulogne.

IV

Upon his arrival in London Marx stayed with Karl Blind, a refugee journalist, who lodged at – or perhaps used only as an accommodation address – Peterson's Coffeehouse in Robert Street, near Grosvenor Square. Almost at once Marx went down with a most inconvenient if mild illness, known as cholerine, which prevented him from househunting for his family or preparing for their reception. Mrs Marx, after severe difficulties and harassment by the police, had been permitted to stay in Paris until 15 September, by which time she was almost eight months pregnant again, ill and exhausted.

When she reached London, penniless, with Lenchen and the three children, she was met by her husband's colleague, George Weerth, who found temporary shelter for them all in a small Leicester Square boarding house. With the birth of the fourth child imminent it was clear that more suitable quarters were a necessity and, at the end of a week, Marx having recovered, they moved into what they hoped would be a fairly permanent home in semi-furnished lodgings at 4 Anderson Street, a little turning off the King's Road in Chelsea.

Here, on 5 November, was born a second son, named Henry Edward Guy and known as Guido, or Föxchen. As a friend wrote to Weydemeyer:

> The young Communist who has put in an appearance at the Marxes is called Henry Edward Guy Fawkes. He was born on the anniversary of the Gunpowder Plot ... So far the little fellow bores everyone with his screaming; however, in time no doubt he will listen to reason.

It is hardly surprising that, the fourth child in five-and-a-half years arriving so soon after the mother's stressful flight to an entirely unknown country in an ailing and anxious condition, he should have been sickly and difficult to rear. Although she knew it to be inadvisable Mrs Marx insisted upon breast-feeding the infant – indeed, she saw no alternative since wet-nurses in London were far beyond her means – and, with sore and bleeding nipples, she suffered torments; while the baby, she said, not only drank in her suppressed anxieties with her milk but 'in his pain sucked so hard ... that blood often poured into his little quivering mouth'. With this start in life, he made but poor progress.

> Since he came into the world he has not had a single night's sleep, at best two or three hours. Recently, too, he has had violent convulsions and has perpetually hung between pitiful life and death ...

When the rent – of about £2 a week – had been paid for some five months to the resident caretaker, herself under notice to quit, it was agreed that the landlord should be paid direct in future. But he was not; and one cold, wet spring morning when the rent had fallen into arrears, while the mother was engaged in trying to feed the unhappy Guido, the caretaker charged into the room, denied the agreement, claimed that she was owed £5 and demanded payment on the spot. The money was simply not there; whereupon bailiffs were sent for and distrained all the family's sparse possessions.

beds, linen, underclothes, dresses, everything [wrote Mrs Marx], down to the very cradle of my poor baby and the best toys of the girls who stood there shedding tears.

The men threatened to come back in two hours' time to take the things away.

I should then have had to lie on the bare boards with my trembling children and streaming breasts.

In this emergency a friend offered to go for help and took a cab whose horse bolted so that he jumped out, in fear of his life, and was brought back to the house, badly injured. Meanwhile, since it was plain that they would have to leave Anderson Street the next day, Marx was wildly seeking other quarters, only to find that nobody was willing to take the family in once the four children were mentioned. At last another friend, better endowed than most, gave them the necessary £5, while Mrs Marx in all haste sold the beds to pay off the chemist, the baker, the butcher and the milkman who, alerted by the news of bailiffs on the premises, now besieged the place, brandishing unpaid bills. Mrs Marx continued the tale:

The beds that had been sold were taken out and loaded on to a cart – and what happened? It was well after sunset, which contravenes English law; the landlord turned up and forced his way in with two police constables, alleging that among the things sold there could be some of his property and that we planned to flee abroad. In less than five minutes there were more than two or three hundred people at our door: the whole Chelsea rabble. The beds were unloaded and brought back in: only next morning, after sunrise, could they be handed over to the buyers. As we were now, thanks to the sale of all our belongings, able to settle everything down to the last farthing, I moved with my children into two small rooms in the German Hotel at 1 Leicester Street, Leicester Square, where, for £5.10 a week, we were humanely welcomed.

The humane welcome did not last long: at the end of a week 'our worthy host refused to serve us breakfast and we were obliged to look for other lodgings'. These they found nearby, at

64 Dean Street in Soho where they stayed for six wretched
months.

> We live, all six of us, in one small room and a very small closet, for
> which we pay more than for the largest house in Germany; and pay
> weekly into the bargain,

wrote Mrs Marx to Weydemeyer that summer. It was of this
time that she also told him:

> ... my husband is almost overwhelmed by the pettiest domestic
> worries of so hideous a nature that it has taken all his energy, all his
> calm, sane, quiet fortitude to sustain him in this daily, hourly
> struggle ... Never, even in the most dreadful moments, did he lose
> his confidence in the future, nor yet his good humour, being
> perfectly content if he saw me happy with our beloved children
> snuggling close to their mama ...

In August, now pregnant with her fifth child, Mrs Marx made
the desperate move of going to Zaltbommel in Holland to beg
help from Lion Philips, a businessman married to Marx's
maternal aunt, Sophia. Still suffering from the effects of the
recent upheavals in Europe, Philips was in no mood to
sympathise with needy revolutionaries, albeit his kin. He refused
to give any financial aid though, on parting, he pressed into Mrs
Marx's hand a small tip for her youngest child, which she
charitably interpreted as regret that he was not able to do more.

> With despair in my heart [she wrote], I turned back home. Little
> Edgar, with his friendly face, came bounding towards me and my
> Föxchen held out his tiny arms to me.

At the end of October Marx entreated Weydemeyer to
borrow enough cash from somewhere or other to redeem the
silver so recently pawned by his wife in Frankfurt, to sell it to a
jeweller or anyone else who would buy it, repay the loan and
send him the surplus.

> The lender [he said], runs no risk, because if you can't sell the

things at a profit you have only to take them back to the pawnbroker. On the other hand, my situation is now such that I absolutely must raise some money if only to be able to go on working.

He asked Weydemeyer to make an exception and to leave in pawn Jenny's little silver mug, plate, knife and fork: 'which in any case have no selling value.'

One cannot but be awed by the reflection that, in this period of domestic tribulations in England, what Marx wrote was *Class Struggles in France, 1848-1850*.

It was in these circumstances, with this work completed, that, a month later, on 19 November, the little Guido having contracted a lung infection, died, barely more than a year old. Marx wrote to Engels on the same day:

Just a couple of lines. This morning at 10 o'clock our little gunpowder plotter Föxchen died. Suddenly, in one of the convulsions he so frequently had. A few minutes before he was still laughing and playful. It was totally unexpected. You can imagine the state of things here. Owing to your absence[8] we happen to be very isolated just now ... Should you be in the mood, drop a few lines to my wife. She is quite beside herself.

Engels immediately complied and Marx wrote to him a few days later:

Your letter did my wife good. She is in a really dangerously nervous and exhausted condition. She had suckled the child herself and paid for his life in the most difficult circumstances at the cost of the utmost sacrifice. Added to that is the thought that the poor child was the victim of domestic poverty, although he did not want for care in any particular ...

At the beginning of December Mrs Marx answered Engels' letter, saying how deeply she appreciated his sympathy in the loss of 'our darling, my poor little child of sorrows'. Later she was to write:

'My woe was great. He was the first child I had lost.' Looking back over the years she added: 'I had no inkling then of the greater woe in store for me beside which all else paled into insignificance.'

Before the turn of the year, but a few weeks after Guido's death, the family moved again, this time into rooms at 28 Dean Street, a little further north on the same side of the road, where they were to remain for close on six years.

Here another daughter was born on 28 March 1851. She was named Jenny Eveline Frances and known as Franziska. This year and the following one were later pronounced by Mrs Marx to have been

> the years of the greatest and, at the same time, the most paltry troubles, worries, disappointments and privations of all kinds.

Nevertheless, the new baby was put out to nurse because, not only were living conditions already overcrowded, but Mrs Marx ever since the birth – an easy one – had been ill, 'owing to domestic rather than physical causes', as Marx wrote to Engels at the end of March. There was literally not a farthing in the house, he said, but a pile of bills from the small local shopkeepers.

Three months after Franziska's arrival, on 23 June, Helene Demuth gave birth to Marx's illegitimate son, named Henry Frederick and usually called Freddy. He was nurtured by foster parents. This episode is not at all well documented.[9] In her reminiscences Mrs Marx alludes to it obliquely – 'In the early summer of 1851 an event occurred which I do not wish to touch upon more closely but which greatly increased our domestic and external troubles' – while Marx in letters to Engels refers to a '*mystère*' – 'in which you too play a part' – but is at pains to put nothing explicit on paper, intent, rather, on arranging a personal meeting:

> ... about the *mystère* I shall not write because, come what may, I shall without fail come to see you ...

Marx indeed spent a few days in Manchester towards the end of April and Engels came to London for the first fortnight in June.

Engels's part was to assume, until he lay on his deathbed, the fictitious paternity of Freddy Demuth.

In August of that year 1851 Charles Dana, the editor of the *New York Daily Tribune*, invited Marx and Freiligrath to become paid contributors to his paper. This should have made for a more promising future, but family misfortune struck again. At Easter, 11 April 1852, the baby Franziska not yet 13 months old, developed bronchitis and on the 14th she died. Hard as it must have been throughout that past year to keep four small children, their parents and servant alive and well in those cramped surroundings, this situation had a special poignancy. Franziska's

> lifeless little body rested in the small back room [wrote Mrs Marx], while we all moved into the front room and, when night fell, we lay down on the floor, the three living children beside us, and we wept for the little creature who lay cold and pallid in the next room. Our dear child's death occurred at a time of the harshest privations ...

With anguished feelings, everyone else's promises having failed, she approached a French refugee of their acquaintance who lived in the neighbourhood and openly appealed for help in their distress. He gave her £2, which paid for the child's coffin.

> She had no crib when she came into the world [wrote the mother], and for long was also denied a last little vessel in which to be laid. It went hard for us when we saw it carried out to its last resting-place ...

After the tragic loss of these two babies, the parents clung even more closely to the three who remained to them.

V

Before he came to England, probably in Germany, a drawing of Edgar was made, the only portrait known to exist. He was not yet three and, though admittedly no Adonis, the young child's face is shown as full of character with large, intelligent dark eyes, a prominent nose, lofty forehead and shapely mouth. He appears to have an abnormally large head, but whether this was a sign of ill-health, of heredity – Marx's head was exceedingly large for his height – or the artist's incompetence, is open to question.

To be sure, Wilhelm Liebknecht, writing some forty years after Edgar's death, spoke of this 'very gifted' little boy whose 'promising head' seemed too heavy for his weak body and claimed that he had been ailing since birth; but there is no contemporary evidence to support this. Not only Edgar but also Jenny and Laura must have had a fairly sound constitution to withstand the vicissitudes of their tenderest years. Before the eldest child had much passed her fifth birthday the family had lived, under less than favourable conditions, in four different countries, while during their first eighteen months in England they had moved from one unsatisfactory lodging to another no less than six times. Yet in May 1850, at the depth of their miseries, Mrs Marx could write:

> Our three eldest children are doing splendidly despite everything. The girls are pretty, healthy, sunny, good little creatures and our stout little boy is full of fun and the most amusing notions ...

At that age – three-and-a-half – he was said to be fond of singing revolutionary songs, in German, at the top of his voice until the whole house shook. His merry disposition gave rise to ingenious stratagems, admiringly recounted by his mother. When he was five Mrs Marx told Engels:

> You may remember that Pieper[10] gave the lad his nice valise as a present. Yesterday he threatened to take it back and buy him something else instead. This morning the boy hid the valise and said 'Mohr,[11] I've hidden it so well that if Pieper wants it I shall say I've given it to a poor man.' The slyboots!

A year later his mother was reporting how Edgar had outwitted the baker who, refusing further credit or supplies until he was paid, called at the house asking for Mr Marx, to which the six-year-old at the door replied 'No, he ain't upstairs', snatched three loaves and darted away in triumph. Though in the habit of composing three letters a day to 'Frederick in Manchester', conscientiously sticking used stamps on them, one of his few known contributions to Marxist writings is a letter he left on his father's desk in March 1854 which read:

> My dear Devil, I hope you are quite well because I am coming to see you and I forgot to tell you that lupus[12] went out to drink as he generally does and got quite drunk and as he was going a long the streets there came some thieves and stole him his watch and his spectacles and five pounds and his Palleto and beat him dreadfully and garotted him. I am your friend Muchla-brassel.

It may be remarked that, although Musch had now been in England for four-and-a-half years, his first language was French, while he must certainly have heard more German than English in the home to which all the Marxes' refugee friends regularly flocked. Marx himself, it is known, despite his exceptional facility with languages, did not take too readily to English.

All his work during those first years in London was written in German. Following Louis-Napleon's *coup d'état* of December 1851[13] until March 1852 he wrote *The 18th Brumaire of Louis Bonaparte*, published in the German language paper *Die Revolution* by Weydemeyer, who had now emigrated, in America; though *Revolution and Counter-Revolution* – with other articles for the *New York Daily Tribune* bearing Marx's name – was in fact Engels' work.

This has been generally known since 1913, but not, of course, by Eleanor Marx when she edited a volume of those articles for English publication in 1896, with a preface describing life in the two rooms at 28 Dean Street where, she believed, her father had written them before she was born.

> I have heard tell [she wrote], how the children would pile up chairs behind him to represent a coach, to which he was harnessed as a horse, and would 'whip him up' even as he sat at his desk writing … It may interest readers to know what Marx was paid for his articles … He received £1 for each contribution …

It was this commission that enabled the Marxes to count

upon a regular if minimum income so that, as his wife put it, they were 'relieved from daily nagging worries', after two years of 'the greatest hardship, of continual acute anxiety, great privations of all kinds and actual need'.

In September 1850 the executive authority of the Communist League had transferred from London to Cologne, but in May 1851 its leaders were arrested and, after some 18 months in gaol, eleven of them were brought to a trial that lasted from 4 October to 12 November 1852. Despite the perjured evidence produced in court against them, four were acquitted. The other seven were sentenced to imprisonment varying from three to six years.

This led to an interruption of Marx's paid work as he set about writing his *Revelations Concerning the Communist Trial in Cologne* while that trial was still in progress.

> All the police allegations are lies [wrote Mrs Marx on 28 October]. They steal, forge, break open desks, swear false oaths, give false testimony, claiming that they are entitled to do these things in dealing with Communists who are beyond the pale of society. This and the way the police, in the most blackguardly fashion, take over the functions of the official Ministry of Justice, pushing Saedt' – the Prussian Public Prosecutor – 'into the background, producing as evidence unauthenticated scraps of paper, barefaced rumours, reports and hearsay as judicially proven facts, all this is positively hair-raising. My husband has had to work all day and far into the night ... Then everything has to be copied six or eight times and sent to Cologne by way of Frankfurt, Paris, etc. as all letters to my husband, as well as those from here to Cologne, are opened and confiscated. The whole thing has become a fight between, on the one hand, the police and, on the other, my husband at whose door the blame is laid for everything: the whole revolution, even the conduct of the trial ... I have had my share of the business and my fingers are sore from copying ... The whole place is now turned into an office; two or three write, some run errands, others scrape the pennies together to enable the writers to go on living ... Meanwhile my three lively children sing and whistle, to get a good scolding from their papa now and again ...

That this interruption was untimely, to say the least, is evident from the letter Marx had written to Engels in September when, with Mrs Marx, Jenny and Lenchen laid up, he would not send for the doctor for fear that he might prescribe medicines they could not afford to buy.

> For the past eight to ten days [Marx wrote], I have fed the family on bread and potatoes, and it is even questionable whether I can pay for those today. Clearly not a suitable diet in the present circumstances ...

Sending off a copy of the *Revelations* for publication in America, he wrote in an enclosing letter dated 7 December:

> You will know how to savour the humour of the pamphlet when you realise that its author is as good as interned for want of adequate covering for his feet and his posterior and, what is more, expects at any moment to see his family overwhelmed by truly appalling distress. The trial has driven me still deeper into a mess, because I have had to spend five weeks working for the Party against the government's machinations instead of earning my bread.

It was while Marx was engaged on this task and, possibly, to get the children out of the 'office', that Wilhelm Liebknecht — a young emigrant of 24 who had met the Marxes at a picnic arranged by the German Workers' Educational Society[14] in the summer of 1850, to become thereafter one of their most constant visitors — took the two small girls, Jenny and Laura, to watch Wellington's State funeral on 15 November 1852 and almost lost them in the crowd near Temple Bar.

From his close observation of family life both at 64 and 28 Dean Street — and, after 1856, in the little house at Kentish Town — Liebknecht wrote that, for Marx, 'the society of children was a necessity, whereby he was refreshed and renewed'. Indeed, every one of those contemporaries, friends and relations and colleagues, who later set down their recollections of Marx testified that he was at his best with children. This might be said of many people who could not in fact be bothered with them for more than five minutes at a time but, as one of his own daughters wrote, Marx was their most delightful and tireless playfellow. He stole time from his desk to sail paper boats on tubs of water, staging naval battles that ended in the burning of the flotillas; he read aloud to them; he told them, in instalments, stories of his own invention; and, when they went to Hampstead Heath, he organised wild games, as when, with one child upon his shoulders and another upon Liebknecht's, he mounted daring cavalry charges and steeplechases. He never wearied of their companionship; nor did this trait ever desert him. His grandson, Edgar Longuet, wrote that he would play with him and his brothers 'as though a child himself without any fear of compromising his dignity'. When he was a tired, sick old man, recently widowed, for whom, it was thought, the household containing his four little grandsons would be altogether too boisterous, he wrote that, on the contrary, he hoped to spend many a good day with them to 'fulfil worthily my duties as a grandfather' and that the peace and quiet he needed was that of family life with 'the microscopic world of children's noises'.

VI

In March 1853, at the time when the Crimean War broke out, Marx was visited by a Prussian police spy who gave his masters a detailed and unexpectedly genial account of the impoverished *ménage* in Dean Street and the 'three really handsome children' whose sticky playthings occupied the only chair with four whole legs in that cluttered living space which was courteously offered to the guest.

Marx's sister Louise, three years his junior, was married that year in June to Jan Juta, a Dutch businessman who wished to open a bookshop in Cape Town. Before sailing to South Africa the bridal pair spent a few pleasant days in London with the Marxes. It was a relatively easeful time.

The children flourished [wrote Mrs Marx] and developed both physically and mentally, although we were still in our poky little dwelling.

All that summer Lenchen took the children to one or other of the parks where they romped in the fresh air and everyone enjoyed the plentiful cherries, strawberries and grapes of that season.

The regular payments from America enabled them to settle old debts and live free from money troubles. Marx wrote some of his most important articles at this time, including those penned between October and December against Lord Palmerston,

> responsible for the whole foreign policy England has pursued from the revolution of 1830 to December 1851 ... the most infamous and reactionary epoch of English history ...

As the year drew to a close there was a brief spell of pure happiness. Christmas was, as Mrs Marx wrote, 'the first joyful festivity we had in London'; and, many years after, Jenny wrote to Laura recalling the occasion:

> Do you remember the jolly evening in Dean Street? I picture, as though it were yesterday, the way you, Edgar and I listened impatiently for the bell to summon us into the room where the Christmas tree stood. When at long last the awaited peal rang out, we were almost frightened, because we hadn't been allowed into that mysterious living room for a whole week. You two hung back timidly, while I, I suppose to hide my own misgivings, rushed forward as impetuously as I could. How glorious the living room seemed to us, how elegant and novel the dusty old furniture looked ...

Ernst Dronke had come the night before to decorate the tree and other friends lavished splendid toys upon the children: dolls, guns, cooking utensils, drums and trumpets.

No sooner was the New Year ushered in than coming events cast their shadow before: Edgar showed the first symptoms of the illness that was to destroy him. At the beginning of January the whole family went down with influenza from which Mrs Marx and the girls quickly recovered, while Edgar did not. He was laid up for a long time; and so, too, was Marx, who begged

Engels to write an article in his stead for the *New York Daily Tribune* as he was now three contributions in arrears. By the early spring Edgar was well enough to go to school with his sisters and when, towards the end of May, all three children picked up measles, it was their mother, newly pregnant once more, who suffered most. She was utterly worn out – which Marx attributed to her strenuous duties as day and night nurse – but refused to see the doctor on the pretext that the medicine he had prescribed for her condition on a former occasion had only made her worse.

By the middle of June, while the children went back to school, she took to her bed and now Marx insisted upon a doctor, with the result that she went with Lenchen and the children to stay for a couple of weeks at a friend's house in Edmonton, then a rural Middlesex village. 'The country air may restore her enough to enable her to go to Trier,' Marx told Engels and, on 8 July, obeying the physician, Mrs Marx set off alone to stay with her mother and take a complete rest.

Laura, then nearly ten, greatly interested in her food but indifferent to her prepositions, wrote to her at once:

My dear Mamma, I hope you have safely arrived by Grandmama ... We had such a beautiful dinner at Sunday a beautiful roast beef green peas potatoes and a nice raspberry and red currant[?pudding].

On 5 August both girls wrote to her at some length. Jenny, who went in for being a Pythoness from time to time, had on this occasion nothing prophetic to impart but, always keen on drama, regaled her mother with the tragicomedy of the young Queen Victoria's carriage coming to pieces in 1837 outside the Fox and Crown on Highgate West Hill, at which pub Marx with Liebknecht and the children had refreshed themselves on that hot summer Sunday morning. Beyond wishing that her 'dear Momchen' had been with them to see the glorious mementoes of that episode, she had little else to say.

Laura's letter was altogether more informative and a good deal more effusive.

My dear Mumchen, I am very glad you can eat as much as you like and that you have got a very great appetite and that your little cheeks have got fat and I hope you will come back fatter than when you went ... Dear Mumchen we laughed very much when we read the bill of the Soho theatre that it would be a coffee shop and that young persons, and want to learn there can do so. You must know that Monsieur de Pepers [Pieper] was ill and that he complained of a violent fever because the day before he drank a lot of gin and he lay in bed all day. At Sunday we went to highgate and when we came back he said he was better, but that he would not come out yet however the next day he got up at eleven o'clock more charming than ever and the hump on his back. I must tell you that last Friday Moor [Marx] was frightened with a bill for the income tax but Moore intends not to pay a single fhating. Now Mummchen how do you like it in Thrieves' [Trier, Trèves] 'I think feel very funny because you have been a very long time in London and that it is very big as to Thrieves. Dear Mumchen the street is very nasty they every moment open it again. first they made a cellar by Cross and Blackwell, When they finished it the gaz broke and they had to make that and so they go on from one thing to another.[15] and My dear Mumchen Helen asks if you would sent something to her sister, if you would ask whether the 5 Thalers she sent for Liesschen were arrived.' [Probably meant was Helene Demuth's niece, Elisabeth, one of the four illegitimate children of her older sister Katherine.] 'When Moor sent dear Friend' [their doctor, Freund] 'the 8 pounds he said he was very much obliged and just that day Jenny was not quite well and Moor thought it was the Cholera so he told Helen you ask what it was and Friend came the same day and he was very creeping(?) and he said it was nothing at all, and Mumchen it is all over now. Mumchen you will soon be here again and then we shall go to many places, and I must tell you Mumchen that I would be very glad if you were here because we would have a great deal of fun and I should like to see your little cheeks and my dear Mumchen I hope you will soon be here to make the little Glassman move Mumchen I have written enough I am your affectionate Laura.

Ever since her last visit to Trier in 1849 Mrs Marx had found the narrow provincial life there, with its gossip and petty local interests, oppressive, as she had written to her friend Lina Schoeler. Added to which her mother, to whom she had always been much attached, had greatly changed. The effects of this 'twaddling mean society', her relative isolation and advancing age – she was now in her sixties – had induced in an erstwhile mild and benevolent character a new harshness and an egotism that wounded her daughter. Daily life with the old lady had given rise to endless small brushes and Mrs Marx declared that she never breathed freely in that atmosphere. However, on this visit, she recuperated her health and returned to London on 10 August in a tranquil state of mind to await the birth of her last child, named Jenny Julia Eleanor, on 6 January 1855. (Another child, of sex unknown, was born to live but a few hours in July 1857.)

The baby – whose sex was a disappointment to Marx – though always yelling, was healthy enough and no more than a vexation; but on 3 March Marx wrote to Engels enumerating the family's several afflictions of which the first, and by far the worst, was Edgar's persistent gastric fever. He added:

> ... the doctor says I need a change of air as I haven't left the precincts of Soho Square for two years. So I should like to visit Manchester before my wife goes to Trier again ... At all events, I must – naturally not until everything here is in order – just for once and for a short spell get away from here, because the physical stuffiness is also stultifying my brain ...

Thereafter came a series of letters to Engels.

> [8 March] I can't leave here until Colonel Musch is visibly restored. All the same, he has made rapid strides towards recovery this week, the doctor was exceedingly pleased today and perhaps everything will be all right next week. As soon as I can leave with a clear conscience I shall write. Next week, I think ...
> [16 March] I don't believe the good Musch will pull through his illness. You will understand the effect this prospect has here at home. My wife is completely down again. However, the matter must now be decided soon, one way or another ...
> [27 March] In the last few days Musch has noticeably improved and the doctor expressed the highest hopes. If all goes well Musch must go into the country at once. Of course he is terribly weak and

emaciated. The fever is got rid of and the constipation much relieved. The main question now is only whether his constitution is strong enough to stand the whole treatment. However, I believe it is. As soon as the doctor says that there is no longer any danger, I shall come to you ... I am dog-tired as a result of my long night vigils as Musch's nurse ...

[30 March] I postponed sending you a daily health bulletin because the illness fluctuated so much that my own opinion changed almost hourly. But finally the disease has taken on the character of the mesenteric tuberculosis hereditary in my family[16] and even on the medical side, hope seems to be abandoned. For the past week my wife has been more unwell than ever before with mental anxiety. My own heart bleeds and my head is on fire, although naturally I have to keep my countenance. Not for an instant during his illness has the child belied his original, good-humoured and at the same time self-reliant character. I cannot thank you enough for the friendship with which you work in my stead and for the concern you show for the child. Should there be a turn for the better, I shall write to you at once.

[6 April, Good Friday] Poor Musch is no more. He closed his eyes (in the literal sense) in my arms today between 5 and 6 o'clock. I shall never forget how your friendship in this terrible time comforted us. You will understand my anguish about the child. My wife sends you the friendliest greetings. Possibly I shall bring her with me for a week when I come to Manchester. In any case I must find some way of getting her over the first days.

Liebknecht came at once to offer his sympathy.

I shall never forget the scene [he wrote]. The mother, bowed over the dead child, weeping silently, Lenchen standing by and sobbing, and Marx, in fearful agitation, rejecting vehemently, almost angrily, every attempt to console him, the two girls crying quietly, pressed close to their mother who, in her agony, clutched them to her convulsively, as though to clamp them to herself, to defend them against death which had robbed her of her boy ...

Two days later Musch was buried in the graveyard of Whitefield Tabernacle.[17] Half a dozen of the Marxes' refugee friends attended the funeral, Liebknecht riding in the carriage with Marx, who sat speechless, his head buried in his hands. I stroked his forehead: 'Mohr, you have your wife, your children and us, we who are all so fond of you' – 'You can't give me back the boy,' he groaned and without a word we drove to the churchyard ... As the coffin was about to be lowered into the grave, Marx became so agitated that I went and stood next to him, afraid that he would leap into the grave ...

On 12 April Marx wrote to Engels:

The house is naturally quite desolate and forlorn since the death of the dear child who was its life and soul. The way we miss him at every turn is quite indescribable. I've been through all kinds of misfortune in my time, but it's only now that I know what real unhappiness is. I feel myself broken down. It's a good thing that since the day of the burial I've had such furious headaches that I can't think or see or hear. In all the terrible agonies I've experienced these days, the thought of you and your friendship has always sustained me, and the hope that, together, we may still do something sensible in the world.

Marx and his wife went to Manchester a few days later for three weeks; but on their return to London he reported that she was in extremely bad health and shortly she collapsed. 'The whole household is still very stricken,' he wrote. The weeks passed, but the burden of grief was not lifted. On 3 July Marx said:

... we are still a sorrowful household here. My wife is still very unwell. The memory of the poor beloved child torments us and even obtrudes upon his sisters' play. One can get over such blows only slowly and with the passage of time. For me the loss is still as fresh as on the first day, so I can share my wife's sufferings ...

Time coursed slowly indeed for Mrs Marx. In September, writing to condole with a newly-widowed friend, Marx wrote:

... the news of this fresh bereavement has so vividly reawakened in my wife the memory of our only little son that her state of mind prevents her from writing to you just now. She weeps and wails like a child ...

More than a year later, when Mrs Marx was once again in Trier with the children at the time of her mother's death and when Marx was stopping with Engels in Manchester, he wrote her — after thirteen years of married life — what can only be described as a love-letter in which he said:

> … Where would I ever find a face whose every feature, yes, every wrinkle, revives the greatest and sweetest memories of my life. Even my everlasting pain, my unappeasable sense of loss, I read in your sweet countenance, and I kiss away the pain when I kiss your lovely face …

Not until the end of 1857 could Mrs Marx say that her husband's former capacity for work and his facility were regained, as were his intellectual vigour and serenity of spirit,

> destroyed for years, ever since his great grief, the loss of our beloved darling for whom my heart will always mourn.

Certainly the heartbroken family took comfort from the little Eleanor.

> The child was just born [wrote her mother], when my poor beloved Edgar went from us and all the love for the little brother, all the tenderness for him, were now transferred to the little sister whom the older girls looked after and cared for with almost maternal solicitude. Still, there can hardly be a more lovable child, as pretty as a picture with an artless and lively sense of fun … The child is Karl's real pet and laughs and chatters many of his cares away …'

Nevertheless, Edgar's sweet young boyhood remained always in mind and his death an abiding sorrow. Eleven years after, when Ferdinand Cohen, Karl Blind's stepson, a student of 24, made an attempt on Bismarck's life, was arrested and committed suicide in gaol, Marx wrote:

> He was a very nice (if not particularly gifted) boy for whom I feel a special sympathy because he was an old friend of Musch …

VII

There can be no question but that Marx would have preferred to father sons rather than daughters. No better proof exists than his openly expressed dismay at the birth of Franziska in 1851 – 'my wife has unfortunately been delivered of a girl, not a boy' – and of Eleanor in 1855 – 'had it been a male the event would have been more acceptable'. Even in later life, hard-driven by poverty and the outlay which he thought necessary for the up-bringing of young girls, he deplored the fact that they were not young men. Yet it is doubtful whether over the years, with his constant and unconditional affection for his children, he would have relished their company and cherished their concerns as dearly, or as intimately, had they been sons and not daughters.

Eleanor, the youngest, was perhaps the most fortunate of all the six children born to the family. Arriving in January 1855, three months before the death of Edgar, she was never forced to leave her native country nor to live the 'vagabond life' of her mother and sisters. Of even greater importance to a stable childhood, the family moved in the autumn of 1857 away for good from their miserable lodgings in the centre of London to the comparative haven of 'the attractive little house', as Mrs Marx called it, at 9 Grafton Terrace in Kentish Town, then a pleasant enough suburb surrounded by fields and gardens, where they spent the next seven years, only to move into even more spacious quarters in Modena Villas in Maitland Park, just across the boundary of Kentish Town, in Hampstead.

The two elder girls, dark-eyed Jenny and blond Laura – separated in years by almost a decade from the youngest by the deaths of the three other children – grew up to marry from that house, while Eleanor remained with her parents until their death in their last home, barely a stone's throw away, then known as 9 Maitland Park Crescent, to which they went in 1875. There, nursed in her last illness by Eleanor and Helene Demuth, Mrs Marx died on 2 December 1881. Two years later, on 11 January 1883, it was Jenny in France who passed away at the age of 38, a few months after giving birth to her sixth child and only daughter, the shock of which bereavement hastened Marx's own end on 14 March.

> To those who knew Karl Marx, [wrote Eleanor], no legend is funnier than the common one which pictures him a morose, bitter, unbending, unapproachable man ... This picture of the cheeriest, gayest soul that ever breathed, of a man brimming over with humour and good humour, whose hearty laugh was infectious and irresistible, of the kindliest, gentlest, most sympathetic of companions, is a standing wonder — and amusement — to those who knew him ...

Jenny's photograph, together with that of his wife and his father, was found in Marx's breast-pocket when he died. Engels laid them in his coffin.

Notes

1. François-Pierre-Guillaume Guizot (1787-1874), historian and politician, briefly Ambassador to the Court of St James, recalled to become Prime Minister of France in 1840. As the King's chief advisor he fled with him to England in February 1848, returning to Paris a year later, only to retire from public life after Louis-Napoleon's *coup d'état* of 1851.
2. Leopold I (1790-1865), Prince of Saxe-Coburg, brother of the Duchess of Kent and thus an uncle of Queen Victoria, accepted the Belgian crown in June 1830.
3. Engels's *Condition of the Working Class in England*, written in the winter and spring of 1844/5, had been published in Leipzig in May 1845.
4. In fact, Mrs Schmalhausen bore five children and outlived Marx by three years, dying in 1886 at the age of 70.
5. Mrs Marx senior, who had borne nine children, was then 57 and died in 1863, aged 75.
6. It appeared anonymously and, although an English translation, published in Julian Harney's *Red Republican* in November 1850, attributed the work to Charles Marx and Frederic Engels, it was not until the 1872 German edition, when it was retitled *The Communist Manifesto*, that, as a separate publication it bore the authors' names.

The term 'scientific socialism' was first used in Engels' Introduction to the 1892 edition.
7.   Louis-Philippe, Duke of Orleans (1773-1850) who adopted the name Philippe-Egalité on accepting the crown in August 1830.
8.   Engels had just left London to work in the office of his father's cotton mill in Manchester.
9.   For the little that is known about Freddy Demuth (1851-1929) see Yvonne Kapp *Eleanor Marx*, Vol. I, pp. 259-297 and Vol. II, pp. 435-439, 535-536 and 597.
10. Wilhelm Pieper, then aged 24, a philologist and journalist, who was a member of the Communist League, emigrated to London in 1850 where he acted briefly as Marx's secretary — until Mrs Marx took over that function — and the constant butt of the children.
11. The children commonly called Marx by his nickname: Mohr, or Moor.
12. Wilhelm Wolff.
13. By which his presidency was prolonged for 10 years. A year later he proclaimed himself Emperor.
14. Founded in London in 1840 by members of the League of the Just.
15. 'The now significantly reduced cholera in our district seems to have been so severe because the sewers made in June, July and August, were driven through the pits where those who died of the plague 1668 (?I think) were buried,' wrote Marx to Engels on 22 September 1854.
16. Marx's father, two of his sisters and two of his brothers died of tuberculosis. Marx himself, at the age of 20, had suspected lung disease and three years later was declared unfit for military service on those grounds.
17. Where also Guido and Franziska were thought to have been buried. Built in 1756 by Matthew Pearce for George Whitefield, one of the founders of Methodism, the chapel, or Tabernacle, was rebuilt in 1899. The present structure is the third on the site in Tottenham Court Road. The graveyard became the scene of disorderly behaviour and was closed in the mid-1890s. In 1898 most of the coffins were disinterred and reburied in Chingford Mount cemetery.

Sources

Bottigelli, Emile, *Marx-Engels: Manifeste du Parti Communiste*, Aubier Montaigne, Paris, 1971.

Dornemann, Louise, *Jenny Marx,* Dietz, Berlin, 1968.

Institute of Marxism-Leninism, Berlin.

Institute of Marxism-Leninism, Moscow.

International Institute of Social History, Amsterdam.

Kapp, Yvonne, *Eleanor Marx*, Volumes 1 & 2, Lawrence & Wishart, 1972 and 1976.

Liebknecht, Wilhelm, *Karl Marx zum Gedächtnis*, Nuremberg, 1896.

Longuet, Edgar, *Some Aspects of Karl Marx's Family Life*, from *Cahiers du Communisme*, March 1949, in *Reminiscences of Marx and Engels*, Foreign Languages Publishing House, Moscow n.d. (*c.* 1956).

Marx, Eleanor, *Karl Marx*, from *Österreichischen Arbeiter Kalender*, 1895, in *Reminiscences of Marx and Engels*.

Marx, Eleanor, Preface to *Revolution and Counter-Revolution*, Allen and Unwin, 1896.

Marx, Jenny (Mrs), *Kurze Umrisse eines bewegten Lebens*, from the MS in *Mohr und General*, Dietz, 1964.

Marx, Jenny (Mrs), Letter to Louise Weydemeyer, 11 May 1861, from *Die Neue Zeit*, 1906/7, in *Mohr und General*.

Marx, Karl, Engels, Frederick, *Collected Works*, Volumes 3-13, Lawrence & Wishart 1975-1980.

Marx, Karl, Engels, Friedrich, *Werke,* Bände 27-31, Dietz, 1963-1969.

Monz, Heinz, *Karl Marx: Grundlagen der Ertwicklung zu Leben und Werk*, Neu & Co., Trier, 1973.

Müller, Manfred (editor), *Familie Marx in Briefen*, Dietz, 1966.

Worobjowa, Olga and Sinelnikowa, Irma, *Die Töchter von Marx*, from the Russian 1961, Dietz, 1963.

Notes on Contributors

Michèle Barrett teaches sociology at the City University, London, and is a member of the *Feminist Review* Collective. Her publications include *Women's Oppression Today: Problems of Marxist-Feminist Analysis* and, with Mary McIntosh, *The Anti-Social Family*.

G.A. Cohen is Reader in Philosophy at University College, London. He is the author of *Karl Marx's Theory of History: A Defence* and of numerous articles on Marx and on social philosophy.

Peter de Francia is Professor of Painting at the Royal College of Art (London). One man exhibitions of his work have been held in galleries in Britain, Czechoslovakia, Holland, Hungary, Italy and the USA. In the fifties he was in charge of Fine Arts programmes for BBC television. He is the author of *Leger – The Great Parade*, and of a forthcoming comprehensive study of Fernand Leger's life and work.

Ben Fine is Reader in Economics at Birkbeck College, University of London. He is the author of *Marx's 'Capital'*, *Rereading Capital* (with Laurence Harris), *Economic Theory and Ideology*, and *Theories of the Capitalist Economy*. Currently he is working with Laurence Harris on a book for Lawrence and Wishart, *The Peculiarities of the British Economy*.

Stuart Hall is Professor of Sociology at the Open University. He is the co-author of *Resistance through Rituals* and *Policing the Crisis*. He was Director of the Centre for Contemporary Cultural Studies in Birmingham and has published widely on race, youth culture, Marxist theory, and the media.

Alan Hunt is Head of the Law School at Middlesex Polytechnic. He is on the editorial boards of *Marxism Today* and *Politics and Power*. He is the editor of a number of books, including *Class and Class Structure* and *Marxism and Democracy*, and co-author of *Marx and Engels on Law*.

Yvonne Kapp worked for refugees from Nazi persecution. She was a research officer of the AEU (now AUEW). For many years she was on the editorial board of the Labour Research Department. She is a writer and translator and is the author of *Eleanor Marx*, a two-volume biography.

Gregor McLennan is Fellow in Sociology at the Open University. He is the author of *Marxism and the Methodologies of History*, and co-author of *On Ideology, Making Histories* and of the Open University reader, *Crime and Society: Readings in History and Theory*.

Betty Matthews is on the editorial board of *Marxism Today*. Her commitment to Marxism dates from participation in the anti-fascist struggles of the mid-thirties, when a student. She has lectured widely on the subjects of Marxism and Politics.

Göran Therborn is Professor of Political Science at the Catholic University in Nijmegen, in the Netherlands. Previously he held a Readership in Sociology in Sweden. His books include *Science, Class and Society, What Does the Ruling Class Do When it Rules?, The Ideology of Power and the Power of Ideology*.

George Rudé is Professor of History at Concordia University, Montreal. His books include *The Crowd in the French Revolution, Wilkes and Liberty, The Crowd in History 1730-*

1848, Revolutionary Europe, 1783-1815, Europe in the Eighteenth Century, Robespierre, Captain Swing (with E.J. Hobsbawm), *Protest and Punishment, Ideology and Popular Protest.*

Gwyn A. Williams is Professor of History, University of Cardiff. His books include *Artisans and Sans-Culottes, Proletarian Order: Antonio Gramsci and the Origins of Italian Communism, The Merthyr Rising, Madoc: The Making of a Myth*, and *The Welsh in their History.* He is now working on a one-volume history of Wales and a television history of Wales (13 episodes, Channel 4).

Index